WITHDRAWN

POWERS, POSSESSIONS, AND FREEDOM

Essays in honour of

C.B. Macpherson

Powers
Possessions
and
Freedom

edited by Alkis Kontos

UNIVERSITY OF TORONTO PRESS

Toronto Buffalo London

© 1979 University of Toronto Press
Toronto Buffalo London
Printed in Canada

Canadian Cataloguing in Publication Data
Main entry under title:

Powers, possessions and freedom

Bibliography: p.
Contents: Hill, C. Covenant theology and the
concept of "A public person". –
Mansfield, H.C. On the political character of property in Locke. –
Taylor, C. Atomism. –
Pateman, C. Justifying political obligation. [etc.]
ISBN 0-8020-5474-9
1. Macpherson, Crawford B., 1911–
– Addresses, essays, lectures.
2. Macpherson, Crawford B., 1911–   – Bibliography.
3. Political science – Addresses, essays, lectures.
I. Macpherson, Crawford B., 1911–
II. Kontos, Alkis, 1937–
JA36.P68   320   C79-094875-3

The photograph of C.B. Macpherson
is by Ashley & Crippen, Toronto

Preface

C.B. Macpherson's seminal study of Hobbes and Locke, his paradigmatic possessive individualists, is an original intellectual achievement. His comprehensive, epigrammatic, critical conceptual category, 'possessive individualism', captures the spirit of the whole of his intellectual endeavour – to humanize individualism.

Remaining faithful to the truth of the central maxim of liberal-democratic theory which affirms self-realization as an end in itself, while drawing inspiration from the Marxian critique of capitalism, Macpherson proceeds to reform liberal-democratic theory. His synthesis of the two traditions, liberal-democratic and Marxian, provides the context within which he elaborates his theoretical analysis of the human predicament: his study of powers, possessions, and freedom. He proposes to extricate individualism from the dehumanizing and negating effects of capitalism, the possessive passions of market society. Macpherson has been performing this task over the years in his solitary, dignified fashion. His scholarship is impeccable; his challenge constant.

The essays in this volume do not, in the main, attempt to analyse or evaluate his achievement. Here, friends and fellow-scholars, fully cognizant of his thought and intellectual concerns, pursue their authentic, independent paths of thought. Homologies and departures in our indirect dialogue with Macpherson are easily discernible.

In the classroom and outside it, Macpherson always attempts to persuade, not to proselytize. Therefore, this volume does not subscribe to a delivered doctrine. I believe that he would not have wished it otherwise.

ALKIS KONTOS

Athens, Greece
Fall, 1978

Acknowledgments

Professor David B. Cook, University of Toronto, has given invaluable assistance during the preparation of this volume. I thank him for his generosity.

Mr R.I.K. Davidson, University of Toronto Press, helped in the genesis of this volume. He combines talent, experience, and diligence. Working with him is a pleasure and a challenge. I am deeply grateful.

This book has been published with the aid of a grant from the University of Toronto Press.

A.K.

Contents

POWERS, POSSESSIONS, AND FREEDOM

CHRISTOPHER HILL

Covenant Theology and the Concept of 'A Public Person'

My subject is the theological concept, which we encounter in England during the sixteenth and seventeenth centuries, of the representative person, or public person, or common person: the phrases seem to be used interchangeably. Adam was a representative of the whole of mankind; it was in consequence of his sin that all Adam's descendants were condemned to eternal death. From this predicament some men were rescued by the second principal representative person, Jesus Christ, who paid the penalty due from all mankind for Adam's sin. The idea that Adam and Christ were in this sense representative persons was shared by a large number of protestants from Luther onwards, though the phrase is not Biblical in any of its variants. Luther criticized the view, which he attributed to 'the Schoolmen and almost all the Fathers', that Christ was 'innocent and, as a private person,... holy and righteous for himself only'. Christ, Luther thought, was a high priest as well as a suffering servant, 'taking thy sinful person upon him'.[1]

This theory was held especially by exponents of the covenant theology, a theology which seems to derive in England from William Tyndale. It was also developed by Calvin and at Heidelberg in the 1580s by Ursinus and others.[2] Its origin coincides in time with a new emphasis on contract in political theory and with new attitudes towards contract among businessmen and lawyers. We cannot be precise about causal links, since the feudal contract, with its very different social context (the oath of loyalty and the coronation oath), had been familiar long before the rise of protestantism. The *Vindiciae contra tyrannos*, for instance, drew upon this body of ideas

---

1 *Commentary on Galatians* (Eng. trans., 1807), I, 304. The 1575 translation of this work was approved by Edwin Sandys, Bishop of London.
2 Tyndale, *Expositions and Notes on Sundry Portions of the Holy Scriptures* (Parker Society, 1849), 9, 76, 87, 96, and *passim*; L.J. Trinterud, 'The Origins of Puritanism', *Church History*, xx (1951), 48. I am indebted to Mr David Zaret of St Antony's College, Oxford, for help with the covenant theology.

perhaps more than upon protestant theories of the covenant, and this tradition had its influence in England. Nevertheless, the actual content of the covenant theology suggests that it was influenced by the growing significance of contracts, and of the debtor-creditor relationship, in the economic life of society as capitalism developed. The Swedes, Bulstrode Whitelocke observed during his embassy of 1653–4, 'have but few contracts, because they have but little trade'.[3]

At about the same time, too, was developing the sectarian church covenant by which men voluntarily associated with other members of the elect to form gathered congregations. There is an analogy here with the Leveller Agreement of the People. Just as baptism is the symbol of entry into church covenant, of access to the means of grace, so acceptance of the Agreement of the People was the means by which men (or some men) would have contracted into the refounded English state if the Leveller program had been accepted.[4]

Medieval sacramental theory was rooted in the symbolism which accompanies, and seals, economic or political transactions in primitive society. Livery of seisin is accompanied by (or rather is) the transfer of a piece of earth; homage is symbolically 'done'; the Lord Treasurer is appointed by handing him the white staff of office. So the ring in matrimony, water in baptism, laying on of hands in confirmation, the elements in the mass, are all means whereby grace is bestowed. Richard Hooker quoted St Bernard with approval: 'God by sacraments giveth grace ... even as honours and dignities are given, an abbot made by receiving a staff, a doctor by a book, a bishop by a ring.'[5]

Protestant sacramental theory evolved in a much more sophisticated social atmosphere. Livery of seisin was already a trifle old-fashioned. Not only were written contracts long established, but verbal agreements were becoming legally more binding; and credit in various forms, by written or verbal bond, was also familiar. Slade's Case in 1602, extended by Warbrook *v.* Griffin in 1610, meant that 'the law was now ready to enforce promises other than those formally recorded', provided there was 'some evidence that a contract really existed ... The consideration or inducement must be shown, in return for which the unfulfilled promise was made.' This important new development of the law of contract gave the individual much more freedom

3 B. Whitelocke, *Journal of the Swedish Embassy* (1855), II, 438; cf. Alan Everitt, 'The Development of Private Marketing', in *The Agrarian History of England and Wales*, IV, *1500–1640*, ed. J. Thirsk (Cambridge, 1967), esp. 543–63.
4 Perry Miller, 'The Marrow of Puritan Divinity', *Publications of the Colonial Society of Massachusetts*, XXXII (1935), 292–3. See p. 12 below for the significance of 'or some men'.
5 *Of the Laws of Ecclesiastical Polity* (Everyman ed.), II, 506

of manoeuvre in regulating his business affairs.[6] Similarly the relationship of serf and lord, mesne lord and overlord, was being replaced by the dual relationship between king and subject, employer and labourer. Voluntary associations, gilds, companies, and partnerships already had their place in the towns.

Now the protestant emphasis on faith as against works, its denial that sacraments are the vehicles of grace, spiritualizes worship and strips it of its symbolical-magical-materialist character. Protestant sacramental doctrine bears the same relation to medieval catholic doctrine as credit does to a metal currency, Marx long ago pointed out.[7] Faith becomes the more important as external material aids to grace (the counters of salvation) lose their usefulness. The relationship between God and man is direct, and emphasis is placed upon promises, mutual covenants between the two parties. That is why the inner state of mind of the Christian was so significant. God is not mocked: in entering into or renewing a covenant it was essential that the intention should be sincere. In feudal law, by contrast, it was precisely the external forms that counted: livery of seisin was livery of seisin, and its proper performance was all that mattered. A good deal of this attitude entered into popular conceptions of the efficacy of sacraments, whatever the more sophisticated theologians might say. Failure to distinguish between symbol and thing symbolized explains much in the reformation controversy over indulgences.

'Without a promise there can be no faith', declared Tyndale. 'The devil hath no promise: he is therefore excluded from Paul's faith.' 'If when thou seest the sacrament, or eatest his body or drinkest his blood, thou have this promise fast in thine heart, that his body was slain and his blood shed for thy sins, and believest it, so art thou saved and justified thereby.'[8] 'The sacraments', wrote Calvin, 'are a kind of mutual contract, by which the Lord conveys his mercy to us, and by it eternal life, while we in our turn promise him obedience.'[9] That Calvin's attitude to justification is remarkably legal has often been noticed; it has been attributed to his training as a lawyer, but he is a lawyer dealing with property and economic relationships. Many shared Calvin's emphases. 'Even infants may contract and covenant with God', wrote the judicious Hooker.[10] 'God deals with men', declared Richard Sibbes, 'as we do by way of commerce one with another, propounding mercy

---

6 A. Harding, *A Social History of English Law* (Penguin ed.), 104–6; D. Little, *Religion, Order and Law* (Oxford, 1970), 204–5

7 *Capital*, III (Chicago, 1909), 696

8 *Doctrinal Treatises* (Parker Society, 1848), 224, 252–3

9 *The Institutes of the Christian Religion*, trans. H. Beveridge (London, 1949), II, 477; cf. 39.

10 *Ecclesiastical Policy*, II, 287. Contrast Hobbes, quoted p. 21 below.

by covenant and condition.'[11] *The Whole Duty of Man* speaks in terms of a bargain with God.[12]

The direct covenant with God does away with the need for mediating saints: 'the master is bound to be just to [his servants] in performing those conditions on which they were hired.'[13] By covenant 'God bindeth himself to fulfil that mercy unto thee only if thou wilt endeavour thyself to keep his laws.'[14] The employer in a family workshop deals directly with his employees: serfs had approached their lord through his bailiff or steward. But the relationship to God is conceived not only as a hiring contract: it is also thought of as debtor-creditor relationship – a relationship perhaps even more frequent in sixteenth-century England than the wage relationship. This is the classical form of the covenant as elaborated by the puritan preachers, Perkins, Ames, Preston, and Sibbes. The covenant of works has been replaced by the covenant of grace, under which God enters into obligations to his elect. The covenant of works is with Adam as representative of all mankind; the covenant of grace is with Christ as representative of the elect only. As Perry Miller pointed out, the covenant theology postulates a law-abiding universe. After the Fall and the Flood, God bound himself to an orderly and perpetual succession of the seasons of the year: he also accepts law in his relations with his elect. This is the world of Bacon and Descartes, looking forward to the mechanical philosophy and the mechanistic universe.[15] The fact that God bound himself to the elect by an explicit bond was a means of overcoming the absolute decrees of high Calvinism, and of smuggling free will back into theology. Since God had limited his arbitrary power by covenant, his operations became predictable, comprehensible to human reason. The elect could appeal to his promise if they kept their part of the bargain. 'All the evidence we have to show for our inheritance ... is our faith.'[16]

The effect was to re-establish moral obligation on a clearer, more rational basis, to free men under normal circumstances from the incomprehensible decrees of an unknowable God. The transition was from the ineluctable inheritance of sin, and with it impotence to comply with God's law, to a definable contractual relationship. Men are born owing God a debt, but

11 *Works* (Edinburgh, 1862–4), IV, 122; cf. III, 394.
12 (1704; first published in the 1650s), 1; cf. 12–23.
13 Ibid., 314
14 Tyndale, *Doctrinal Treatises*, 403; cf. 470.
15 W. Gouge, *A Commentary on the Whole Epistle to the Hebrews* (Edinburgh, 1866–7), II, 187; G. Hakewill, *An Apologie or Declaration of the Power and Providence of God in the Government of the World* (3rd ed., 1635), II, 147; Miller, 'The Marrow of Puritan Divinity', 292–7
16 S. Hieron, *Sermons* (1624), 221, 293, 352, 356

depraved sinners can now claim their rights under the contract which their representative has entered into on their behalf. The element of choice, of freedom of the will, is restored.[17] Milton hoped by education to repair the ruins of the Fall.[18] As Bulkeley put it, 'the covenant which passeth between God and us is like that which passeth between a king and his people; the king promiseth to rule and govern in mercy and righteousness, and they again promise to obey in loyalty and faithfulness.'[19] Hence the activism which is such an apparently paradoxical feature of puritanism. Sibbes expressed this again in economic terms: 'Thou hast a title in the common ... How do men strive with their landlord for their commons? They will raise a mutiny, do anything, keep somewhat on it for possession's sake, rather than lose it, if it were but to keep one poor cow upon it ... In Christianity, if we be entered as freemen, where is our scot and lot? Where are our prayers offered up for king, our country, for religion?'[20]

It is against this background that we must see the idea that Adam and Christ were representative persons. The covenant of works between God and Adam was replaced by a covenant of grace between God and Christ, 'made anon after the former covenant was broken'.[21] The covenant of grace was revealed to Adam, promised to Abraham, and renewed to Moses (all public persons).[22] But the formal covenant between God and his elect was entered into on behalf of the latter by Jesus Christ in his capacity as representative person.

This doctrine was elaborated by William Perkins, the greatest English puritan theologian, and was developed by the covenant theologians who were his followers – Preston, Sibbes, Ames, William Gouge, Thomas Goodwin, William Bridge, John Owen.[23] Preston's contribution was especially to emphasize the legal aspects of Adam's breach of contract, his role as a representative person rather than as a father from whom we inherit physically. Man is born in debt to God: Christ has obtained easier terms for his

17 Cf. Perry Miller, *The New England Mind: The Seventeenth Century* (New York, 1939), 401–8; P. Miller and T.H. Johnston, *The Puritans* (New York, 1938), 188–91; my *Puritanism and Revolution* (Panther ed.), 240–3.
18 *Complete Prose Works* (Yale ed., 1953–), II, 366–7
19 P. Bulkeley, *The Gospel-Covenant: Or The Covenant of Grace Opened* (1646), 345–6
20 *Works*, VII, 249
21 Gouge, *Commentary*, II, 185; T. Goodwin, *Works* (Edinburgh, 1861–3), I, 70–1, 74–6; cf. 123, 330, 435; Sibbes, *Works*, VI, 350
22 Z. Ursinus, *The Summe of Christian Religion* (1645), 124–7; J. Owen, *Works* (1850–3), VI, 76–9; Sibbes, *Works*, VI, 1–25; Bulkeley, *The Gospel-Covenant*, 38
23 See esp. J. Preston, *The Breastplate of Faith and Love* (5th ed., 1634), 4 (sermons preached 1625); Sibbes, *Works*, III, 571, IV, 462, VII, 192; K.L. Sprunger, *The Learned Dr. William Ames* (Urbana, IL, 1972), 148–52.

clients.[24] The covenant theology was summarized succinctly by the Larger Catechism (1648) of the Westminster Assembly of Divines: 'the covenant being made with Adam as a public person not for himself only but for his posterity' was replaced by a new covenant made by Christ 'as a public person'.[25]

What exactly was understood by a public person in the seventeenth century? John Davies of Hereford assumed that 'a great lord' was a public person:

> And public persons (if they mighty be)
> The public state, and theirs, they still must eye.[26]

Samuel Morland, writing to Secretary Thurloe in December 1655, took it for granted that an ambassador was a public person, who could not travel incognito.[27] But the analogy most frequently used by those who spoke of Adam and Jesus Christ as public persons was a member of the House of Commons. Perkins said that all Adam's posterity sinned with him 'as in a Parliament whatsoever is done by the burgess of the shire is done by every person in the shire'.[28] 'As the king, his nobles, knights and burgesses do represent the whole realm in Parliament', declared Thomas Tuke in 1609, 'even so did Adam represent the persons of his whole posterity.'[29] Thomas Hooker echoed Perkins: 'Adam in innocency represented all mankind; he stood (as a Parliament man doth for the whole country) for all that should be born of him.'[30]

We note, in passing, that for Thomas Tuke the concept of representation does not necessarily imply election in the modern sense. Nor indeed does the concept of election: 'The word election intendeth the taking out of the best not of the worst out of things', wrote George Wyatt in the 1590s.[31] Election means selection. In this sense the Western Circuit Assizes in February 1640 could order that 'John Spenser, ... yeoman, is to be elected constable of

---

24 *The Saints Qualification* (2nd. ed., 1634), 38; Miller, 'The Marrow of Puritan Divinity', 281–3; cf. my *Puritanism and Revolution*, 240–2, for Preston and the covenant theology.
25 *The Larger Catechism* (Edinburgh, 1865), 110, 122
26 *The Complete Works*, ed. A.B. Grosart (1878), II, *The Scourge of Folly*, 81
27 *Thurloe State Papers* (1742), IV, 281
28 W. Perkins, *Works* (Cambridge, 1616–18), I, 161, II, 214–15
29 Quoted by C.A. Patrides, *Milton and the Christian Tradition* (Oxford, 1966), 103
30 Quoted by Miller, *The New England Mind: The Seventeenth Century*, 401; cf. pp. 10–11 below.
31 *The Papers of George Wyatt*, ed. D.M. Loades (Camden Fourth Series, vol. 5, 1968), 71

Barton Stacey Hundred'.[32] We must beware of carrying modern conceptions back into the seventeenth century.

More important for our purposes is the legal fact that the public person is accepted as representing his clients. Speaking of Christ as a common person, Goodwin observed that 'the notion of a public representative to do acts that in law are counted as theirs whom he represents, is common among all nations'.[33] 'A common person ... is one who represents, personates and acts the part of another, by the allowance and warrant of the law, so as what he doth as such a common person and in the name of the other, that other whom he personates is by the law reckoned to do.' Christ is like an attorney at law, who has the power to act in our stead. Goodwin instanced receiving money, giving possession of an estate, acting as an ambassador. Christ is also a surety, who binds himself to pay our debts, something that Adam could not be.[34] As the Shorter Catechism of 1647 put it, God must punish 'all sin, either in the sinner or in Christ the surety'.[35]

The legal consequences of this analogy were drawn with unpleasant thoroughness: 'God having once arrested Christ, and cast him into prison and begun a trial against him and had him to judgment, he could not come forth till he had paid the very uttermost farthing.'[36] But 'by the law, if the surety hath discharged the debt, the debtor is then free.' Christ's 'death was but the satisfaction and payment'; but 'in that he rose again as a common person this assures us yet further that there is a formal, legal and irrevocable act of justification of us passed and enrolled in that court of heaven between Christ and God.' 'For he hath engaged, and if he should fail, [he] might ever lose that honour which he hath now in heaven.'[37] 'When Christ arose, he rose as our head, and as a common person ... God accounts that we rose also with him.' 'In Christ as a common person, and as a pattern of us, we may be said to have done what Jesus Christ did or doth, or what befalleth him; and we are reckoned by God to have done it. ... This is one of the greatest hinges of the gospel.' '"I will", saith Christ, "represent them; they are all virtually

32 *Western Circuit Assize Orders, 1629–1648*, ed. J.S. Cockburn (Camden Fourth Series, vol. 17, 1976), 186; cf. 209 (JPs to elect a constable), 235, 286 (the assize court 'electing' a constable).
33 *Works*, II, 239; cf. Bunyan, *Works* (1860), I, 304.
34 Goodwin, *Works*, IV, 27. For Christ as surety as well as public person, cf. Paul Bayne, *An Entire Commentary upon the Whole Epistle of St. Paul to the Ephesians* (Edinburgh, 1866), 82 (first published in 1643; Bayne died in 1617); Owen, *Works*, X, 358; Sibbes, *Works*, V, 326–7, 345; VI, 245; Bunyan, *Works*, I, 525, 564.
35 *The Shorter Catechism* (1897), 22
36 Goodwin, *Works*, IV, 30; cf. 31–41 *passim*.
37 Ibid., IV, 30, 39, 71, 87–8; cf. 32–5.

in me; and do thou, O Father, reckon them as having a subsistence in me.''
... So a covenant was truly struck, through Christ's representing us, as the
covenant of works was between God and Adam.' The gift of the Holy Ghost
was an earnest of this bargain.[38]

The doctrine of the public person, like the whole covenant theology, was
often expressed in terms that drew on economic realities familiar to
seventeenth-century congregations. Christ, Thomas Goodwin told his readers, 'was truly and indeed God's hired servant in his work [of satisfaction],
and God covenanted to give him the salvation of those he died for as his wages
and reward. ... So that, if God be just, he must give forth salvation,
otherwise Christ's obedience would cry as the work of a hireling doth for
wages.'[39] Goodwin speaks much of sureties, earnest money, pawns, and
pledges. Gerrard Winstanley in his early pamphlets refers to Christ as the
pledge and earnest-penny.[40] The covenant, said Jeremiah Burroughs, is
'God's insurance office', at which we have to pay no premium.[41] 'You may
sue him of his bond written and sealed, and he cannot deny it.'[42] God is
'willing to indent with us, to make himself a debtor to us'. We must 'extort,
... oppress the promises, that as a rich man oppresseth a poor man, and gets
out of him all that he is worth, he leaves him worth nothing; ... after that
manner deal thou with the promises, for they are rich.'[43] Johnston of
Wariston demanded of Christ: 'show then thy satisfaction applied to me
before thy Father, and tell him he cannot take twice payment for one debt ...
Thy credit is now engaged, let me know that thy Father denieth thee
nothing.'[44]

The most recent historian of representation in seventeenth-century England
tells us that in Elizabethan parliaments assertions that MPs were 'public men'
in a special relationship to their electors were 'unconsidered and relatively
infrequent'. But under James I there developed a 'stridently assertive, if
incoherent, emphasis on the fact of representation'.[45] It was at this time that
John Preston called on electors 'to keep their minds single and free from all
respects, so that when they come to choose they might choose him whom in

38 Ibid., I, 254–5, IV, 33, 244; cf. 265; I, 75; and Bunyan, Works, I, 525–6, 564
39 Goodwin, Works, IV, 215
40 The Mysterie of God, Concerning the Whole Creation, Mankind (1649; first
    published 1648), 28; The Saints Paradise (n.d. ?1649), 53, 119
41 The Rare Jewel of Christian Contentment (1964; first published 1648), 79–80,
    201
42 Quoted in Miller, The New England Mind: the Seventeenth Century, 289–90
43 Preston, The New Covenant (5th ed., 1630), 331, 477–8
44 Sir A. Johnston of Wariston, Diary (Scottish History Society, 1917–40), I, xvi
45 Derek Hirst, The Representative of the People? (Cambridge, 1975), 8

their consciences and in the sight of God they think fittest for the place ... Do nothing for fear or favour of men, or for any sinister respect.'[46] Such an attitude would strengthen the resistance of freeholders and burgesses faced with the pressures of landlords and courtiers; it would contribute to the growing independence of the electorate which Dr Hirst traces. The covenant theology made man a partner with God and God a debtor to man, so creating 'a kind of equality between us'. A point of faith is 'when the will of a man claims God's statutes'.[47]

But even under Elizabeth MPs had drawn attention to their claim to be public persons and therefore in a special relationship to the government. It was argued that an arrested member of Parliament should not be held in custody, 'forasmuch as he was not now a private man, but to supply the room, person and place of a multitude specially chosen'. Or as Peter Wentworth put it in 1575: 'I am now no private person. I am a public, and a counsellor to the whole state.'[48] In a Fast Sermon of March 1642 Cornelius Burges pressed home the analogy with Adam and Christ, telling members of the House of Commons to look upon themselves 'as public persons, that must both bear the sins of others whom you represent, and purge out the sins of others, or be guilty of them yourselves'.[49] In later Fast Sermons Obadiah Sedgwick, Daniel Cawdrey, and Thomas Hill addressed MPs as public persons.[50] Peter Sterry distinguished between the two capacities of his audience, 'as private Christians' and as 'public persons and magistrates',[51] glancing no doubt at the Calvinist doctrine that revolt might be justified if led by the magistrate.

In Adam all men died; in Christ the elect were free. Christ died for all men, but for some more than for others. When the covenant theologians are careful they speak, as Goodwin did in the passages quoted on p. 10 above, of 'those he died for', those 'whom he represents'. But very often they speak ambiguously of 'us'; 'we' were condemned because of Adam's sin, 'we' were saved by Christ. This ambiguity at the heart of the covenant theology, and indeed of Calvinism generally, has its political parallels.

'The church' for a Calvinist sometimes means the whole people, some-

46 Preston, *Life Eternal* (4th ed., 1634), Sermon XII, 67; cf. my *Puritanism and Revolution*, 240–1, 255–6.
47 T. Hooker, *The Soules Vocation* (1638), 460. I owe this reference to Mr David Zaret.
48 Sir S. D'Ewes, *The Journals of All the Parliaments during the Reign of Queen Elizabeth* (1682), 175, 241; L.F. Brown, 'Ideas of Representation from Elizabeth to Charles I', *Journal of Modern History*, II (1939), 26–7
49 *Two Sermons Preached to the Honourable House of Commons* (1645), 37
50 Sedgwick, *England's Preservation* (1642), 25; Cawdrey, *The Good Man* (1643), 36; Hill, *The Season for Englands Selfe-Reflection* (1644), 22
51 *The Spirits Conviction of Sinne* (1645), 29–30

times the elect only. Adam represents all men, Christ the elect only; but both are public persons. When Christ is considered in his representative character, the reprobate slip out of sight. Exactly the same slide occurs in seventeenth-century uses of 'the people'. Ireton defined them, precisely, as 'the persons in whom all land lies, and those in corporations in whom all trading lies'. Colonel Rich and Captain Baynes distinguished between 'the people' and 'the poor'.[52] Some, even among the Levellers, would have excluded servants and paupers from the franchise (compare the analogy between entry into a gathered congregation and acceptance of the Agreement of the People).[53] Yet Parliament represented 'the people', and of course its decisions were binding on the poor as well as on the electors. Locke's original contract was made between 'the people'. Yet some of the contracting people already had servants. The state exists for all Englishmen, but for some more than others. The theory of the representative person must have assisted this slide, of which we appear today to be so much more conscious than our seventeenth-century predecessors.

Emphasis on the representative character of the 'public men' in the House of Commons came just about the time that questions were being asked about the precise way in which Adam and Jesus Christ 'represented' humanity, questions which no doubt arose from the legal analogies we have been considering. For Perkins 'Christ, because he is the head of the faithful, is to be considered as a public man sustaining the persons of all the elect'.[54] Anthony Burges supposed that Adam 'knew himself to be a common parent, and that he received a common stock for all mankind'. His sin may be said to be ours 'by way of delegation, as if we had chosen him to be our common parent, and had translated our wills over to him, as amongst men it is usual in arbitrations'.[55] But that was written in 1659, after men had had a good deal of experience of representation. 'As if we had chosen him' betrays uneasiness, since of course we hadn't. Goodwin tried to face this difficulty. There are three ways in which you may come to be a common person, he tells us: either 1/ 'by choice of the parties themselves, as you choose the burgesses in Parliament'; or 2/ they are chosen by another – we did not choose Christ; or 3/ 'by God's appointment founded upon a law of nature'. 'Adam was by the

52 *Puritanism and Liberty* ed. A.S.P. Woodhouse (London, 1938), 64; *The Parliamentary Diary of Thomas Burton*, ed. J.T. Rutt (1828), III, 147
53 C.B. Macpherson, *The Political Theory of Possessive Individualism* (Oxford, 1962), chap. III; K.V. Thomas, 'The Levellers and the Franchise', in *The Interregnum: The Quest for Settlement*, ed. G.E. Aylmer (London, 1972), 57–78
54 *Works*, I, 78
55 *Of Original Sin* (1659), 38–9; cf. 2, 46.

law of nature a common parent, and therefore we come to be guilty of that first act by which our nature was defiled.' 'Generation is but the channel.'[56]

By the time Burges and Goodwin were writing, the mere inheritance of sin was being challenged: it must be shown that Adam's posterity were more directly involved in his actions than by physical inheritance of his tainted blood. 'A sinful man must beget a sinful man', wrote Thomas Goodwin. But 'Adam was a public person ... which no other parent is.'[57] The covenant theology had endeavoured to meet this difficulty. Burges wrote that Adam 'as our head being in covenant with God, when he became a covenant breaker then we all forfeited all in and by him. So that it's the covenant of God that is the foundation of communicating original sin, as far as sin can be communicated to all mankind, yet natural generation is the medium or way of conveying it.'[58]

This is precisely what was being challenged. The Quaker, Edward Burrough, in 1654 answered the question: 'Whether did not the man Christ suffer as a public person in the elect's stead?' by saying 'Thou makest it manifest that thou dost not know the man Christ at all; ... for a public person Christ is not to thee, but a mystery which thou knowest nothing of, and for the redeeming of the elect from under such mouths as thine did and doth Christ suffer.'[59] The covenant theology had striven to replace Adam as our common parent by Adam as our representative, our attorney, just at the time that election to the House of Commons was being stressed, when constituencies were refusing to accept MPs nominated by their betters, whether peers or town oligarchies.

Perry Miller pointed out that the developed covenant theology, by postulating a 'conditional covenant' into which men could enter freely, achieved almost all that Arminians sought to achieve by the heresy of conditional election. Both are safeguards of propertied society against the antinomian possibilities latent in revolutionary Calvinism. The conditions attached to the covenant are like those imposed on 'a free man of a corporation' by apprenticeship, Cotton suggested: there is no admission to the corporation of the godly by purchase.[60] Bulkeley in 1646 declared that 'the Apostle saith *The promise is made unto Abraham*. ... He stands as a public person, as the common parent of all the faithful to the world's end ... receiving the promise

---

56 *Works*, II, 126–33
57 Ibid.
58 *Of Original Sin*, 165
59 'Answer to several Queries put forward by Philip Bennett, who calls himself minister of Christ but is found a deceiver', in *Works* (1672), 31
60 J. Cotton, *The Covenant of Gods Free Grace* (1645), quoted by Miller, 'The Marrow of Puritan Divinity', 285–6

of faith not only for himself but for all that should *imitate* him in his faith.'[61] Imitation implies voluntary action. That was the activism which the covenant theology insinuated into traditional Calvinism.

But in the course of the Revolution political activism came to be expressed in the radical Arminianism which Milton and others were to adopt in the name of human freedom. God could not be just if man were not free.[62] Even the elective principle did not satisfy the extremer wing; there must be a closer link between Christ and his elect than mere representation. Thomas Goodwin denied that Christ was a common person in his incarnation and intercession. Like Milton, he had little interest in the atonement.[63] 'We are said to be risen in Christ as in a common person, and to sit in heavenly places in him ... because we are one with him. ... When a man is thus quickened and turned to God, the state of that man is altered; ... he doth now actually sit with Christ in heaven.' Christ is 'a common person, ... the first fruits of a company of members that are raised with him as a common head'.[64] The patriarchs, Goodwin told the House of Commons in February 1646, 'may be understood as common persons, representing indeed the nation of the Jews. All the saints are their successors.'[65]

All the saints then are common persons? The elect represent the nation? Here in explicit form is the slide from 'the people of England' to 'the good people'. The good people represent the rest, as Christ represented the good people. 'The Son and the saints make one perfect man', declared William Erbery, who took over many of Thomas Goodwin's theological ideas. 'Though there shall be but one king in all the earth, yet all the saints shall reign on earth also.' The Second Coming is when God 'appears in glory in us. ... God appearing in the saints shall punish kings of the earth upon the earth.'[66]

But if Adam represented humanity, some radicals thought that Christ should do so too. The scales of justice would not be held even if Christ represented only the elect. A century earlier the radical sectary Henry Hart had rejected absolute predestination on the ground that 'it putteth away the covenant between God and man ... in that Christ is denied to be a general Saviour to all men'. Salvation depends on actively putting oneself under 'the

---

61 *The Gospel-Covenant*, 38. I have italicized the word 'imitate'.
62 Milton, *Complete Prose Works*, VI, 160–6, 397
63 *Works*, IV, 70–1, I, 98–9
64 Ibid., I, 462, II, 241–2, 244
65 *The Great Interest of States & Kingdoms* (1646), 4. Goodwin meant something very different from Richard Montague when he provocatively described St Peter as a public person in *A New Gagg for an Old Goose* (1624), 64.
66 *The Testimony of William Erbery* (1658), 8, 40; cf. 3–4, 10–11, 15, 18, 23

covenant of God.'[67] Such ideas no doubt survived underground, to be picked up by the radical Arminianism of the revolutionary decades.

Winstanley as usual produced the most radical version of this doctrine. 'As the body of the first man was a representation of the whole creation, and did corrupt it, so the body of Christ was a representation of the whole creation, and restores it from corruption and brings all into the unity of the Father again. In this particular lies the mystery of the Fall and the restoration of all things again.' All mankind is 'but the one first Adam', the mighty power of flesh. '*The whole bulk of mankind*, when they shall be drawn up to live in the unity of the one spirit, is the second man [i.e. Christ] and every son and daughter of this spirit is of the lineage of the second man.' 'Mankind ... shall be the mystical body of Christ.' Hitherto the second man did never rule in earth, being held down and kept as a servant by the first man. But now things are changing.[68] The oligarchy of grace which the covenant theology expressed is being explicitly democratized. Christ no longer represents the elect only: he incorporates – indeed he is – all mankind.

Lords were public persons; MPs were public persons; the House of Commons in April 1643 'took the Lord General to be a public person', who might have lands voted to him as an individual.[69] George Wither in 1652 described how he had served the commonwealth 'otherwhile as a private, and sometimes as a public person'.[70] He had been a justice of the peace in the 1640s, but he more probably refers to his service as captain and colonel, first in Charles I's army against the Scots in 1639 and then in the Parliamentary army during the civil war. In 1649 the officers of the New Model Army were drawn from a lower social class than when the Earl of Essex had been Lord General, but it was claimed that they too 'are public persons', and that the Presbyterian ministers who aspersed them '(though presumed public) are in civil things private'.[71] The theory of the public person thus made possible an extension of the Calvinist doctrine that revolt might be justified if led by the magistrate.

67 *The Writings of John Bradford* (Parker Society, 1848), 322–3, where Bradford quotes Hart in order to refute him; J.W. Martin, 'English Protestant Separatism at Its Beginnings: Henry Hart and the Free-Will Men', *Sixteenth Century Journal*, VII (1976), esp. 70–2
68 *The Works of Gerrard Winstanley*, ed. G.H. Sabine (Ithaca, NY, 1941), 116–17, 120–1, 162–3, 225, 486. My italics. Cf. *Paradise Lost*, V, lines 609–10.
69 *Mercurius Aulicus*, 30 April 1643
70 *Parallelogrammaton* (1652), 8
71 Anon., *The True Primitive State of Civil and Ecclesiasticall Government* (March 1648–9), 15

The preachers had called on MPs to act as public persons. When after the summer of 1647 the Army effectively took over power from Parliament, it was natural that it, or its leaders, should succeed to the claim to be public persons representing the people. We may see such a claim in the New Model Army's declaration of June 1647: 'We were not a mere mercenary army, hired to serve any arbitrary power of a state, but called forth and conjured by the several declarations of Parliament to the defence of our own and the people's just rights and liberties ... against all particular parties or interests whatsoever.'[72] God, Milton wrote in the first *Defence of the People of England*, has 'handed over to the state and with it all its officers not patience but laws and arms to avenge wrong and violence'. When *Ecclesiastes* asks, Who may say to the King 'what doest thou?' he is 'instructing neither the Great Sanhedrin nor the Senate, but private persons'; and Milton draws the appropriate conclusions for England. David would not slay Saul 'being a private citizen'. But public persons are liable to no such limitations: 'shall a senate therefore fear to touch a tyrant?'[73] A century earlier Christopher Goodman had argued that kings were public persons, but that they might lose this public capacity and 'be taken of all men as private persons' if they became tyrants or murderers.[74]

'What makes a public person above a private', William Sedgwick asked in 1649, 'but that he hath the civil sword in his hand to administer justice?' This led him to reflect that the Army was superior to Parliament because it had a sharper sword: Parliament lost its authority when it turned England into an armed camp. The Army was composed of 'men of the common and ordinary rank of people, most of them of trades and husbandry (with a small mixture of the gentry) which are the body and strength of the kingdom, in which the common interest most lies'. 'This Army is truly the people of the kingdom', not 'in a gross heap' but by the ordinance of God.[75] Just as the elect might be public persons representing the rest, so the New Model was 'the Army of God, as public persons and not for a particular interest'. As early as 1646 Thomas Edwards reported that John Hitch, former soldier turned preacher, told the incumbent of a Buckinghamshire parish that he, Hitch, 'was as public a person as himself'.[76]

72 *The Leveller Tracts, 1647–1653* eds. W. Haller and G. Davies (New York, 1944), 55
73 *Complete Prose Works*, IV, 346–7, 398, 402; cf. *Ecclesiastes* VIII : 4.
74 *How Superior Powers Ought to be Obeyed of Their Subjects* (Geneva, 1558), 187–8, quoted by Q. Skinner, *The Foundations of Modern Political Thought* (Cambridge, 1978), II, 223. Goodman may be relying on John Major, *History of Greater Britain* (1521), quoted by Skinner in II, 121.
75 *A Second View of the Army Remonstrance* (1649), 6, 11–13
76 *The Testimony of William Erbery*, 25; *Gangraena* (1646), I, 70

We see the culmination of this process in Milton's *Samson Agonistes*. Adam and Eve were public persons in *Paradise Lost*: so was the Son of God in *Paradise Regained*; so was Samson. In *Areopagitica* the poet had seen the people of England as a Samson, 'shaking his invincible locks'; in the *Defence of the People of England* Samson was a rebel who 'thought it not impious but pious to kill those masters who were tyrants over his country'.[77] In *Samson Agonistes* Milton carefully prepared the identification of Samson with the New Model Army. In his first speech Manoa referred to his son as 'himself an army', and later he spoke of

> those locks
> That of a nation armed the strength contained ...
> Garrisoned round about him like a camp
> Of faithful soldiery.[78]

Harapha denounced Samson as 'a murderer, revolter and a robber', since his nation was

> subject to our lords.
> Their magistrates confessed it when they took thee
> As a league-breaker and delivered bound
> Into our hands.

The regicides and Army leaders were subject to similar accusations after 1660, when they too had been 'delivered bound' to 'unjust tribunals under change of times' by men who still claimed that the Solemn League and Covenant was binding on them. Samson's reply was

> I was no private but a person raised
> With strength sufficient and command from heaven
> To free my country.[79]

This echoes the New Model Army's declaration of June 1647, quoted on p. 16 above. That Army, like Samson, was representative not so much 'as you choose the burgesses in Parliament', but 'by God's appointment founded upon a law of nature': justice and force well met. Milton endorsed the argument which John Cook had intended to use against Charles I in his trial: that the High Court of Justice 'was a resemblance and representation of the

77 *Complete Prose Works*, II, 558, IV, 402
78 Lines 346 and 1493–8. For other similar comparisons, see my *Milton and the English Revolution* (London, 1977), 429–30, 435.
79 Lines 1178–85, 1211–13. 'Subject to our lords' refers to the radical theory of the Norman Yoke, to which the free English people had been subjected. See my *Puritanism and Revolution*, 58–125.

great day of judgment, when the saints shall judge all worldly powers'.[80] The godly were public persons because Christ was a public person, and they were part of Christ. So they could not only oppose but even judge their sovereign.

But when the doctrine of the public person could be extended to justify a revolution of which the men of property had lost control, the covenant theology itself became less attractive – in old England if not in New England. Part of the original point of seeing Adam as a public person was to substitute the representative for the hereditary principle. 'Adam's offence in eating the forbidden fruit is not to be reputed as a personal offence, but he being a public person it was a public sin, even the sin of all mankind.' So Samuel Hieron, who died in 1617. Sin is inherited: heaven is an inheritance, owing nothing to merit.[81] 'Adam, the parent and head of all men, either stood or fell as a representative of the whole human race.' So Milton tells us in the *De doctrina christiana*: he repeated it in *Paradise Lost*.[82] By this time Milton was aware that the justice of visiting the sins of the fathers upon the children was being challenged, by Socinians and others, and he himself disliked the hereditary principle in politics. But the Bible is clear on this matter, as Milton abundantly showed, adding examples of 'a very ancient law among all races and all religions', and quoting Thucydides, Virgil, and the English law of treason.[83] He clearly felt a little uneasy on the subject. Bunyan had no doubts. 'All had transgressed in the first Adam, as he stood a common person representing both himself and us in his standing and falling.' Adam and Christ were 'the two great public persons or representators of the whole world, as to the first and second covenants'.[84]

But others were even more uneasy than Milton, and some of them put the inner light before the letter of the Bible. I quoted Edward Burrough. Another Quaker, Robert Barclay, flatly rejected the *hereditary* implications of the theory. 'That Adam is a public person is not denied,' but it does not follow from this that all infants share Adam's guilt.[85] When we get to Locke the

80 Cook, *King Charls his Case* (1649), in *Somers Tracts* (1748–51), II, 196; cf. Milton, *Complete Prose Works*, III, 597, VI, 499–501, and John Canne, *A Voice From the Temple to the Higher Powers* (1653), 14.
81 Hieron, *Sermons*, 373, 420; cf. Hakewill, *An Apologie*, 601.
82 *Complete Prose Works*, VI, 384. Cf. Addison: 'the principal actors' in *Paradise Lost* 'are not only our progenitors but our representatives. We have an actual interest in everything they do.' *The Spectator*, no. 273, 12 January 1712
83 *Complete Prose Works*, VI 385–8. Cf. Preston: 'It is true Adam ran in debt, but do not we pay many debts of our grandfathers and fathers, which we never drunk for?' *The Saints Qualification*, 38
84 John Bunyan, *Law and Grace* (Oxford, 1976; first published 1659) 28, 55, 94; cf. 166. Bunyan cites I John III: 4; Romans V : 12; I Corinthians XV : 22.
85 *Apology*, Proposition Fourth, para. 5. For Burrough see p. 13 above.

covenant has become totally Arminian: repentance was an absolute condition of the new covenant. For Locke, as for Bulkeley,[86] as for Milton in *Paradise Lost* and *Paradise Regained*, what Christ gives us is a clearer perception of the reality of God, of the *reasons* for behaving morally. We are no longer bound by traditional ceremonies. But once we have reached that stage the covenant theology itself becomes superfluous.[87] Morality is self-validating.

In its secular form the doctrine of the original contract was not always liberating. In 1628 Sir Robert Philips declared that 'it is well-known that the people of this state are under no other subjection than what they did voluntarily assent unto by their original contract between king and people'.[88] He was arguing against the great anti-puritan, Roger Mainwaring. Here the appeal to the past set men free in the present: the contract was used to call existing authority in question. But when in New England John Winthrop said that men were not to be brought under any rule otherwise 'than according to their will and covenant; ... the foundation of the people's power is their liberty',[89] his intention was to restrict some men's freedom by means of a contract known or alleged to be known. The Levellers were soon to hear Ireton at Putney telling them in Hobbist terms that they must keep their covenants made. The appeal to the past could be used to impose new chains. Uncertainty concerning what the original contract had said meant that it could be twisted either way.

Consequently many radicals became dissatisfied less with the ambiguities of the conception of the public person than with the whole idea of the dependence of the present on the past. When the Levellers proclaimed that 'whatever our forefathers were, or whatever they did or suffered or were enforced to yield unto, we are the men of the present age, and ought to be absolutely free from all kinds of exorbitancies, molestations or arbitrary power',[90] they were no doubt thinking primarily of liberation from the Norman Yoke. But the principle that men were bound only by agreements into which they themselves had freely entered was to undermine the whole idea of a covenant made once for all in remote antiquity by representative persons. It is another example of the dissidence of dissent: puritan individualism dissolved its own central doctrine of the covenant.[91] By 1738 John Taylor could reject the idea of inheritance of original sin as expressed in the

86 See pp. 13–14 above.
87 G.R. Cragg, *From Puritanism to the Age of Reason* (Cambridge, 1950), 127–9
88 Quoted by S.R. Gardiner, *The History of England, 1603–1642* (1884), VI, 237
89 Quoted by Miller, *The New England Mind: the Seventeenth Century*, 408
90 *Leveller Manifestoes of the Puritan Revolution*, ed. D.M. Wolfe (New York, 1944), 114; cf. 157–8.
91 Trinterud, 'The Origins of Puritanism', 53

contract theology's picture of Adam as a public person. It is unreasonable, he declared, for any man 'without my knowledge and consent' so to represent me that I become guilty of his sin.[92] This line of argument would undermine any theory which based political obligation on a supposedly historical social contract.

So the theory of the public, common, or representative person helped to liberate from the constraints of a traditional status society those who believed themselves to be the elect. If such men could demand their rights from God, could extort the promises from him, they would hardly be more deferential to princes. The theory helped, perhaps, to dissociate the idea of representation from the idea of election (in the political sense, election from below). The slide from Adam representing all men to Christ representing the elect reinforced mental attitudes which saw the church as the whole of society and yet more particularly as the elect members of it, which saw the people as the whole populace and yet more particularly as the men of some substance in that society. The elect were chosen by God; MPs were not elected by the headless multitude. During the Revolution the idea of the public person helped both the godly and the Army to see themselves as in the truest sense representatives of the people, even though not elected by them.

The doctrine faded out after the revolutionary decades, as Arminianism replaced Calvinism, as secular contract theory replaced religious theories, as 'natural' rights replaced pseudo-historical rights, as a morality of internal conviction replaced a morality of external observance.

When we ask ourselves what the influence of the idea of the public person was on the evolution of political thinking in seventeenth-century England, it does not appear to be very great. I find no significant trace of the idea in the writings of Filmer, Hunton, Henry Parker, the Levellers, Winstanley, Milton, Harrington, or Baxter. Its direct influence on modern theories of representation, which assume the election of representatives, seems to be nil. But it is worth perhaps pausing for a moment over the greatest seventeenth-century political thinker of all – Thomas Hobbes.

The sovereign in *Leviathan* is a public person – the only public person. 'A person is he whose words or actions are considered either as his own or as representing the words or actions of another man, or of any other thing to whom they are attributed, whether truly or by fiction. When they are considered as his own, then is he called a natural person; and when they are considered as representing the words and actions of another, then is he a feigned or artificial person.'[93] Hobbes steers very carefully round the cove-

---

92 Quoted in Perry Miller, *Jonathan Edwards* (Toronto, 1949), 277–8
93 *Leviathan* (Penguin ed.), 217

nant theology's doctrine of the public person. 'The true God may be personated', as he was first by Moses and secondly by Jesus Christ. But 'to make covenant with God is impossible but by mediation of such as God speaketh to, either by revelation supernatural or by his lieutenants that govern under him and in his name'. Hobbes' object here is to substitute Leviathan for Jesus Christ. None represents God's person 'but God's lieutenant, who hath the sovereignty under God'. Any other 'pretence of covenant with God is so evident a lie, even in the pretenders' own consciences, that it is not only an act of an unjust but also of a vile and unmanly disposition'. Moses was a political sovereign.[94]

In *Leviathan* Hobbes repeatedly emphasizes that 'a Commonwealth is but one person', and that the sovereign, whether a man or a body of men, 'is the absolute representative of all the subjects'. 'And therefore no other can be representative of any part of them, but so far forth as he shall give leave.'[95] Parliament in a monarchy like England cannot be considered the representative of the people. The sovereign is called 'the representative person of a commonwealth'.[96] Private men have no political authority 'without permission from the representative of the commonwealth'. Those who are employed by the sovereign 'in any affairs, with authority to represent in that employment the person of the commonwealth' – viceroys, treasurers, generals, authorized preachers, judges, JPs, ambassadors – are very carefully called 'public ministers'.[97]

In *The Elements of Law* (published 1650, but written in 1640) and in the *De Cive* (1642) there is no elaborate description of the sovereign as a representative person such as is fundamental to *Leviathan*.[98] In both the earlier works Hobbes stresses the impossibility of covenanting with God 'further than it hath pleased him to declare who shall receive and accept of the covenant in his name', and describes the sovereign in passing as 'a person civil'. But that is all. What had happened between 1640–2 and 1651 to cause this change of emphasis? It seems to me possible that Hobbes' insistence that the sovereign is the only true representative of the people may owe something to the popularity of the covenant theology, and in particular of the claims made in the 1640s that Parliament and the Army were public

94 Ibid., 197, 220, 230, 503
95 Ibid., 405, 220–1, 228, 275–6; cf. 381, 524.
96 Ibid., 241, 307, 317; cf. chap. xxx *passim*.
97 Ibid., 700, 289–94. Hobbes uses the words 'public person' only once and in the negative: councillors without executive authority are not public persons.
98 *The Elements of Law*, ed. F. Tönnies (Cambridge, 1928), 60–1, 97; cf. 84, 133, 138. See also Hobbes, *English Works*, ed. Sir William Molesworth (1839–45), II, 20–2, 69–73 – the *De Cive*; and F.C. Hood, *The Divine Politics of Thomas Hobbes* (Oxford, 1964), 146–9.

persons. Hobbes naturally wished to refute those who 'have pretended for their disobedience to their sovereign a new covenant made not with men but with God'. But the violence of his language against covenant theologians in general ('so evident a lie', 'a vile and unmanly disposition') suggests that he regarded them as significant enemies even though he failed to name them.[99] The covenant theologians had argued that the elected should also be the elect.[100] But the Long Parliament had proved disappointing in this respect, at least to the radicals. Theories of Fifth Monarchism or of the dictatorship of the godly were a natural consequence, as we have seen. The more activist version of the elect as public persons, the version of Thomas Goodwin, John Cook, John Milton, and the Fifth Monarchists, was sufficiently prevalent in 1651 for Hobbes to wish to refute it.

The frontispiece to *Leviathan* shows the public person of the sovereign incorporating all individual subjects. This may have been inspired by the contemporary concept of the composite Christ: for radical theologians Christ was a representative person compounded of all the faithful.[101] The doctrine that the godly were part of Christ and therefore entitled to act for him in earthly affairs was as dangerous for Hobbes as the claims to inspiration which he so fiercely lampooned.[102] It was characteristic of him to twist his opponents' arguments to suit his own purposes.

The time indeed was propitious. As the godly discredited themselves in the 1650s, as they fragmented into a welter of competing sects, so the ungodly rule of Leviathan came to seem more and more attractive to men who had property to lose.[103] It mattered less who the sovereign was – the Long Parliament, the Lord Protector, Charles II – or how he had acquired his office, than that he should maintain law, order, property, and social security, and be accepted by the bulk of his subjects. For Hobbes the best way to get him accepted seemed to be to say that he represented them: he and no one else.[104] If I am right, then the doctrine of the public person may have had at least a negative influence on Hobbes, making him think out more carefully his own theory of representation. And from there modern political thinking begins.

99 *Leviathan*, 230
100 Cf. Preston, quoted on p. 11 above.
101 See pp. 14–15 above.
102 *Leviathan*, 440–2, 691–2; cf. 205–6. 'To speak by inspiration, like a bagpipe', wrote Hobbes in his *Answer* to Davenant's *Preface before Gondibert*, in *Sir William Davenant's Gondibert*, ed. D. Gladish (Oxford 1972), 49. Cf. also Hobbes, *English Works*, II, 277–9: the mystical body of the church, of which Christ is the head, is not one person.
103 Cf. W. Lamont, *Godly Rule: Politics and Religion, 1603–1660* (London, 1969), esp. 125–9, 175–6.
104 *Leviathan*, 227–8

On the Political Character
of Property in Locke

It is a curious fact that Marx, who elaborated the labour theory of value, had little to say of Locke, who originated it. Only in the manuscript called *Theories of Surplus Value* does he comment on Locke's theory; and although as usual acute, his comment is brief – much briefer than his treatment of Adam Smith and his successors – and it is given in the context of Locke's dispute with Sir Dudley North on the cause of the high rate of interest. Marx concludes his comment promisingly: 'Locke's view is all the more important because it was the classical expression of bourgeois society's ideas of right as against feudal society, and moreover his philosophy served as the basis for all the ideas of the whole of subsequent English political economy.'[1] But Marx never made the study implied by this note to himself, as it might seem. Nor did he acknowledge Locke's theory as the origin of his own. Although it was 'the classical expression' of the undeveloped Hobbesian insight that 'labour is the sole source of all wealth',[2] Marx did not compare his theory with Locke's.

Such disregard cannot be put down to Marx's enmity for bourgeois private property. For Locke, of course, 'labour ... puts the difference of value on every thing.' But since value to humans is enjoyment or advantage to separate humans, human value, for Locke, is necessarily private. Marx thought, however, that the value of a product or commodity was more truly its exchange value with other commodities, socially determined; and he

---

1 Karl Marx, *Theories of Surplus Value*, E. Burns trans., 3 vols. (Moscow, 1963), I, 367. For other comments of Marx on Locke, see *Capital*, trans. S. Moore and E. Aveling, 3 vols. (New York, 1967), I, 36, 90, 101, 125, 390n, 617n; Marx and Engels, *Die Deutsche Ideologie* (Berlin, 1953), 431, 434–5; S.W. Ryazanskaya, *A Contribution to the Critique of Political Economy* (New York, 1970), 77–8, 160, 164; Marx, *The Eighteenth Brumaire of Louis Bonaparte*, in D. Fernbach ed. *Political Writings*, 3 vols. (New York, 1974), II, 148, 252.
2 *Theories of Surplus Value*, I, 365

concluded in favour of communism, which would give effect to the essential sociality of human value. Yet communism can acknowledge its debt to capitalism, like child to parent, with no abatement of hostility. If Marx's doctrine on the labour theory of value was the culmination of Locke's, so also was communism in general the culmination of capitalism, because culmination, in Marx's view, includes or rather requires correction and revolution. Since Marx was so far from denying that he asserted the progressive character of capitalism and its theoreticians, why did he overlook Locke?

C.B. Macpherson can be said to have supplied the missing Marxian critique of Locke in his notable work, *The Political Theory of Possessive Individualism*. In what follows I do not purport to give an analysis of his work, which would have to be done in the context of Locke scholarship today. Clearly he brought two benefits to scholars which were the more useful as they were less welcome: recognition of the fundamental similarity of Hobbes and Locke and attention to the bourgeois content of Locke's system of rights, duties, laws, and powers. Both points had the effect of reducing Locke's political philosophy to the reflection of nascent bourgeois society, of a 'market society' determined by 'market assumptions'. In Macpherson's view, which was also the view of Marx in so far as Marx disclosed it, Locke is a proto-political economist. Although Locke's 'achievement' was in political philosophy – to have based property right on natural law, and then to have removed the natural law limits on property right[3] – it was bounded by contradictions that can only or best be explained by his 'preconceptions', the bourgeois 'market assumptions'. These assumptions are still at the stage of preconceptions in Locke, and Locke's achievement could also be described as the refutation of traditional economic doctrine in its own terms of natural law. Locke's theoretical importance, therefore, lies in his preparation of bourgeois society unadorned with political philosophy, and in his preparation of the ascendancy of economics, when market assumptions are used consciously and determinedly to construct and reform market society.

Against this Marxian interpretation of Lockean politics in the service of Lockean economics, my intent in this essay is to show that Lockean economics served Lockean politics, and to suggest that Locke's political philosophy is the foundation, not the scaffolding or superstructure, of political economy.

Marx gave the subtitle 'Critique of Political Economy' to his major work, indicating that his solution appears from a critique of the society of whose ideas Locke was the 'classical expression'. We may, then, usefully begin our inquiry into the place of politics in Lockean economics by asking: what did

---

3 C.B. Macpherson, *The Political Theory of Possessive Individualism* (Oxford, 1962), 199; Marx, *Capital*, I, 390n

Marx mean by 'political' in 'political economy'? Marx himself begins *Capital* at some distance from politics, with the analysis of a commodity. A commodity has both use value and exchange value. Although at first the use of a commodity seems to be its value, in the course of investigation it develops that the value of a commodity is expressed *only* in the form of its exchange value.[4] The course of Marx's investigation follows the course of human history, however, as can be seen from the first sentence of *Capital*: 'The wealth of those societies in which the capitalist mode of production prevails presents itself as an "immense accumulation of commodities".'[5] To explain what a commodity is he must explain what it is in the most developed society, in which value is fully manifested in exchange; but to do this, he must begin with the apparent value of a commodity in use and show how use value, which at first seems to be intrinsic to the commodity, is replaced by its true exchange value, which seems at first to be accidental. This beginning in use value is not merely hypothetical for the purpose of analysis; it is also historical, because men at one time actually lived in societies in which non-capitalist modes of production prevailed and value was measured in terms of apparent use. Marx's science is both non-historical and historical: non-historical in that exchange value is true value and that the society of exchange value, where commodities are exchanged freely without the compulsion of scarcity and political power, is the perfect society; historical in that the analysis of value follows the actual development of societies from use value to exchange value.[6]

There is, then, a fundamental contrast in Marx between capitalist societies based on exchange value and the evanescent, but actual, non-capitalist societies based on use value, which capitalist societies succeeded. Non-capitalist societies include feudal societies, but to reveal this fundamental contrast more fully, Marx returns to ancient cities, particularly to the ideologists or interpreters of ancient cities, 'the writers of classical antiquity, who hold exclusively by quality and use value',[7] and of these, especially to Aristotle. Aristotle, Marx says, lacked a concept of value, i.e., exchange value, because he did not see how things unequal in quality could be made commensurable for exchange except by some partly arbitrary equalization. He was prevented from seeing that human labour is the requisite non-arbitrary measure of exchange value by the fact that Greek society was

---

4 *Capital*, I, 38
5 Ibid., I, 35
6 'Political Economy, which as an independent science, first sprang into being during the period of manufacture, views the social division of labor only from the standpoint of manufacture.' Ibid., I, 364; and see I, 8–10, 18–20, 169.
7 Ibid., I, 365. Marx also makes a discerning reference to Xenophon's 'characteristic bourgeois instinct.'

founded on slavery, hence on the natural inequality of men and their labour-power.[8] Since no society could be entirely free, according to Aristotle, every society had to decide, in part arbitrarily, who would be free and who slave. Such a decision was political; it was based on an opinion as to who should rule rather than derived from an analysis of what a commodity is.

An opinion as to who should rule implies choice of rule within the necessity of rule. The economy described by Aristotle might therefore be called (though Marx does not so call it) the 'natural economy', as it is determined by the different qualities of men that nature presents to us, as it seems, beyond our capacity to change. It might also be called the 'conventional economy' in so far as opinions of those differing qualities and their political relevance differ. Societies in which use value predominates over exchange value are both natural, because the needs men find useful to satisfy are imposed by nature, and conventional, because useful goods do not exchange according to laws of nature or of economics. Nature forces men to use the force of convention and to satisfy their needs by exchange, in which they must resort to politics.

Marx believed that men could overcome this enslavement in politics, where they serve as nature's jail-keepers and their own task-masters. His solution might be called quantification, and it can only be outlined here. In Part I of *Capital* he shows that commodities can be exchanged for one another not because of some convention but because each commodity has a form that makes it relative and equivalent to all other commodities. This form is money, but money is not what makes commodities exchangeable; rather, it is because commodities are exchangeable that money is possible and is invented. Through money, but because of the relative and equivalent forms of commodities, the different qualities of commodities corresponding to their different use values are transformed into quantities, and the commodities themselves are thereby brought into a whole, 'the whole world of commodities'.[9] Value to humans, use value, is in invisible forms that can be abstracted from the bodies of commodities, thus disembodied, and re-embodied in other, indeed in all other, commodities.

This means that things in themselves are not useful to men. Things in themselves, that is, as they are given by nature, are distinct by their different qualities; and with this distinctness they enslave men who make their livings in compartments fixed by the different qualities of things – for example, as farmers are determined by the nature of their crops. When men's lives are determined in this way by the qualities of things in a division of labour, they seek vainly to overcome the one-sidedness of their condition and attempt to

8 Ibid., I, 59–60. For Aristotle, exchange has a natural basis in human need; *Nicomachean Ethics*, 1133a26–29.
9 *Capital*, I, 63.

impose the conditions of their own lives on the whole. This is religion. Religion is the conventional political formalism that Marx believes he can replace with the scientific analysis of the money-form. It is the spurious political whole he will replace with the true economic whole.

In order to turn Hegel's dialectic right side up, and return the ideal to a reflection of the material,[10] Marx was compelled to acknowledge the wholesomeness of natural needs, hence of nature. Nature could not be understood merely as the enslaver of men if human freedom consists in the satisfaction of needs or in furnishing use value. Nature supplies men with a 'wealth of human needs'[11] that permits them to live independent of any one of them. Without human labour to produce exchange values, men would be enslaved; but in view of nature's contribution of manifold needs (which is potential freedom), human labour must be considered co-operation with nature as well as the overcoming of natural enslavement. Natural enslavement was imposed through the rule of conventions; now that one-sided conventions favouring particular commodities and the ways of life they determine have been replaced by the undistorted Marxian science, men can live in an easy relationship with nature and with each other.

Thus, Marx, after departing from the natural economy of Aristotle, returns to it – just as exchange value, after departing from use value, returns to it. Marx agrees with Aristotle that man is a political animal, except that he corrects 'political' to social.[12] For 'political' refers to the Greek city, and cities or states are variable and historically determined, and as such bound to disappear. In Marx's rational society, the political and the conventional are no longer required by nature. He can omit to say that man is *by nature* a social animal because it is by human labour that nature is rendered wholesome to men. But in his own analysis of commodities, he says: 'we go back to the great thinker who was the first to analyze so many forms, whether of thought, society or Nature, and among them also the form of value. I mean Aristotle.'[13]

Going back to Aristotle means returning to his thought, and to the intelligibility of the things Aristotle thought about. The natural economy described by Aristotle is evanescent, but it requires only to be corrected by Marx's discovery of the concept of value supposedly indiscernible to Aristotle.[14] Marx's correction of Aristotle presupposes Aristotle. In *Capital*,

---

10 Ibid., I, 20.
11 Marx, *Economic and Philosophical Manuscripts*, in L. Colletti ed., *Early Writings* (New York, 1975), 348, 356, 358
12 *Capital*, I, 326n
13 Ibid., I, 59. High-flying Plato is ignored.
14 In fact, Aristotle's discussion of slavery is more open-minded than any modern lecture on the subject that merely asserts the possibility of freedom. *Politics*, 1253b15–18, 1255b4–6.

Aristotle, not Hegel, appears to be Marx's main antagonist; and the principal distinction appears to be between the ancients, who believed that man is in part enslaved to nature, and the moderns, who did not.[15] It is true that political economy sprang into being as an independent science only 'during the period of manufacture' and that 'its accentuation of quantity and exchange value' is to be contrasted with 'the attitude of the writers of classical antiquity, who hold exclusively by quality and use value'.

But the 'political' in political economy is a remainder and a reminder of the natural economy. The 'political' is exploitation through formalism, by the extension of form in commodities to the conventions that rule men's lives according to distinct qualities. Formalism occurs when men fail to quantify the qualitative forms by means of the concept of value, which is homogeneous human labour, and instead elevate one quality to the quality of qualities, personified in God or reified in a concept such as freedom. Bourgeois formalism is less disguised than that of Aristotle or of 'Aristotelity' because it promises more freedom than do the classical writers, and so reveals itself by trying to conceal itself.[16] It is none the less derived from Aristotle; and Marx's 'critique of political economy' is the same as his correction of Aristotle: the removal of 'political' from political economy. As we turn to Locke, there will be opportunity to judge the accuracy of Marx's understanding of this 'political.'

Locke, like Marx, engages in a critique of religion to establish his doctrine on property, but unlike Marx, he does not carry it to the length of expelling politics, as being indissolubly allied with religion, from that doctrine. Locke's critique of religion is, of course, subdued; he did not and could not indulge in the competitive, strident atheism characteristic of Left Hegelianism which has become routine in our day and has taken all the fun out of free-thinking. Locke's critique of religion was, indeed, unmistakeable to any age but our own, which, partly by the influence of Marxism, has lost all understanding and respect for sound convention. Locke proposed to replace the unsound conventions or superstitions of religion with sound, political conventions. In this attempt he followed Aristotle, for in the first book of the *Politics* Aristotle attempted to replace reliance on the gods (who are not discussed[17]) with the opinion that the city is self-sufficient, i.e., self-sufficient without the gods. This opinion had the consequence that economic acquisition could be limited by political and moral requirements,

15 See esp. *Capital*, I, 364–8.
16 Marx, *On the Jewish Question*, in Colletti ed., *Early Writings*, 218–21; Georg Lukács, *History and Class Consciousness*, R. Livingstone trans. (Cambridge, MA, 1971), 83–110
17 Aristotle, *Politics*, 1252b2, 25–8; 1252a2–5, 29; 1253b36; 1259b14

and hence that economics could be subordinated to politics. But Locke, in repeating Aristotle's attempt to replace religion with politics, did it differently. As opposed to Aristotle, Locke denied that the city could be made self-sufficient and that economics could be ruled by politics. He emancipated economic acquisition to the point that he made it appear – and he certainly said – that government is formed to preserve property rather than *vice versa*. None the less, for Locke as for Aristotle, economics serves political ends.

In the *First Treatise*, Locke shows that the question of property is the question of religion. For the fundamental question in regard to property is whether man has a right to property or not: not whether some men have a right of property against other men, or whether property is private or social. If any particular man or men are to have property, man himself must have property, and this is disputable. As for Marx religion is the means and effect of political force, so for Locke the necessity of political power reflects the priority of the religious question: is man such a creature as belongs, together with everything that belongs to him, to his Creator? It is only after answering this question negatively in the *First Treatise* that Locke is ready to consider at length in the *Second Treatise* what political power is and how private property may be acquired.[18]

This is not to say that Locke gives his negative answer to the question whether man is the property of God definitively. On the contrary, as is his habit in matters of religion, he leaves one trail for the sceptical and another for the pious, the latter more plainly marked but leading in circles, so that eventually the pious will have to follow the sceptics' trail if they wish to get anywhere. On the one hand, he says to the pious (and to those suspicious of his own piety) that man is the workmanship of God and hence God's property (I, 39, 40, 52, 53; II, 6, 56); on the other, he says that 'every Man has a *Property* in his own *Person*' (II, 27, 44). In accordance with the conclusion that man is God's property, Locke reminds us that in the Bible, Noah, and not Adam, was permitted the full power to use or enjoy other creatures in the sense of destroying them, i.e., of eating them[19]; but in accordance with his assertion that man is his own property, Locke announces that he 'doubts not' that 'Man had a right to a use of the Creatures' before the verbal donation to Noah (I, 86). Why does Locke not doubt his correction of the Bible on this point?

Man being the 'Image of his Maker', he, 'the whole species of Man', is the chief inhabitant of the Earth and has 'Dominion over the other Creatures' (I, 40). But it appears that men (even including philosophers and anatomists)

18 Political power is defined in Locke, *Two Treatises of Government*, I, 48, but see I, 129 and II, 3–4.

19 Ibid., I, 27, 39, 40, 92, 97; II, 31. There is no right to destroy in the sense of spoil.

are ignorant of the structure and working of this image, or 'admirable engine', and especially of 'that Operation wherein Life consists in the whole' (1, 52). While deprecating the power of fathers over the children they beget, because begetting a child is so much less than making a human being, Locke makes one wonder what power the Creator has over His creatures. Man was made as an 'admirable engine' and then, it seems, was in addition given a 'living soul' or a 'living and rational soul' or a 'rational soul' (1, 53, 55).[20] Despite this possession or implantation, Locke stresses in the same context that man, misled by fancy and passion, is often not guided by reason, 'his only Star and compass,' and acts contrary to both nature and God. And even when man uses his reason, also called *'the voice of God in him'* (1, 86), it is to serve his 'strong' desire, nay his 'first and strongest desire' (1, 88), for self-preservation.[21] For in serving this desire with his reason, he cannot but suppose that he follows 'the Will of his Maker' when he exercises his property in other creatures, which 'was founded upon the right he had, to make use of those things, that were necessary or useful to his Being' (1, 86, 97). What is necessary and useful to Man's being, therefore, considering that each man is a whole and has a self to preserve, is in accordance with God's will. Though making might seem far more original than begetting, God cannot have property in an image He made of Himself any more than a parent can have property in a child. On the contrary, as making is more original than begetting, the duty of the Maker to preserve his creatures is greater than the duty of parents to preserve their children. God seems to have performed this duty by implanting in man a strong desire of self-preservation, as in all other animals, and to have distinguished man by the gift of reason instead of instinct. Man uses this gift to learn the will of God in so far as God's will is assumed to allow man to pursue his natural inclination for self-preservation, which is what reason 'could not but teach him and assure him' (1, 86). Locke does not say that reason enables man to pursue an end that distinguishes him from all other animals. Reason is man's star and compass, part natural and part artificial, his guide in taking him where he wants to go or in showing him what he wants to have (II, 30). We may conclude that God made men for the sake of their own self-preservation,[22]

20 On the soul, see also ibid., II, 212, 239; and *An Essay Concerning Human Understanding*, II, 1, sections 9–21; II, 27, section 27; IV, 3, section 6. The question of the soul's immateriality has political importance in so far as it affects the question whether men have 'mean Souls fitted ... for slavery' (*Two Treatises*, II, 239).
21 Death is the 'severest penalty.' *Two Treatises*, I, 56.
22 And for propagating their like, which may get in the way of self-preservation (ibid., I, 56, end) or may not. (I, 27, 57).

and that they follow the will of their Maker when they regard themselves as their own property.

Man, then, not being the property of God, has received no property from God. Man's only gifts are the desire for self-preservation and the reason to effect it which are in his own nature and could not have been withheld by any Maker of such as himself. Above all, man's divine inheritance does not include government by Providence; and, as Locke makes clear in his arguments against Filmer, no human government can claim to rule by divine right. First, God gave the earth to 'the whole Species of Man' (I, 23, 24, 29–39), not merely to Adam and not merely to Noah and his sons (I, 27). God, therefore, did not establish either monarchy or aristocracy (the latter we infer); on the contrary, He made men free, or so that they were naturally free, of government.

Second, when God did give some men government over other men in paternal power, He confused paternal power with parental. Locke is obliged to scold Filmer again and again for forgetting to honour his mother, contrary to divine command, because of his eagerness to join or identify paternal and monarchial power. Moreover, paternal power, like the power of creating human beings, is limited by the character of the product. Men are bound to preserve what they have begotten, but since they have begotten their own like, and their own like are each an equal, separate whole, they are not awarded rule merely for 'the bare *act of begetting*' (II, 65), as Locke calls it. Hence paternal power, a power to preserve, cannot reach to political power, the power of life and death. God did not supply men with rule when He gave them fathers.

Third, God did not provide for an orderly succession of government in men, which is the conclusion of the last chapter of the *First Treatise* (chap. 11), quaintly entitled 'Who Heir?' God gave the earth to all mankind, but then He suffered mankind to become divided into distinct nations with independent governments established by conquest rather than inheritance. Similarly, mankind is divided into families where the children have a natural right of inheritance of property over the rest of mankind outside the family (I, 89); but among those children God left no sign of preference,[23] and primogeniture as a rule of succession in government must be accounted a human institution (I, 140), if perhaps the kind of custom that becomes sacred (I, 58). If God had prescribed the manner of human inheritance, He would have left a rule (i.e., a sign that is a rule) to determine who precisely inherits: 'For the word *Heir*, without a Rule to know who it is, signifies no more than

---

23 See ibid., I, 111, where we discover Locke not as kind to daughters as he is elsewhere to mothers.

somebody, I know not whom' (I, 128). To say, then, that God has appointed no recognizable inheritance among men is also to say that God has appointed no Heir among men; and the two kinds of divine providence, personal and at a distance, are denied.

The premise of these arguments is a state of nature, mentioned once in the *First Treatise* (I, 90) but expressly presented as the foundation of political power or civil society in the *Second Treatise* (II, 4), where men may or may not have been placed by Creation, but where they surely live each separate and independent, a whole to himself, unranked with his like. In order to ensure that men's right of property in animals does not extend to property in or government over other men, Locke sees to it that the distinguishing property of men from animals, their reason, is not used to distinguish men from men. Wisdom is no title to rule, as it is with Plato and Aristotle.[24] 'Thus we are *born Free*, as we are born Rational' (II, 61): as free as rational, but none so rational as to destroy the freedom of other men. There is no heir to govern us,[25] but rather a law of nature that is a rule of reason; and that rule of reason, accessible to all, teaches equality to all in the state of nature. The law of nature may be studied, Locke says,[26] implying unequal rationality in the studiers and so also in the law they study. But at least in the state of nature it is plain that, all being equal, each has a right to defend himself and at the same time a duty to punish others, on behalf of mankind, for transgressing the law of nature, because any offence against each is thereby 'a trespass against the whole Species' (II, 8).

The condition, however, in which each is executioner of the law of nature for all is fraught with inconveniences 'which must certainly be Great' (II, 13). Each man is naturally his own property, but all are equally; and so the property that is man's must be defended by each man. It is not hard to imagine that the property each man defends he will come to consider his own, and the easy identification of the whole of each man with the whole of the species will not succeed. What is needed is a new whole that secures property for mankind as well as property for each. It will have to be a conventional whole, created by men, because God's Creation or nature's provision leaves men in great inconveniences. But because it is conventional, some arbitrariness will have to be accepted, especially the dividing of mankind into distinct nations (which God had permitted anyway). Yet still more arbitrariness will be removed by convention, especially the levelling of mankind imposed by the pretence that all are equally rational.[27] In civil

24 Plato, *Republic*, 473d; *Laws*, 690b–c; Aristotle, *Nicomachean Ethics*,
   1140b10–11; *Politics*, 1287a29–34. Locke, *Two Treatises*, II, 54
25 Consider the summary of the *First Treatise* in II, 1.
26 Ibid., II, 12, 124
27 Macpherson, *The Political Theory of Possessive Individualism*, 232–8.

society, inequality will flourish and men will be ranked, roughly of course, according to the standard by which they are distinguished from other animals. But the ranking will preserve freedom: what gives men property in other animals will not give them property in each other but only more property for some of them, than for others. Fundamental equality in the desire for self-preservation, or better to say, in the desire for freedom, will be maintained because the possession of reason (as man's property) is not allowed to become the reason for ruling.

If a convention is accepted as necessary for freedom, perhaps it would be well to have men regard each other as God's property so that they will respect each other because they respect God. Locke considers this possibility, but advances it only to the extent that regarding other men as God's property is consistent with regarding oneself as one's own property, 'when [one's] own preservation comes not in competition' (II, 6). Regarding himself as God's property may remind a man 'not to quit his Station wilfully', but Locke does not ask anyone to become a martyr against his own preservation or even to make a sacrifice to his loss. It is rather that Locke does not scorn the force of divine command as it may operate to recommend all convenient charity[28] and every exertion of industry.[29] Duty is not rejected, but it is scaled down to right, and right made identical with self-preservation. More than this is dangerous, for when men are regarded as God's property, one must contend with the claims of the guardians of God's property, the priests. They are very inclined to seize 'an occasion of working upon another's necessity, to save his Life, or any thing dear to him, at the rate of his Freedom' (I, 43).

Locke, therefore, constructs the necessary convention, in the chapter on property in the *Second Treatise*, on the ground that 'every *Man* has a *Property* in his own *Person*', which 'no Body has any Right to but himself' (II, 27). God, then, does not have property in men, unless God is not a body; but God's agents are surely excluded. Locke proceeds to show how 'Men might come to have a *property* in several parts of that which God gave to mankind in common, and that without any express Compact of all the Commoners' (II, 25). That is, he explains the origin of property, and after it the origin of society, without reliance on divine providence or on man's distinctive rationality. His account omits both the Garden of Eden and the Fall, sliding them into a condition of necessity which forces men to appropriate from nature by labour.[30] Labour appears to be distinctively human, but Locke does not say so expressly. He does not say why the labour of man's body is properly his (II, 27) but the labour of a horse is not properly its (II,

28 Locke, *Two Treatises*, I, 42, II, 5–6
29 Ibid., II, 32, 34–5
30 Leo Strauss, *Natural Right and History* (Chicago, 1953), 215–16, 238

28). Human labour is no doubt rational, and human beings, it turns out, must be rational in addition to industrious (II, 34); but Locke's reliance is on labour rather than rationality. This allows him to find a beginning for property in a capacity all humans can exercise, which indeed, in the penury of their condition, they *must* exercise, without undue pride toward each other. If men had instituted property with an express compact, their rationality would have been ahead of their necessity and their distinctiveness would have been too divisive for themselves. Locke wants a human but not a teleological explanation of property.

Labour, then, is a beginning principle that is distinctively human without being divisive. Because labour is the work of one's own body, it creates private property; and in labouring in the state of nature, one man, if he does not *take* from other men, at least secures his property from other men. Property right at this time requires that there be 'enough and as good left' (II, 33), for if there were not, it would require an express compact; but the difference in value between unimproved common property and improved private property may be so great (Locke implies that labour will make an infinite approximation to all value[31]) that a great supply of nature's 'almost worthless materials' (II, 43) will still leave the lazy and incompetent in need. In so far as labour makes private property, it would seem to be divisive, at least potentially.

But labour, in making property private, also improves it. Such improvement is an addition to the stock of all mankind, because one cannot improve one's private property without improving others' property; improvement or increase is the correction of the inevitable privateness of property. Improvement would not be possible if men could not sell their labour, as distinguished from their bodies. No owner can improve his property very much by himself, and the alienation of labour gives effect to human sociality, allowing men to work together peaceably, again without emphasizing rationality as the basis of community.

Not emphasizing rationality as the basis of community is compatible with, or the same as, recognizing equal pretensions to rationality as the basis of community. Locke allows himself to be impressed more with men's common possession of the faculty of reason in their 'State of Maturity' (II, 59) than with inequality in the extent or use of it. To repeat, although Locke does not deny the superior right of those with more rationality, he denies that their superior right gives title to rule and confines that right to the acquistion of unequal property. He couples together 'the Industrious and

31 Locke, *Two Treatises*, II, 40, 43. On 'increase' see Robert A. Goldwin, 'John Locke', in Leo Strauss and Joseph Cropsey eds., *History of Political Philosophy* (Chicago, 1963), 450–3.

Rational' (I, 34) as much to constrain the potential tyranny of reason as to give reason a profitable occupation.[32]

When men improve on nature with their labour to make property, they *appropriate* from nature. To lay due stress on appropriation, Locke discusses food and agriculture, rather than arts and manufacture, in the chapter on property. He says that the *'chief matter of property'* is 'the Earth it self' (II, 32) and that improving the Earth meant subduing it.[33] Labour is the beginning principle that subdues nature; it comes out of necessity but it appropriates necessity for the benefit of human life. Accordingly, Locke's example of a modern, sophisticated commodity is not a coat, which is Marx's example in *Capital*, but a loaf of bread. Locke lists a 'strange *Catalogue*' of materials industry makes use of for a loaf of bread, including those made use of in the ship that brought any of them (II, 43), for even this product of the earth is assembled across waters. Locke's point is not the division of labour but the mixing and reconstitution of natural materials in a human product that sums them up. In his example he stays away from arts (if bakery is an art) that induce one to suppose that the task of human industry is the perfection of nature. Men do not seek out and assume the purposes of nature so as to carry them out; they appropriate nature to supply their needs, as if swallowing it. The human economy is made universal through exchange, as with Marx, but exchange value is clearly subordinated to use value and the Lockean commodity does not become a fetish.[34] Behind it the power of man remains visible.

So much is the right of property that labour gave in the beginning (II, 45). It is a natural right as opposed to a divine right, and it does not rest on convention. But this is not the property right that prevails in civil society, which is to be found in settled laws. Before laws are settled, indeed before society is agreed to, men have consented to the convention of money. Money is necessary for improvement, for without money industry is limited to the quantity of perishables that will not spoil. With money, men will enlarge, in order to improve, their possessions of land; so money becomes the object of those who enclose land, which was said to be the chief matter of property. And as money makes improvement possible (by making it reasonable for men who regard themselves as their own property), it also makes unequal property just, since the one who gets more need not, and will not, take away from others.

Since money is a convention, depending on 'Fancy or Agreement', and

32 On the superiority of mental labour to physical labour in Locke, see J.E. Parsons Jr., 'Locke's Doctrine of Property', *Social Research*, vol. 36 (1969), 409; and Giuseppe Zarone, *John Locke; Scienza e forma della politica* (Bari, 1975), 49.
33 Cf. Spinoza, *Political Treatise*, VII, 19.
34 Marx, *Capital*, I, 72

necessary to improvement, it can no longer be said that labour determines value (though it remains 'in great part, *the measure*,' II, 50); for one thing, the labour of 'the Industrious and Rational' is now duly and unequally rewarded. Yet, although money is adopted by a 'tacit and voluntary consent' (II, 50), it is not deliberately chosen by express compact and Locke seems to allow that money is almost inevitable because it will be adopted wherever there is some thing that could serve as money (II, 48). He plots a careful course between arriving at property without human agency and achieving it by the full exercise of human reason, since either extreme could imply a gift by divine providence.[35] The result is consent to unequal property which is said to be without controversy. Throughout the chapter on property Locke emphasizes the lack of controversy in establishing property right, beginning with labour that requires no consent and proceeding to money that requires no express compact.[36] This evident exaggeration[37] is corrected later (II, 123); here it serves to show that men can determine property on their own.

Conflict, when it comes, is made to arise out of 'paternal power', the subject of the chapter following which prepares the seventh chapter of the *Second Treatise*, 'Of Political or Civil Society'. In discussing paternal power, Locke rehearses the arguments of the *First Treatise* and quickly arrives at an emphatic distinction between paternal and political power which is immediately applied to the inheritance of property. Whether paternal power is considered as an obligation on fathers to provide or on children to obey, it is incomplete without inherited property, which must be settled by laws, that is, by political power. While money is the convention that permits property to be passed around, inheritance is the convention that permits it to be passed along. Locke has civil society and political power arise out of the settlement of inheritance, not, as he might easily have done, out of disputes over the inequalities introduced by money. One may discern the reason for this in the opportunity afforded by the topic of inheritance to contrast the shortcomings of divinely instituted paternal power to the advantages of humanly instituted political power. While money is the non-divine convention of property, inheritance is the anti-divine convention.

In the seventh chapter Locke says for the first time, and incidentally to a remark on slaves, that 'the chief end [of Society] is the preservation of Property' (II, 85). That capacity for property is the mark or perhaps even the definition of a free man as opposed to a slave, and that society is necessary to property, were at most implicit in the discussion of the chapter on property;

35 Note especially the ambiguity in 'his own' between a man's and Man's. *Two Treatises*, II, 44
36 Ibid., II, 31–4, 39, 45, 50, 51
37 Note the present tense in ibid., II, 50, which brings men to the present without controversy, followed by the past tense in II, 51, which returns this idyllic state of affairs to the beginning.

now we are abruptly informed of the need for political power. Moreover, we are also given, for the first time, the enlarged definition of property as 'Life, Liberty and Estate' (II, 87), no notice of which was given in the chapter on property.[38] Property is suddenly announced to be the human good, to preserve which is the end of civil society. The preservation of property means 'the preservation of the property of all the Members of ... society, as far as is possible' (II, 88). This is done when 'any number of Men, in the state of Nature, enter into Society to make one People, one Body Politick, under one Supreme Government' (II, 89).

Men 'incorporate' to make one body politic.[39] They agree, or pretend, that they are one body, an artificial, conventional body that makes each not merely a number in all but also a member (though not a part) of the whole. The whole to which men belong is bodily, the end of which is announced to be external goods inflated to include all human goods. The body politic has its soul, the legislative power[40] that passes laws settling property. To settle property, it will be necessary to take some of it in taxation[41]; but taxing is justified to preserve the whole, so long as taxpayers consent to the government that represents them as a whole. In society, men consent by majority rule because 'the *act of the Majority* passes for the act of the whole' (II, 96); the will of society is the will of the majority.

Property is the protection of consent, not because property will be inviolate in Locke's society but because it cannot be taken without the consent of the majority. Property is therefore not merely or chiefly what supplies men's needs; it is what keeps men free. Security of property protects freedom even against conquerors (II, 193–4), and freedom is the fence to life (II, 17). The difference between political and despotical power can be stated in terms of property: political power is 'where Men have Property in their own disposal; and *Despotical* over such as have no property at all' (II, 174).[42] This does not mean that property (in the narrow sense) is more valuable than life or liberty; it means that property is the convention that best protects them. For when life and liberty are at stake, they are already in jeopardy. Locke's reasoning, one may assume, is that it is better to elevate a lesser good, and to pay the price of an increased love of gain and a somewhat arbitrary status for property and the propertied than to endanger the greater goods by endeavouring to protect them directly.

Freedom will always have to be defended with strong government, and this is as true of Locke's society as of any previous one. Although the law of nature makes all mankind into one community, civil society incorporates

38 See also ibid., II, 123, 173.
39 Ibid., II, 38, 89, 95, 99, 101, 120, 121, 128, 145, 178, 211
40 Ibid., II, 212
41 Ibid., II, 138, 140, 170
42 See Xenophon, *Cyropaideia*, VIII, 1, 20, 2.8, 15–19.

men into distinct communities opposed to one another.[43] But government can be kept from invading freedom, or resisted when it does, by property understood as an effectual whole: when anyone's property is taken without his consent, property as a whole is attacked and the people as a body can see or can be made to see this clearly.[44] In this way property, having its origin prior to society, can serve in the dissolution of society, when government acts contrary to its trust, to facilitate mutual defence without and against government. Property is a pre-political convention with, but not created for, a political end. In civil society property has its own laws, the laws of 'natural market value' which resist political intrusion and maintain the independence of property from government despite its need of protection by the government.[45] Property can be pre-political and so have its political end because of its natural basis in human labour, but for Locke, human labour and the laws of human labour do not issue of necessity in laws of distribution. Thus they cannot quantify or overcome the qualitative distinction between the state of nature and civil society, between necessity and freedom. To be free, men must make use of their reason, but at the cost of tolerating their unreason.

Marx's aim was to complete and purify political economy by finally creating, or announcing, what is known today as 'the economy'. But he did not intend merely to refurbish a part of society. He meant to usher in the economy in the sense of a universal non-political whole of free exchange, operating according to its own laws which in turn operate according to human will. Following the post-Lockean political economists, he abandoned Locke's distinction between the state of nature and civil society, in his attempt to find autonomous laws determining the economy and to expel every trace of convention that would be political in origin. He believed, of course, that the bourgeois conventions of property had become, not the defender, but the chief enemy of freedom, and he could think of no other way to restore freedom than to abolish convention altogether. Proletarian class consciousness, derived from Marxian science, was to be truly reflective of the fundamental reality of human control. Whether he was successful in this may be judged, in part, from the fact that class consciousness as a force in itself – as a convention necessary to political action – has been the point of departure for neo-Marxism.

43 Locke, *Two Treatises*, II, 128, 145, 217, 239. See Willmoore Kendall, *John Locke and the Doctrine of Majority Rule* (Urbana, II, 1959), 79.
44 Locke, *Two Treatises*, II, 221, 222. Cf. the distinction between political and civil law in Montesquieu, *De l'esprit des lois*, XXVI, 15.
45 Locke, *Some Considerations of the Consequences of the Lowering of Interest and Raising the Value of Money*, in *Works*, 3 vols. (London, 1740), II, 19–23, 51. Locke did not put these restrictive laws into the *Second Treatise*, his justification of political power. Zarone, *John Locke*, 131–4.

Atomism

I would like to examine the issue of political atomism, or at least to try to clarify what this issue is. I want to say what I think atomist doctrines consist in, and to examine how the issue can be joined around them – that is, how they might be proved or disproved, or at least cogently argued for or against, and what in turn they may be used to prove.

The term 'atomism' is used loosely to characterize the doctrines of social contract theory which arose in the seventeenth century and also successor doctrines which may not have made use of the notion of social contract but which inherited a vision of society as in some sense constituted by individuals for the fulfilment of ends which were primarily individual. Certain forms of utilitarianism are successor doctrines in this sense. The term is also applied to contemporary doctrines which hark back to social contract theory, or which try to defend in some sense the priority of the individual and his rights over society, or which present a purely instrumental view of society.

Of course, any term loosely used in political discourse can be defined in a host of ways. And perhaps one should even leave out of philosophical discourse altogether those terms which tend to be branded as epithets of condemnation in the battle between different views. One might well argue that 'atomism' is one such, because it seems to be used almost exclusively by its enemies. Even extreme individualists like Nozick don't seem to warm to this term, but tend to prefer others, like 'individualism'.

Perhaps I am dealing with the wrong term. But there is a central issue in political theory which is eminently worth getting at under some description. And perhaps the best way of getting at it is this: what I am calling atomist doctrines underlie the seventeenth-century revolution in the terms of normative discourse, which we associate with the names of Hobbes and Locke.

These writers, and others who presented social contract views, have left us a legacy of political thinking in which the notion of rights plays a central part in the justification of political structures and action. The central doctrine of this tradition is an affirmation of what we could call the primacy of rights.

Theories which assert the primacy of rights are those which take as the fundamental, or at least a fundamental, principle of their political theory the ascription of certain rights to individuals and which deny the same status to a principle of belonging or obligation, i.e., a principle which states our obligation as men to belong to or sustain society, or a society of a certain type, or to obey authority or an authority of a certain type. Primacy-of-right theories in other words accept a principle ascribing rights to men as binding unconditionally,[1] binding, that is, on men as such. But they do not accept as similarly unconditional a principle of belonging or obligation. Rather our obligation to belong to or sustain a society, or to obey its authorities, is seen as derivative, as laid on us conditionally, through our consent, or through its being to our advantage. The obligation to belong is derived in certain conditions from the more fundamental principle which ascribes rights.[2]

The paradigm of primacy-of-right theories is plainly that of Locke. But there are contemporary theories of this kind, one of the best known in recent years being that of Robert Nozick.[3] Nozick too makes the assertion of rights to individuals fundamental and then proceeds to discuss whether and in what conditions we can legitimately demand obedience to a state.

1 The words 'conditional/unconditional' may mislead, because there are certain theories of belonging, to use this term for them, which hold that our obligation to obey, or to belong to a particular society, may in certain circumstances be inoperative. For instance, medieval theories which justified tyrannicide still portrayed man as a social animal and were thus theories of belonging in the sense used here. But they allowed that in certain circumstances our obligation to obey that authority by which our society cohered was abrogated, and that when the ruler was a tyrant he might be killed. In this sense we could say that the obligation to obey was 'conditional'. But this is not the same as a theory of the primacy of right. For in theories of belonging it is clear that men *qua* men have an obligation to belong to and sustain society. There may be a restriction on what kind of society would fulfil the underlying goal, and from this a licence to break with perverted forms; but the obligation to belong itself was fundamental and unconditional; it held 'by nature'. In primacy-of-right theories the notion is that simply by nature we are under no obligation to belong whatever; we have first to contract such an obligation.

2 This may not be true of all doctrines which found a political theory on an affirmation of natural right – a point which is particularly relevant in the context of this collection. For the new doctrine of human rights which Professor Macpherson envisages in, for example, *Democratic Theory: Essays in Retrieval* (Oxford, 1973) 236, and which would free itself of 'the postulate of the inherent and permanent contentiousness of men' would seem to involve an affirmation of individual rights which presuppose society, rather than merely setting the boundary conditions of its possible legitimacy.

3 *Anarchy, State and Utopia* (Boston, 1974)

Primacy-of-right theories have been one of the formative influences on modern political consciousness. Thus arguments like that of Nozick have at least a surface plausibility for our contemporaries and sometimes considerably more. At the very least, opponents are brought up short, and have to ponder how to meet the claims of an argument, which reaches conclusions about political obedience which lie far outside the common sense of our society; and this because the starting point in individual rights has an undeniable *prima facie* force for us.

This is striking because it would not always have been so. In an earlier phase of Western civilization, of course, not to speak of other civilizations, these arguments would have seemed wildly eccentric and implausible. The very idea of starting an argument whose foundation was the rights of the individual would have been strange and puzzling – about as puzzling as if I were to start with the premise that the Queen rules by divine right. You might not dismiss what I said out of hand, but you would expect that I should at least have the sense to start with some less contenious premise and argue up to divine right, not take it as my starting point.

Why do we even begin to find it reasonable to start a political theory with an assertion of individual rights and to give these primacy? I want to argue that the answer to this question lies in the hold on us of what I have called atomism. Atomism represents a view about human nature and the human condition which (among other things) makes a doctrine of the primacy of rights plausible; or to put it negatively, it is a view in the absence of which this doctrine is suspect to the point of being virtually untenable.

How can we formulate this view? Perhaps the best way is to borrow the terms of the opposed thesis – the view that man is a social animal. One of the most influential formulations of this view is Aristotle's. He puts the point in terms of the notion of self-sufficiency (*autarkeia*). Man is a social animal, indeed a political animal, because he is not self-sufficient alone, and in an important sense is not self-sufficient outside a polis. Borrowing this term then we could say that atomism affirms the self-sufficiency of man alone or, if you prefer, of the individual.

That the primacy-of-rights doctrine needs a background of this kind may appear evident to some; but it needs to be argued because it is vigorously denied by others. And generally proponents of the doctrine are among the most vigorous deniers. They will not generally admit that the assertion of rights is dependent on any particular view about the nature of man, especially one as difficult to formulate and make clear as this. And to make their political theory dependent on a thesis formulated in just this way seems to be adding insult to injury. For if atomism means that man is self-sufficient alone, then surely it is a very questionable thesis.

What then does it mean to say that men are self-sufficient alone? That they would survive outside of society? Clearly, lots of men would not. And the best and luckiest would survive only in the most austere sense that they would not succumb. It would not be living as we know it. Surely proponents of the primacy of rights don't have to deny these brute facts. Just because one would fail a survival course and not live for a week if dropped north of Great Slave Lake with only a hatchet and a box of (waterproof) matches, does one have to stop writing books arguing for the minimal state on the basis of the inviolable rights of the individual?

Under the impact of this rhetorical question, one might be tempted to conclude that the whole effort to find a background for the arguments which start from rights is misguided. They don't seem to have anything to do with any beliefs. If we take the widely held view that normative questions are autonomous and not to be adjudicated by factual considerations, then why shouldn't a normative position in which rights are the ultimate standard be combinable with any set of factual beliefs about what men can and cannot do, and what society does or does not do for them?

From this point of view it would be a matter of uninteresting historical accident that the great classical theorists of atomism also held to some strange views about the historicity of a state of nature in which men lived without society. Indeed, one could argue that even they were not committed to the self-sufficiency of man as we defined the issue in the above paragraph. It was not only Hobbes who saw man's life in the state of nature as nasty, brutish, and short. All social contract theorists stressed the great and irresistible advantages that men gained from entering society. And in the case of Locke, one could claim that even his state of nature was not one of self-sufficiency in the sense of our survivor north of Great Slave Lake; rather it was clearly a condition of exchange and fairly developed and widespread social relations, in which only political authority was lacking.

Perhaps then we shouldn't look for a background at all, and the whole enterprise of this paper is misguided. Readers who are convinced by this argument should, of course, stop here. But I am convinced that there is a lot more to be said.

To begin with, what is at stake is not self-sufficiency in the Great Slave Lake sense, but rather something else. What has been argued in the different theories of the social nature of man is not just that men cannot physically survive alone, but much more that they only develop their characteristically human capacities in society. The claim is that living in society is a necessary condition of the development of rationality, in some sense of this property, or of becoming a moral agent in the full sense of the term, or of becoming a fully responsible, autonomous being. These variations and other similar ones represent the different forms in which a thesis about man as a social animal have been or could be couched. What they have in common is the view that outside society, or in some variants outside certain kinds of society, our distinctively human capacities could not develop. From the standpoint of this thesis, too, it is irrelevant whether an organism born from a human womb would go on living in the wilderness; what is important is that this organism could not realize its specifically human potential.

But, one might argue, all this too is irrelevant to the individual-rights argument. Such argument is as independent of any thesis about the conditions of development of human potential, whatever this is, as it is of the conditions of survival in the wilderness. The argument simply affirms that justification of political authority ought to start from a foundation of individual rights. The proof of this independence is usually taken to be this: that plainly we do not deny rights to beings born of woman who lack the fully developed human potential, for instance infants. And if one objects that these are on the way to develop to full humanity, the reply is that we accord rights to lunatics, people in a coma, people who are irreversibly senile, and so on. Plainly, in our ordinary attribution of rights, we accord them to human beings as such, quite regardless of whether they have developed such potential or not. And so why should any thesis about the conditions for developing such potential be relevant to arguments about such rights?

The answer is that the question is not closed by the reflection that we attribute rights to idiots. It can nevertheless be the case that our conception of the human specific potential is an essential part of the background of our ascription of rights. Why, for instance, do we ascribe them to human beings, and not to animals, trees, rocks, and mountains? Someone might reply that some people do want to ascribe them to animals. Nozick himself is among their number, in fact. But an examination of this position will help make the case I want to plead.

Why ascribe rights to animals? Or if this sounds too bizarre, why claim that it is wrong to kill or inflict pain on animals? The answer commonly given is that they are sentient beings. But this concept of sentience is not as simple as it looks, as those who have argued this position readily acknowledge. We can't take it to mean simply 'capable of feeling pain', and argue from that common factor that we ought not to inflict pain on any sentient being; because in fact we want to claim more: we would not agree, if there were some utterly painless way of killing, say by a laser-ray, that vegetarians ought to drop their objections to killing cattle for food, let alone that it would be licit to kill people for the convenience of others or for the demands of progress (though in the human case, the argument would be complicated by the anxiety about being a potential victim of the laser-ray).

'Sentience' here has to mean something more; it has to mean something like 'capable of enjoying life and one's various capacities', where 'enjoying' has something like its old-fashioned or legal sense, as in 'enjoying the use of one's limbs', rather than its narrower colloquial sense of having a good time. Sentience in this sense involves some kind of self-awareness or self-feeling; and the intuition underlying a prohibition on killing animals is that this capacity ought to be respected wherever it exists and that one ought not to snuff it out or seriously impair it in beings who have it.

The point that emerges from this reflection is that attributing rights to animals is bound up with discerning in them a capacity which we sense we must respect, in the sense of 'respect' used in the previous paragraph, i.e., that it is something which we ought to foster and which we are forbidden to impair. Nor is the relation simply this, that the content of the rights we accord (e.g., to life or to the unimpaired use of limbs) restricts them to these beings, since others (e.g., rocks and mountains) couldn't exercise these rights. For that a given being has capacity c is not a sufficient condition of our according it a right to c. The sand on certain beaches tends to form in dunes, but no one would claim that in levelling it out for the tourists we are violating any rights.

Rather the intuition, if we want to call it such or whatever we want to say lies behind the conviction that certain beings have rights to a, b, or c, is that these beings exhibit a capacity which commands respect, which capacity helps determine the shape of the rights, or what the rights are rights to. Once we accept that beings with this capacity command respect, then indeed, it is sufficient that we identify a as possessing this capacity to make a a bearer of rights. And it is clearly always a necessary condition as well of bearing those rights, if only because what the rights are to will be defined in relation to the capacity. But the mere possession of the capacity will have no normative consequences at all for us if we do not share the conviction that this capacity commands respect.

I apologize to the non-vegetarian for this long excursus into the rights of animals. But perhaps it will help us to make clear the point about the rights of man, that they too are ascribed in virtue of a capacity which also helps to determine their shape. Even the strongest defenders of animal rights will agree that men have different rights – e.g., the right to free choice of their religious or metaphysical convictions, to will their property, and so on. And it is not a sufficient explanation of this difference that animals cannot do these things; most animals cannot scratch themselves in the small of their backs, but this doesn't induce us to inscribe this capacity in the UN Charter. Rather, the intuition that men have the right to life, to freedom, to the unmolested profession of their own convictions, to the exercise of their moral or religious beliefs, is but another facet of the intuition that the life-form characterized by these specifically human capacities commands our respect.[4]

Beings with these capacities command our respect, because these capacities are of special significance for us; they have a special moral status. And from this we can see why the schedule of rights is what it is: life, of course, is protected, because these beings are life-forms, and so are integrity of limb and freedom protected from molestation for the same reason. But the schedule also includes protection for those activities which realize the specifically human capacities; and hence we have a right to our own convictions, the practice of our religion, and so on.

In other words, our conception of the specifically human is not at all irrelevant to our ascription of rights to people. On the contrary, there would be something incoherent and incomprehensible in a position which claimed to ascribe rights to men but which disclaimed any conviction about the special moral status of any human capacities whatever and which denied that they had any value or worth.[5]

But, an opponent might object, what if we do admit that in asserting a right we affirm that a certain form of life or certain capacities command our respect? What are we allowing over and above the conviction that these capacities are the basis of right? What else does this commit us to? For surely,

---

4 I don't pretend to have given a satisfactory formulation here to what it is in human beings which commands our respect. That is far from an easy task. Cf. the interesting discussion in ibid., chap. 3, 48–51, and also the discussion preceding. But while a satisfactory general formulation eludes us, we can readily agree on some of the specifically human capacities, and this is enough to state my argument.

5 There is indeed a position which is approached by utilitarians which makes sentience the ground of right (or rather its weak utilitarian analogue, the status of a being whose desires and interests are to be weighed in moral calculations) and thus would in its extreme form deny any special consideration to humans as against other animals. But this is linked to the conviction that sentience commands our respect, that it enjoys this special moral status. And indeed, in a position of this kind the incoherence will break out elsewhere, in the schedule of human rights which will be difficult to square with the reduction of human beings and animals to the same level. How to justify the assertion of the right to one's own moral or religious convictions? Perhaps with drugs of a certain kind people could be made very happy, even euphoric, while they were induced to profess almost anything to please whomever they were with. We would still feel that injecting them with these drugs was a violation of their rights. Cf. an analogous point by Nozick – 'the experience machine' in ibid., 42–5. But this right to one's own convictions cannot be squared with the notion that sentience alone is the basis of right. And this difficulty of extreme utilitarianism shows how the affirmation of rights is bound up with the conviction that certain capacities are of special worth.

the normative consequences in either case are the same: viz., that we should refrain from violating the rights of any beings with these capacities.

But in fact the normative consequences are broader, and this is what the second formula brings out. To say that certain capacities command respect or have worth in our eyes is to say that we acknowledge a commitment to further and foster them. We do not just acknowledge people's (and/or animals') right to them, and hence the negative injunction that we ought not to invade or impair the exercise of these capacities in others. We also affirm that it is good that such capacities be developed, that under certain circumstances we ought to help and foster their development, and that we ought to realize them in ourselves.

It is true, of course, that the scope of this affirmation of worth will not be very great in the limiting case where we take sentience as the basis of right, because sentience is a capacity which, broadly speaking, either exists or does not in a given being; it is not a potential which needs to be developed and which can be realized to greater or lesser degree. Even here, however, the affirmation of worth still says something more than the assertion of right; it says, for instance, that other things being equal it is good to bring sentient beings into the world.

In the case where we are dealing with the full schedule of human rights, the scope of the affirmation of worth becomes significantly greater. To affirm the worth of the human capacity to form moral and religious convictions goes far beyond the assertion of the right to one's convictions. It also says that I ought to become the kind of agent who is capable of authentic conviction, that I ought to be true to my own convictions and not live a lie or a self-delusion out of fear or for favour, that I ought in certain circumstances to help foster this capacity in others, that I ought to bring up my own children to have it, that I ought not to inhibit it in others by influencing them towards a facile and shallow complaisance, and so on. This is because we are dealing with a characteristically human capacity which can be aborted or distorted or underdeveloped or inhibited or, alternatively, can be properly realized or even realized to an exemplary degree.

The claim I am trying to make could be summed up in this way: 1/ To ascribe the natural (not just legal) right of x to agent A is to affirm that A commands our respect, such that we are morally bound not to interfere with A's doing or enjoying of x. This means that to ascribe the right is far more than simply to issue the injunction: don't interfere with A's doing or enjoying x. The injunction can be issued, to self or others, without grounds, should we so choose. But to affirm the right is to say that a creature such as A lays a moral claim on us not to interfere. It thus also asserts something about A: A is such that this injunction is somehow inescapable.

2/ We may probe further and try to define what it is about A which makes the injunction inescapable. We can call this, whatever it is, A's essential property or properties, E. Then it is E (in our case, the essentially human capacities) which defines not only who are the bearers of rights but what they have rights to. A has a natural right to x, if doing or enjoying x is essentially part of manifesting E (e.g., if E is being a rational life-form, then A's have a natural right to life and also to the unimpeded development of rationality); or if x is a causally necessary condition of manifesting E (e.g., the ownership of property, which has been widely believed to be a necessary safeguard of life or freedom, or a living wage).

3/ The assertion of a natural right, while it lays on us the injunction to respect A in his doing or enjoying of x, cannot but have other moral consequences as well. For if A is such that this injunction is inescapable and he is such in virtue of E, then E is of great moral worth and ought to be fostered and developed in a host of appropriate ways, and not just not interfered with.

Hence asserting a right is more than issuing an injunction. It has an essential conceptual background, in some notion of the moral worth of certain properties or capacities, without which it would not make sense. Thus, for example, our position would be incomprehensible and incoherent, if we ascribed rights to human beings in respect of the specifically human capacities (such as the right to one's own convictions or to the free choice of one's life-style or profession) while at the same time denying that these capacities ought to be developed, or if we thought it a matter of indifference whether they were realized or stifled in ourselves or others.

From this we can see that the answer to our question of a few pages ago (why do we ascribe these rights to men and not to animals, rocks, or trees?) is quite straightforward. It is because men and women are the beings who exhibit certain capacities which are worthy of respect. The fact that we ascribe rights to idiots, people in a coma, bad men who have irretrievably turned their back on the proper development of these capacities, and so on, does not show that the capacities are irrelevant. It shows only that we have a powerful sense that the status of being a creature defined by its potential for these capacities cannot be lost. This sense has been given a rational account in certain ways, such as for instance by the belief in an immortal soul. But it is interestingly enough shared even by those who have rejected all such traditional rationales. We sense that in the incurable psychotic there runs a current of human life, where the definition of 'human' may be uncertain but relates to the specifically human capacities; we sense that he has feelings that only a human being, a language-using animal can have, that his dreams and fantasies are those which only a human can have. Pushed however deep, and however distorted, his humanity cannot be eradicated.

If we look at another extreme case, that of persons in a terminal but long-lasting coma, of the kind exhibited by the recent plight of Karen Quinlan, it would seem that the sense that many have that the life-support machines should be disconnected is based partly on the feeling that the patient herself, should she *per impossibile* be able to choose, would not want to continue, precisely because the range of human life has been shrunk here to zero.

How does the notion then arise that we can assert rights outside of a context of affirming the worth of certain capacities? The answer to this question will take us deep into the issue central to modern thought of the nature of the subject. We can give but a partial account here. There clearly are a wide number of different conceptions of the characteristically human capacities and thus differences too in what are recognized as rights. I will come back to this in another connection later.

But what is relevant for our purposes here is that there are some views of the properly human which give absolutely central importance to the freedom to choose one's own mode of life. Those who hold this ultra-liberal view are chary about allowing that the assertion of right involves any affirmation about realizing certain potentialities; for they fear that the affirming of any obligations will offer a pretext for the restriction of freedom. To say that we have a right to be free to choose our life-form must be to say that any choice is equally compatible with this principle of freedom and that no choices can be judged morally better or worse by this principle – although, of course, we might want to discriminate between them on the basis of other principles.

Thus if I have a right to do what I want with my property, then any disposition I choose is equally justifiable from the point of view of this principle: I may be judged uncharitable if I hoard it to myself and won't help those in need, or uncreative if I bury it in the ground and don't engage in interesting enterprises with it. But these latter criticisms arise from our accepting other moral standards, quite independent from the view that we have a right to do what we want with our own.

But this independence from a moral obligation of self-realization cannot be made good all around. All choices are equally valid; but they must be *choices*. The view that makes freedom of choice this absolute is one that exalts choice as a human capacity. It carries with it the demand that we become beings capable of choice, that we rise to the level of self-consciousness and autonomy where we can exercise choice, that we not remain enmired through fear, sloth, ignorance, or superstition in some code imposed by tradition, society, or fate which tells us how we should dispose of what belongs to us. Ultra-liberalism can only appear unconnected with any affirmation of worth and hence obligation of self-fulfilment, where people have come to accept the utterly facile moral psychology of traditional empiricism, according to which human agents possess the full capacity of choice as a given rather than as a potential which has to be developed.

If all this is valid, then the doctrine of the primacy of rights is not as independent as its proponents want to claim from considerations about human nature and the human social condition. For the doctrine could be undermined by arguments which succeeded in showing that men were not self-sufficient in the sense of the above argument – that is, that they could not develop their characteristically human potentialities outside of society or outside of certain kinds of society. The doctrine would in this sense be dependent on an atomist thesis, which affirms this kind of self-sufficiency.

The connection I want to establish here can be made following the earlier discussion of the background of rights. If we cannot ascribe natural rights without affirming the worth of certain human capacities, and if this affirmation has other normative consequences (i.e., that we should foster and nurture these capacities in ourselves and others), then any proof that these capacities can only develop in society or in a society of a certain kind is a proof that we ought to belong to or sustain society or this kind of society. But then, provided a social (i.e., an anti-atomist) thesis of the right kind can be true, an assertion of the primacy of rights is impossible; for to assert the rights in question is to affirm the capacities, and granted the social thesis is true concerning these capacities, this commits us to an obligation to belong. This will be as fundamental as the assertion of rights, because it will be inseparable from it. So that it would be incoherent to try to assert the rights, while denying the obligation or giving it the status of optional extra which we may or may not contract; this assertion is what the primacy doctrine makes.

The normative incoherence becomes evident if we see what it would be to assert the primacy of rights in the face of such a social thesis. Let us accept, for the sake of this argument, the view that men cannot develop the fullness of moral autonomy – that is, the capacity to form independent moral convictions – outside a political culture sustained by institutions of political participation and guarantees of personal independence. In fact, I don't think this thesis is true as it stands, although I do believe that a much more complicated view, formed from this one by adding a number of significant reservations, is tenable. But for the sake of simplicity let us accept this thesis in order to see the logic of the arguments.

Now if we assert the right to one's own independent moral convictions, we cannot in the face of this social thesis go on to assert the primacy of rights, that is, claim that we are not under obligation 'by nature' to belong to and sustain a society of the relevant type. We could not, for instance, unreservedly assert our right in the face of, or at the expense of, such a society; in the event of conflict we should have to acknowledge that we were legitimately pulled both ways. For in undermining such a society we should be making the activity defended by the right assertion impossible of realization. But if we are justified in asserting the right, we cannot be justified in our undermining; for the same considerations which justify the first condemn the second.

In whatever way the conflict r ˙ ght arise it poses a moral dilemma for us. It may be that we have already been formed in this culture and that the demise of this mode of society will not deprive us of this capacity. But in asserting our rights to the point of destroying the society, we should be depriving all those who follow after us of the exercise of the same capacity. To believe that there is a right to independent moral convictions must be to believe that the exercise of the relevant capacity is a human good. But then it can't be right, if no over-riding considerations intervene, to act so as to make this good less available to others, even though in so doing I could not be said to be depriving them of their rights.

The incoherence of asserting primacy of rights is even clearer if we imagine another way in which the conflict could arise: that, in destroying the society, I would be undermining my own future ability to realize this capacity. For then in defending my right, I should be condemning myself to what I should have to acknowledge as a truncated mode of life, in virtue of the same considerations that make me affirm the right. And this would be a paradoxical thing to defend as an affirmation of my rights – in the same way as it would be paradoxical for me to offer to defend you against those who menace your freedom by hiding you in my deep freeze. I would have to have misunderstood what freedom is all about; and similarly in the above case, I should have lost my grasp of what affirming a right is.

We could put the point in another way. The affirmation of certain rights involves us in affirming the worth of certain capacities and thus in accepting certain standards by which a life may be judged full or truncated. We cannot then sensibly claim the morality of a truncated form of life for people on the ground of defending their rights. Would I be respecting your right to life if I agreed to leave you alive in a hospital bed, in an irreversible coma, hooked up to life-support machines? Or suppose I offered to use my new machine to erase totally your personality and memories and give you quite different ones? These questions are inescapably rhetorical. We can't take them seriously as genuine questions because of the whole set of intuitions which surround our affirmation of the right to life. We assert this right because human life has a certain worth; but exactly wherein it has worth is negated by the appalling conditions I am offering you. That is why the offer is a sick joke, the lines of the mad scientist in a B movie.

It is the mad scientist's question, and not the question whether the person in the coma still enjoys rights, which should be decisive for the issue of whether asserting rights involves affirming the worth of certain capacities. For the latter question just probes the conditions of a right being valid; whereas the former shows us what it is to respect a right and hence what is really being asserted in a rights claim. It enables us to see what else we are committed to in asserting a right.

How would it do for the scientist to say, 'Well, I have respected his right to *life*, it is other rights (free movement, exercise of his profession, etc.) which I have violated'? For the separation in this context is absurd. True, we do sometimes enumerate these and other rights. But the right to life could never have been understood as excluding all these activities, as a right just to biological non-death in a coma. It is incomprehensible how anyone could assert a right to life meaning just this. 'Who calls that living?' would be the standard reaction. We could understand such an exiguous definition of life in the context of forensic medicine, for instance, but not in the assertion of a right to life. And this is because the right-assertion is also an affirmation of worth, and this would be incomprehensible on behalf of this shadow of life.

If these arguments are valid, then the terms of the argument are very different from what they are seen to be by most believers in the primacy of rights. Nozick, for instance, seems to feel that he can start from our intuitions that people have certain rights to dispose, say, of what they own so long as they harm no one else in doing so; and that we can build up (or fail to build up) a case for legitimate allegiance to certain forms of society and/or authority from this basis, by showing how they do not violate the rights. But he does not recognize that asserting rights itself involves acknowledging an obligation to belong. If the above considerations are valid, one cannot just baldly start with such an assertion of primacy. We would have to show that the relevant potentially mediating social theses are not valid; or, in other terms, we would have to defend a thesis of social atomism, that men are self-sufficient outside of society. We would have to establish the validity of arguing from the primacy of right.

But we can still try to resist this conclusion. And this in two ways. We can resist it first of all in asserting a certain schedule of rights. Suppose I make the basic right I assert that to life, on the grounds of sentience. This I understand in the broad sense that includes also other animals. Now sentience, as was said above, is not a capacity which can be realized or remain undeveloped; living things have it, and in dying they fail to have it; and there's an end to it. This is not to say that there are not conditions of severe impairment which constitute an infringement on sentient life, short of death. And clearly a right to life based on sentience would rule out accepting the mad scientist's offer just as much as any other conception of this right. But sentient life, while it can be impaired, is not a potential which we must develop and frequently fail to develop, as is the capacity to be a morally autonomous agent, or the capacity for self-determining freedom, or the capacity for the full realization of our talents.

But if we are not dealing with a capacity which can be undeveloped in this sense, then there is no room for a thesis about the conditions of its development, whether social or otherwise. No social thesis is relevant. We are sentient beings whatever the social organization (or lack of it) of our existence; and if our basic right is to life, and the grounds of this right concern sentience (being capable of self-feeling, of desire and its satisfaction/frustration, of experiencing pain and pleasure), then surely we are beings of this kind in any society or none. In this regard we are surely self-sufficient.

I'm not sure that even this is true – that is, that we really are self-sufficient even in regard to sentience. But it certainly is widely thought likely that we are. And therefore it is not surprising that the turn to theories of the primacy of rights goes along with an accentuation of the right to life which stresses life as sentience. For Hobbes our attachment to life is our desire to go on being agents of desire. The connection is not hard to understand. Social theories require a conception of the properly human life which is such that we are not assured it by simply being alive, but it must be developed and it can fail to be developed; on this basis they can argue that society or a certain form of society is the essential condition of this development. But Hobbesian nominalism involves rejecting utterly all such talk of forms or qualities of life which are properly human. Man is a being with desires, all of them on the same level. 'Whatsoever is the object of any man's desire ... that is it which he for his part calleth good'.[6] At one stroke there is no further room for a social thesis; and at the same time the right to life is interpreted in terms of desire. To be alive now in the meaning of the act is to be an agent of desires.

So we can escape the whole argument about self-sufficiency, it would seem, by making our schedule of rights sparse enough. Primacy-of-rights talk tends to go with a tough-mindedness which dismisses discussion of the properly human life-form as empty and metaphysical. From within its philosophical position, it is impregnable; but this doesn't mean that it is not still open to objection.

For the impregnability is purchased at a high price. To affirm a right for man merely *qua* desiring being, or a being feeling pleasure and pain, is to restrict his rights to those of life, desire-fulfilment, and freedom from pain.

6 *Leviathan*, I, chap. 6

Other widely claimed rights, like freedom, enter only as means to these basic ones. If one is a monster of (at least attempted) consistency, like Hobbes, then one will be willing to stick to this exiguous conception of rights regardless of the consequences. But even then the question will arise of what on this view is the value of human as against animal life; and of whether it really is not a violation of people's rights if we transform them, unknown to themselves, into child-like lotus-eaters, say, by injecting them with some drug.

In fact, most of those who want to affirm the primacy of rights are more interested in asserting the right of freedom, and moreover, in a sense which can only be attributed to humans, freedom to choose life plans, to dispose of possessions, to form one's own convictions and within reason act on them, and so on. But then we are dealing with capacities which do not simply belong to us in virtue of being alive – capacities which at least in some cases can fail to be properly developed; thus the question of the proper conditions for their development arises.

We might query whether this is so with one of the freedoms mentioned above – that to dispose of one's own possessions. This is the right to property which has figured prominently with the right to life in the schedules put forward by defenders of primacy. Surely this right, while not something we can attribute to an animal, does not presuppose a capacity which could fail to be developed, at least for normal adults! We all are capable of possessing things, of knowing what we possess, and of deciding what we want to do with these possessions. This right does not seem to presuppose a capacity needing development, as does the right to profess independent convictions, for instance.

But those who assert this right almost always are affirming a capacity which we can fail to develop. And this becomes evident when we probe the reason for asserting this right. The standard answer, which comes to us from Locke, is that we need the right to property as an essential underpinning of life. But this is patently not true. Men have survived very well in communal societies all the way from paleolithic hunting clans through the Inca empire to contemporary China. And if one protests that the issue is not under what conditions one would not starve to death, but rather under what conditions one is independent enough of society not to be at its mercy for one's life, then the answer is that, if the whole point is being secure in my life, then I would be at less risk of death from agents of my own society in the contemporary Chinese commune than I would be in contemporary Chile. The property regime is hardly the only relevant variable.

But the real point is this: supposing a proponent of the right to property were to admit that the above was true – that the right to property does not as such secure life – would he change his mind? And the answer is, in the vast majority of cases, no. For what is at stake for him is not just life, but life in freedom. My life is safe in a Chinese commune, he might agree, but that is so only for so long as I keep quiet and don't profess heterodox opinions; otherwise the risks are very great. Private property is seen as essential, because it is thought to be an essential part of a life of genuine independence. But realizing a life of this form involves developing the capacity to act and choose in a genuinely independent way. And here the issue of whether a relevant social thesis is not valid can arise.

Hence this way of resisting the necessity of arguing for self-sufficiency (by scaling down one's schedules of rights to mere sentience or desire) is hardly likely to appeal to most proponents of primacy – once they understand the price they pay. For it involves sacrificing the central good of freedom, which it is their principal motive to safeguard.

There remains another way of avoiding the issue. A proponent of primacy could admit that the question arises of the conditions for the development of the relevant capacities; he could even agree that a human being entirely alone could not possibly develop them (this is pretty hard to contest: wolf-boys are not candidates for properly human freedoms), and yet argue that society in the relevant sense was not necessary.

Certainly humans need others in order to develop as full human beings, he would agree. We must all be nurtured by others as children. We can only flourish as adults in relationship with friends, mates, children, and so on. But all this has nothing to do with any obligations to belong to political society. The argument about the state of nature should never have been taken as applying to human beings alone in the wilderness. This is a Rousseauian gloss, but is clearly not the conception of the state of nature with Locke, for instance. Rather it is clear that men must live in families (however families are constituted); that they need families even to grow up human; and that they continue to need them to express an important part of their humanity.

But what obligations to belong does this put on them? It gives us obligations in regard to our parents. But these are obligations of gratitude, and are of a different kind; for when we are ready to discharge these obligations our parents are no longer essential conditions of our human development. The corresponding obligations are to our children, to give them what we have been given; and for the rest we owe a debt to those with whom we are linked in marriage, friendship, association, and the like. But all this is perfectly acceptable to a proponent of the primacy of rights. For all obligations to other adults are freely taken on in contracting marriage, friendships, and the like; there is no natural obligation to belong. The only involuntary associations are those between generations: our obligations to our parents and those to our children (if we can think of these as involuntary associations, since no one picks his children in the process of natural generation). But these are obligations to specific people and do not necessarily involve continuing associations; and they are neither of them cases where the obligation arises in the way it does in the social thesis, viz., that we must maintain the association as a condition of our continued development.

Hence we can accommodate whatever is valid in the social thesis without any danger to the primacy of rights. Family obligations and obligations of friendship can be kept separate from any obligations to belong.

I don't think that this argument will hold. But I can't really undertake to refute it here, not just on the usual cowardly grounds of lack of space, but because we enter here precisely on the central issue of the human condition which divides atomism from social theories. And this issue concerning as it does the human condition cannot be settled in a knockdown argument. My purpose in this paper was just to show that it is an issue, and therefore has to be addressed by proponents of primacy. For this purpose I'd like to lay out some considerations to which I subscribe, but of which I can do no more than sketch an outline in these pages.

The kind of freedom valued by the protagonists of the primacy of rights, and indeed by many others of us as well, is a freedom by which men are capable of conceiving alternatives and arriving at a definition of what they really want, as well as discerning what commands their adherence or their allegiance. This kind of freedom is unavailable to one whose sympathies and horizons are so narrow that he can conceive only one way of life, for whom indeed the very notion of a way of life which is *his* as against everyone's has no sense. Nor is it available to one who is riveted by fear of the unknown to one familiar life-form, or who has been so formed in suspicion and hate of outsiders that he can never put himself in their place. Moreover, this capacity to conceive alternatives must not only be available for the less important choices of one's life. The greatest bigot or the narrowest xenophobe can ponder whether to have Dover sole or Wiener schnitzel for dinner. What is truly important is that one be able to exercise autonomy in the basic issues of life, in one's most important commitments.

Now, it is very dubious whether the developed capacity for this kind of autonomy can arise simply within the family. Of course, men may learn, and perhaps in part must learn, this from those close to them. But my question is whether this kind of capacity can develop within the compass of a single family. Surely it is something which only develops within an entire civilization. Think of the developments of art, philosophy, theology, science, of the evolving practices of politics and social organization, which have contributed to the historic birth of this aspiration to freedom, to making this ideal of autonomy a comprehensible goal men can aim at – something which is in their universe of potential aspiration (and it is not yet so for all men, and may never be).

But this civilization was not only necessary for the genesis of freedom. How could successive generations discover what it is to be an autonomous agent, to have one's own way of feeling, of acting, of expression, which cannot be simply derived from authoritative models? This is an identity, a way of understanding themselves, which men are not born with. They have to acquire it. And they do not in every society; nor do they all successfully come to terms with it in ours. But how can they acquire it unless it is implicit in at least some of their common practices, in the ways that they recognize and treat each other in their common life (for instance, in the acknowledgment of certain rights), or in the manner in which they deliberate with or address each other, or engage in economic exchange, or in some mode of public recognition of individuality and the worth of autonomy?

Thus we live in a world in which there is such a thing as public debate about moral and political questions and other basic issues. We constantly forget how remarkable that is, how it did not have to be so, and may one day no longer be so. What would happen to our capacity to be free agents if this debate should die away, or if the more specialized debate among intellectuals who attempt to define and clarify the alternatives facing us should also cease, or if the attempts to bring the culture of the past to life again as well as the drives to cultural innovation were to fall off? What would there be left to choose between? And if the atrophy went beyond a certain point, could we speak of choice at all? How long would we go on understanding what autonomous choice was? Again, what would happen if our legal culture were not constantly sustained by a contact with our traditions of the rule of law and a confrontation with our contemporary moral institutions? Would we have as sure a grasp of what the rule of law and the defence of rights required?

In other words, the free individual or autonomous moral agent can only achieve and maintain his identity in a certain type of culture, some of whose facets and activities I have briefly referred to. But these and others of the same significance don't come into existence spontaneously each successive instant. They are carried on in institutions and associations which require stability and continuity and frequently also support from society as a whole – almost always the moral support of being commonly recognized as important but frequently also considerable material support. These bearers of our culture include museums, symphony orchestras, universities, laboratories, political parties, law courts, representative assemblies, newspapers, publishing houses, television stations, and so on. And I have to mention also the mundane elements of infrastructure without which we couldn't carry on these higher activities: buildings, railroads, sewage plants, power grids, and so on. Thus the requirement of a living and varied culture is also the requirement of a complex and integrated society, which is willing and able to support all these institutions.[7]

I am arguing that the free individual of the West is only what he is by virtue of the whole society and civilization which brought him to be and which nourishes him; that our families can only form us up to this capacity and these aspirations because they are set in this civilization; and that a family alone outside of this context – the real old patriarchal family – was a quite different animal which never tended to develop these horizons. And I want to claim finally that all this creates a significant obligation to belong for whoever would affirm the value of this freedom; this includes all those who want to assert rights either to this freedom or for its sake.

One could answer this by saying that the role of my civilization in forming me is a thing of the past; that, once adult, I have the capacity to be an autonomous being; and that I have no further obligation arising out of the exigencies of my development to sustain this civilization. I doubt whether this is in fact true; I doubt whether we could maintain our sense of ourselves as autonomous beings or whether even only a heroic few of us would succeed in doing so, if this liberal civilization of ours were to be thoroughly destroyed. I hope never to have to make the experiment. But even if we could, the considerations advanced a few pages back would be sufficient here: future generations will need this civilization to reach these aspirations; and if we affirm their worth, we have an obligation to make them available to others. This obligation is only increased if we ourselves have benefited from this civilization and have been enabled to become free agents ourselves.

But then the proponent of primacy could answer by questioning what all

7 This is what makes so paradoxical the position of someone like Robert Nozick. He presents (cf. *Anarchy, State and Utopia*, particularly chap. 10) the model of an ideal society where within the framework of the minimal state individuals form or join only those associations which they desire and which will admit them. There is no requirement laid down concerning the over-all pattern that will result from this. But can we really do without this? The aim of Nozick's utopian framework is to enable people to give expression to their real diversity. But what if the essential cultural activities which make a great diversity conceivable to people begin to falter? Or are we somehow guaranteed against this? Nozick doesn't discuss this; it is as though the conditions of a creative, diversifying freedom were given by nature. In this respect the standard utopian literature, which as Nozick says is concerned with the character of the ideal community and not just with a framework for any community, is more realistic. For it faces the question of what kind of community we need in order to be free men, and then goes on to assume that this is given non-coercively.

this has to do with political authority, with the obligation to belong to a polity or to abide by the rules of a political society. Certainly, we could accept that we are only what we are in virtue of living in a civilization and hence in a large society, since a family or clan could not sustain this. But this doesn't mean that we must accept allegiance to a polity.

To this there are two responses. First, there is something persuasive about this objection in that it seems to hold out the alternative of an anarchist civilization – one where we have all the benefits of wide association and none of the pains of politics. And indeed, some libertarians come close to espousing an anarchist position and express sympathy for anarchism, as does Nozick. Now it is perfectly true that there is nothing in principle which excludes anarchism in the reflection that we owe our identity as free men to our civilization. But the point is that the commitment we recognize in affirming the worth of this freedom is a commitment to this civilization whatever are the conditions of its survival. If these can be assured in conditions of anarchy, that is very fortunate. But if they can only be assured under some form of representative government to which we all would have to give allegiance, then this is the society we ought to try to create and sustain and belong to. For this is by hypothesis the condition of what we have identified as a crucial human good, by the very fact of affirming this right. (I have, of course, taken as evident that this civilization, could not be assured by some tyrannical form of government, because the civilization I am talking about is that which is the essential milieu for free agency.)

The crucial point here is this: since the free individual can only maintain his identity within a society/culture of a certain kind, he has to be concerned about the shape of this society/culture as a whole. He cannot, following the libertarian anarchist model that Nozick sketched,[8] be concerned purely with his individual choices and the associations formed from such choices to the neglect of the matrix in which such choices can be open or closed, rich or meagre. It is important to him that certain activities and institutions flourish in society. It is even of importance to him what the moral tone of the whole society is – shocking as it may be to libertarians to raise this issue – because freedom and individual diversity can only flourish in a society where there is a general recognition of their worth. They are threatened by the spread of bigotry, but also by other conceptions of life – e.g., those which look on originality, innovation, and diversity as luxuries which society can ill afford given the need for efficiency, productivity, or growth, or those which in a host of other ways depreciate freedom.

Now, it is possible that a society and culture propitious for freedom might arise from the spontaneous association of anarchist communes. But it seems

8 Ibid., chap. 10

much more likely from the historical record that we need rather some species of political society. And if this is so then we must acknowledge an obligation to belong to this kind of society in affirming freedom. But there is more. If realizing our freedom partly depends on the society and culture in which we live, then we exercise a fuller freedom if we can help determine the shape of this society and culture. And this we can only do through instruments of common decision. This means that the political institutions in which we live may themselves be a crucial part of what is necessary to realize our identity as free beings.

This is the second answer to the last objection. In fact, men's deliberating together about what will be binding on all of them is an essential part of the exercise of freedom. It is only in this way that they can come to grips with certain basic issues in a way which will actually have an effect in their lives. Those issues, which can only be effectively decided by society as a whole and which often set the boundary and framework for our lives, can indeed be discussed freely by politically irresponsible individuals wherever they have licence to do so. But they can only be truly *deliberated* about politically. A society in which such deliberation was public and involved everyone would realize a freedom not available anywhere else or in any other mode.

Thus, always granted that an anarchist society is not an available option, it is hard to see how one can affirm the worth of freedom in this sense of the exercise of autonomous deliberation and at the same time recognize no obligation to bring about and sustain a political order of this kind.

The argument has gone far enough to show how difficult it is to conclude here. This is because we are on a terrain in which our conception of freedom touches on the issue of the nature of the human subject, and the degree and manner in which this subject is a social one. To open this up is to open the issue of atomism, which is all I hoped to do in this paper. I wanted to show that there is an issue in the 'self-sufficiency' or not of man outside political society and that this issue cannot be side-stepped by those who argue from natural rights. This issue, as we can see, leads us very deep, and perhaps we can see some of the motivation of those who have waited to side-step it. It seems much easier and clearer to remain on the level of our intuitions about rights.

For we can now see more clearly what the issue about atomism is, and how uncommonly difficult it is. It concerns self-sufficiency, but not in the sense of the ability to survive north of Great Slave Lake. That is a question whether we can fulfil certain causal conditions for our continued existence. But the alleged social conditions for the full development of our human capacities are not causal in the same sense. They open another set of issues altogether: whether the condition for the full development of our capacities is not that we achieve a certain identity, which requires a certain conception of ourselves; and more fundamentally whether this identity is ever something we can attain on our own, or whether the crucial modes of self-understanding are not always created and sustained by the common expression and recognition they receive in the life of the society.

Thus the thesis just sketched about the social conditions of freedom is based on the notion, first, that developed freedom requires a certain understanding of self, one in which the aspirations to autonomy and self-direction become conceivable; and second, that this self-understanding is not something we can sustain on our own, but that our identity is always partly defined in conversation with others or through the common understanding which underlies the practices of our society. The thesis is that the identity of the autonomous, self-determining individual requires a social matrix, one for instance which through a series of practices recognizes the right to autonomous decision and which calls for the individual having a voice in deliberation about public action.

The issue between the atomists and their opponents therefore goes deep; it touches the nature of freedom, and beyond this what it is to be a human subject; what is human identity, and how it is defined and sustained. It is not surprising therefore that the two sides talk past each other. For atomists the talk about identity and its conditions in social practice seems impossibly abstruse and speculative. They would rather found themselves on the clear and distinct intuition which we all share (all of us in this society, that is) about human rights.

For non-atomists, however, this very confidence in their starting point is a kind of blindness, a delusion of self-sufficiency which prevents them from seeing that the free individual, the bearer of rights, can only assume this identity thanks to his relationship to a developed liberal civilization; that there is an absurdity in placing this subject in a state of nature where he could never attain this identity and hence never create by contract a society which respects it. Rather, the free individual who affirms himself as such *already* has an obligation to complete, restore, or sustain the society within which this identity is possible.

It is clear that we can only join this issue by opening up questions about the nature of man. But it is also clear that the two sides are not on the same footing in relationship to these questions. Atomists are more comfortable standing with the intuitions of common sense about the rights of individuals and are not at all keen to open these wider issues. And in this they derive support in those philosophical traditions which come to us from the seventeenth century and which started with the postulation of an extensionless subject, epistemologically a *tabula rasa* and politically a presupposition-less bearer of rights. It is not an accident that these epistemological and political doctrines are often found in the writings of the same founding figures.

But if this starting point no longer appears to us self-evident, then we have to open up questions about the nature of the subject and the conditions of human agency. Among these is the issue about atomism. This is important for any theory of rights, but also for a great deal else besides. For the issue about atomism also underlies many of our discussions about obligation and the nature of freedom, as can already be sensed from the above. That's why it is useful to put it again on our agenda.

Justifying Political Obligation

Political theorists today usually agree that political obligation poses a problem in the sense that it requires justification. Yet they are also almost unanimously agreed that there are no really serious or intractable difficulties in providing a justification for the authority of the liberal-democratic state or the political obligation of its citizens. Indeed, a few theorists have even gone so far as to claim that to suggest that political obligation requires a justification, to suggest that it genuinely does pose a general problem, is to show oneself as conceptually confused and in a state of philosophical disorder. I have taken issue with the latter claim elsewhere.[1] In this paper I shall argue that not only is it a mistake to suppose that few problems exist in justifying political obligation in the liberal-democratic state, but that the justifications most frequently offered do not provide a solution to the problem. Political theorists typically appeal to voluntarist arguments that are, as I shall show, integrally bound up with the valued liberal principles of individual freedom and equality. These arguments cannot provide a justification of political obligation in the liberal-democratic state. Instead, they lead to the conclusion that it is only within a participatory or self-managing form of democracy that a justified political obligation can exist.

In discussing political obligation in the liberal-democratic state, theorists almost invariably rely on some form of voluntarism. Appeal is made to consent, contract, agreement, commitment or promises, or, more broadly, to the voluntary actions of individuals that, it is held, give rise to political obligation. That is to say, political theorists usually assume that political obligation is a form of self-assumed obligation, or a moral commitment

This essay is a slightly revised version of a paper presented to the Annual Meeting of the Australasian Political Studies Association, Armidale, NSW, in 1977.

1 'Political Obligation and Conceptual Analysis', *Political Studies*, XXI (1973), 199–218

freely entered into by individuals and freely taken upon themselves by their own actions. Underlying this assumption is a view of liberal democracy as a certain kind of society, with a specific kind of inhabitant, a view that has been nicely summed up by Rawls who writes that liberal democracy comes 'as close as a society can to being a voluntary scheme ... its members are autonomous and the obligations they recognize self-imposed.'[2] However, a striking feature of contemporary discussions of political obligation is that the question is rarely asked of exactly *why* voluntarism, or the ideas of consent, agreement, and promising, are so important; why must obligations be self-assumed or self-imposed? An answer to this question is required if the magnitude of the problem of justifying political obligation in the liberal-democratic state is to be appreciated.

Political theories in which consent and the associated idea of the social contract were central and fundamental became prominent, as everyone knows, in the seventeenth and eighteenth centuries. Nor is this surprising. Political ideas and concepts, notwithstanding the way in which they are treated by so many political theorists, do not exist in a separate, timeless world of their own, but help constitute specific forms of social life. Social contract and consent theories were formulated at a time of great socio-economic development and change, at a time when the capitalist market economy and the liberal constitutional state were beginning to emerge. As part of these developments, individuals and their relationships began to be seen in a new and revolutionary way. The contract theorists began their arguments from the premise that individuals are 'born free and equal' or are 'naturally' free and equal to each other. Such a conception was in complete contrast to the long-prevailing view that people were born into a God-created and 'natural' hierarchy of inequality and subordination. Within this traditional perspective, although disputes could frequently arise about the scope of specific rulers' right of command, there was scarcely room for general doubts about political obedience; rulers and political obedience were part of God's way with the world. But once the idea gained currency that individuals were born free and equal or were 'naturally' so (and how were they freely to enter contracts and make equal exchanges in the market, and pursue their interests as they saw fit, if they were not?) then a very large question was also raised about political authority and political obedience.

The social contract theorists were very well aware of the problem that liberal individualism brought with it; namely, how and why any free and equal individual could legitimately be governed by anyone else at all. The full implications of this subversive query have not, even today, fully worked themselves out; consider, for example, the argument of the feminists that

2 J. Rawls, *A Theory of Justice* (Oxford 1972), 13

there is no good reason for the widely held belief that a free and equal individual woman should be subject to the authority of the man whom she marries. Moreover, the emergence of this basic question means that the security in which political authority and political obedience were wrapped for so long can never return. To avoid misunderstanding I should note here that I am not, like the philosophical anarchists, arguing that a completely unbridgeable gulf exists between political authority and individual autonomy, or individual freedom and equality.[3] I am not claiming that an acceptable answer to this fundamental question of government is impossible and that political obligation is an irrelevant concept. Rather, I am arguing that political obligation can be justified – and that it always requires justification – but that the only acceptable justification has implications that most writers on the subject neglect to investigate.

Given the initial postulate of individual freedom and equality there is only *one* rational and acceptable justification for political obligation and political authority. Individuals must themselves consent, contract, agree, choose, or promise to enter such a relationship. Political authority must have its basis in individuals' own voluntary actions, or, to put this the other way round, they must freely assume their political obligation for themselves. With the development of liberal individualism the relationship between individual and government has to be transformed from one of mere *obedience*, however engendered, into one of *obligation*, into a relationship in which individuals are bound by their own free acts. But political obligation then becomes a general problem; it can never be taken for granted, and a very specific justification is always required. The frequency with which voluntarist justifications are encountered in discussions of political obligation illustrates how reluctant theorists are to give up the liberal heritage bequeathed by the contract theorists. It also illustrates the widely held assumption that political obligation in the liberal-democratic state can quite easily be justified in the appropriate manner. However, most theorists display an extremely ambiguous attitude to the voluntarist justification of political obligation, although the ambiguity is not usually acknowledged.

It is frequently argued that whether or not individuals have agreed, consented, or promised, they do nevertheless have a justified political obligation in the liberal-democratic state. This claim both upholds the assumption

---

3 A recent example of the philosophical anarchist argument can be found in P. Abbott, *The Shotgun behind the Door* (Athens, GA, 1976). R.P. Wolff, *In Defense of Anarchism* (New York, 1970) is equivocal about his philosophical anarchism. In the final section of the book he suggests that a solution to the problem of autonomy and authority can be found in institutions based on 'voluntary compliance'.

that political obligation in a liberal democracy is unproblematic and avoids
the notorious difficulties of specifying who performed these actions, when,
and how. An especially memorable instance of this line of argument can be
found in Tussman's *Obligation and the Body Politic*. He argues that the
liberal democratic state should be seen as a voluntary association in which
membership is based on consent. But he also states that not all citizens
consent; some (the majority?) are 'child-bride citizens' who, like minors, are
governed without their own consent. Yet these citizens too have a justified
political obligation, although Tussman does not inform us as to its basis. It
appears then, that despite the apparent importance of consent, voluntarism is
of only limited relevance to political life – and that political 'obligation' does
not seem to be the appropriate characterization of the relation between all
citizens and the state after all.

In our everyday lives the paradigmatic way in which we assume an
obligation is by making a promise. When an individual says 'I promise ...' he
or she has assumed an obligation and has committed himself or herself to
perform (or refrain from) certain actions. Political theorists have often
suggested that political obligation is like, or rests upon, or is a special kind of,
a promise. But this is to assume once more that the relationship between
citizens and the liberal democratic state is indeed a form of self-assumed
obligation. The comparison between political obligation and the social practice of promising is usually drawn in very general terms, and is rarely
pursued. Yet it is precisely through a consideration of this comparison that
the full extent of the problem of political obligation in the liberal democratic
state is revealed. In recent years moral philosophers have paid a good deal of
attention to promising. Here, I can mention only some aspects of promising
that are of particular importance for the present argument.[4]

Making promises is one of the most basic ways in which free and equal
individuals can freely create their own social relationships. As part of their
social and moral education individuals learn how to take part in the social
practice of promising and so develop as persons with certain kinds of
capacities. These capacities include the ability to engage in the rational and
reasoned deliberation required to decide whether, on this occasion, a promise
ought to be made, and also the ability to look back and critically evaluate their
own actions and relationships; sometimes a promise may justifiably be
broken or altered or revised in some way. Now, if political obligation is like,
or is a form of, promising there is an important question to be asked; namely,
how can citizens assume their political, like their other, obligations for

4 A detailed discussion of the social practice of promising and its relationship to
  political obligation and to contracts can be found in C. Pateman, *The Problem of
  Political Obligation: A Critical Analysis of Liberal Theory* (Chichester, 1979).

themselves; what form of political system would make this possible? In short, it must be asked what is the political counterpart of the social practice of promising.

In political life voting is the practice that enables individuals to engage in reasoned deliberation and decide for themselves how to order their political lives and environment. The result of a vote, like that of a promise, is a commitment or an obligation, although in the case of voting it will be a collective not an individual commitment. However, this abstract and conceptual connection between voting in general and political obligation does not tell us the specific form that voting must take if a political practice of self-assumed obligation is to exist. Political theorists frequently suggest that a liberal-democratic form of voting is required and I shall present some further objections to this suggestion later. At present it is sufficient to point out that, for the analogy with promising to hold, voting must enable individuals collectively to decide upon their political obligation for themselves. It is a direct or participatory democratic form of voting that allows them to do this. It is within a participatory form of democracy that individuals retain their political decision-making power as citizens. They exercise political authority over themselves in their private capacity as individuals (something which many people find an odd idea, so used are we to thinking of representatives exercising political authority over citizens), and they collectively commit themselves, or freely obligate themselves, to do whatever is necessary to implement their own decisions and to maintain their self-managed political association in being. It is also a participatory democratic form of voting that, like promising, enables citizens politically to exercise their capacity to reflect upon and evaluate their own actions and decisions and, if necessary, to change them. Thus, the liberal principle of individual freedom and equality and its corollary of self-assumed obligation lead towards and provide a justification for participatory, not liberal, democracy.

There are two further points that should be made here. The first, to which I shall return, is that political obligation, in a participatory democracy, is owed to fellow citizens and not to the state or its representatives. To whom else could it be owed? Second, it is important to emphasize that the question now being considered is *not* the question asked in recent discussions of political obligation. Theorists do not usually ask what are the political consequences of the ideal of self-assumed obligation – that would presuppose that there is a problem! Instead, following from their assumption that political obligation is justified in the liberal democratic state, they (implicitly) ask: how is it that individuals voluntarily agree to their political obligation, or what are the voluntary actions that can reasonably be said to, or be inferred to, give rise to political obligation? Before looking at their answers to *this* question, I want to pause to say something about the relation of my argument, and recent discussions, to classical social contract theory, taking Locke's theory as my example.

The hypothesis of the contract is a way of showing how 'in the beginning' free and equal individuals can rationally agree to live under political authority. However, the *liberal* social contract has two stages and the significance of each stage is very different.[5] It is the first part of the contract story that shows how the 'dispersed' individuals form a new political community. This part of the social contract establishes an obligation between, and places authority in the hands of, the members of the community themselves. Thus the first stage of the contract, taken by itself, is related to the question about the comparison with promising. Locke treats the first part of the contract as necessary (a political community must be created) but as an unimportant preliminary. It is the second stage of the contract that is fundamental to liberal theory. The second stage embodies the assumption that it is necessary for the members of the new community to alienate their right to exercise political authority to a few representatives. The free agreement of the contract thus becomes an agreement that a few representatives shall decide upon the content of individuals' political obligation. Self-assumed obligation becomes an obligation to let others decide upon one's political obligation. The comparison with promising now begins to appear misplaced and, furthermore, political obligation is now owed to the state and its representatives, not by citizens to each other.

Locke could not complete his theory with the idea of the social contract. He had to meet the patriarchalists' objection that an agreement of the fathers could not bind sons, not if the latter were truly born free and equal. Locke had, therefore, to introduce the notion of consent into his theory.[6] The sons had, in their turn, voluntarily to consent or agree to the political arrangements made by their fathers. Locke had to answer the same problems as contemporary theorists: given a legitimate political system, how can individuals be said to consent to it? From what aspect of their actions can their political obligation be inferred?

In his discussion of consent, Locke remarks that no one doubts that express consent gives rise to political obligation and makes an individual the subject of government. The difficulty about consent arises 'where he has

5 Rousseau's social contract theory provides a brilliant critique of, and non-liberal alternative to, liberal contract theory. His critique is usually ignored by writers on political obligation.
6 For the distinction between the contract and consent, usually treated as synonymous, see G.J. Schochet, *Patriarchalism in Political Thought* (Oxford, 1975), 9, 262.

made no Expressions of it at all'. Locke solves this problem by his famous claim that the tacit consent of the members of the community can be inferred from their peaceful every-day interactions under the protection of government. But who gives express consent, and how? Locke's treatment of consent is hardly a model of clarity, but the most plausible answer to this question is that express consent is given by the individuals who inherit property, individuals who can also be called the politically relevant members of their society. Locke calls those who expressly consent 'perfect members' of society and indicates that they, unlike individuals who merely consent tacitly, have no right of emigration.[7] It therefore seems that Locke is implying that a differential political obligation exists: those who expressly consent have a greater obligation than the rest.

In this hint of a differential political obligation, as in his other arguments, Locke closely foreshadows more recent discussions of political obligation. But there is also a very important difference between Locke's social contract theory and contemporary arguments. In the seventeenth century Locke could not merely take it for granted that the political obligation of citizens of the liberal state was justified. He argued, in his conjectural history of the state of nature, that the socio-economic developments of his day had rendered unacceptable the claims for the divine right of kings and for patriarchy. Only a liberal, constitutional, representative state could protect individuals' property – and the social contract story provides the necessary voluntarist justification for the authority of such a state. It must be emphasized that it is quite clear that Locke's contract is an answer to a *problem* of political authority and political obligation, whereas in the most recent revival of contract theory, as in other present-day discussions of political obligation, no such problem is admitted. Rawls, in *A Theory of Justice*, assumes that the liberal democratic state exercises a justified political authority over its citizens. His 'original position', and the choices of its 'parties', is a device to show why 'our' considered judgments about liberal democracy are rational and acceptable judgments. It shows us why we are right to regard the relationship of citizens and the state in the way that we do – as embodying a justified political obligation. Rawls' contract exhibits the rationality of the state; unlike classic social contract theory it neither begins from the position, nor admits, that the authority of the state poses a problem. In other words, the liberal democratic state is today entirely taken for granted as if it were a natural feature of the world. This marks a most significant shift from the classic contract theorists' view that the state is conventional.

7 J. Locke, 'Second Treatise of Government', in *Two Treatises of Government*, ed. P. Laslett, 2nd ed. (Cambridge, 1967), paras. 116–22.

That political obligation is no longer seen as a problem means that consent is now treated explicitly 'as a constituent element of democratic ideology'.[8] Criticisms of the ideological character of much liberal democratic theory are now familiar and I shall not pursue this here, but it is worth commenting on one ideological assumption and its relationship to social contract theory.[9] It is widely assumed by liberal-democratic theorists that liberal-democratic voting works in practice as it is held to in theory and, in particular, that voting protects and furthers the interests of all citizens. Locke was able to make his inference about tacit consent because, during the contract, individuals exchange their 'natural' freedom and equality for the civil freedom and legal equality of political subjects. The end of government is protection, and in their new status all citizens' 'property', in both of Locke's senses of the term, is protected (or they would not enter the contract) no matter what substantive social inequalities divide them. Hence, all can be said to continue to give their consent. Since Locke's day, the status of political subject has been transformed and institutionalized as the formally equal political status of liberal-democratic citizenship, which includes civil liberties and the right to exercise the franchise. Voting, it is claimed, protects the interest of all citizens no matter how substantively unequal they are: and so all can be said to consent.

It is therefore not surprising that the most popular recent argument about consent is that it can be said to be given through, or even equated with the existence of, the liberal-democratic electoral mechanism. I have already challenged the assumption that the general conceptual connection between voting and political obligation is given actual expression through liberal-democratic voting (although the general connection helps explain why this may appear 'obvious'). Even fairly cursory reflection on the empirical evidence about voting behaviour casts immediate doubt on the simple identification of consent with liberal-democratic voting. It is argued by Plamenatz, for example, that even electoral abstainers consent, and Gewirth states that the

8 P.H. Partridge, *Consent and Consensus* (London, 1971), 23
9 The continuing ideological importance of the legacy of liberal social contract theory is, rather curiously, overlooked by Marxist and neo-Marxist writers. C.B. Macpherson, in *The Political Theory of Possessive Individualism* (Oxford, 1962), ignores the contract in his interpretation of Hobbes and Locke, and argues that the liberal state was justified by the equal subordination of all individuals to the inevitable laws of the market. Similarly, J. Habermas, *Legitimation Crisis* (London, 1976), 22, argues that 'the bourgeois constitutional state finds its justification in the legitimate relations of production'. They thus neglect the directly *political* justification of the liberal state and the present ideological strength of the idea that all individuals have a common interest as citizens.

meaning of the electoral 'method of consent' is that 'one can participate if one chooses to do so' and, therefore, 'the individual is obligated ... whether he personally utilizes his opportunity or not.'[10] The close relationship of this argument to conclusions drawn about political apathy by empirical theorists of democracy is obvious; and so are its defects. What is ignored, of course, is who abstains and why they do so. The empirical evidence shows that electoral abstainers tend to be drawn disproportionately from lower socio-economic groups and the female sex. The evidence also suggests that they abstain because voting does not seem worthwhile; that is, they do not believe that voting achieves what it is claimed to in liberal-democratic theory. As Verba and Nie have shown, political participation, including voting, 'helps those who are already better off'.[11] It hardly makes sense to insist that individuals are consenting when they refrain from an activity which helps reinforce their disadvantaged position.

Yet, it might be argued, those who vote can surely be said to consent. The question of the 'meaning' of the vote is an extremely complex one and I can only briefly mention two of the major objections to this claim. The first objection concerns the votes of men and women. Political scientists often argue that men and women are doing something different when they vote; they argue that a female vote is 'qualitatively different' from a male vote. Men, acting like good liberals, vote from self-interest; women vote for moral reasons, out of 'a kind of bloodless love of the good'.[12] But, if that is so, then can women's votes 'mean' the same things as men's votes, namely, consent? Either political theorists have to give up their male chauvinist prejudices or they have to construct a sex-differentiated argument about political obligation and voting.

The second objection centres on the requirements of a meaningful or genuine sense of 'consent'. When an individual makes a promise he or she knows what they are committed to and can break or alter the obligation if this is necessary. An acceptable sense of 'consent' also implies that those consenting can have reasonable knowledge of the consequences of their action, or can refuse or withdraw their consent. There are some familiar features of liberal-democratic elections that illustrate how difficult it is for this requirement to be met. I shall leave aside the problems consequent upon attempts by representatives and officials to 'defactualize' the political world,[13] and from

10 J. Plamenatz, *Man and Society* (London, 1963), vol. 1, 238–40; A. Gewirth, 'Political Justice', in R.B. Brandt ed., *Social Justice* (Englewood Cliffs, 1962), 138
11 S. Verba and N.H. Nie, *Participation in America* (New York, 1972), 338
12 R.E. Lane, *Political Life* (New York, 1959), 212
13 The term is H. Arendt's in 'Lying in Politics', in *Crises of the Republic* (Penguin ed., 1973).

systematic lying on their part, and note, first, that parties and candidates are now 'sold' to the electorate through commercial advertising techniques and that citizens are urged to vote on the basis of 'images'; but in what sense can one consent to an image? Second, the crude equation of voting and consent ignores the argument that liberal-democratic voting is no more than a ritual or, at least, contains large ritual elements. Certainly, many citizens see their vote as a 'duty' associated with citizenship and, again, the important question is how far, if at all, this leaves room for anything that could reasonably be called freely and deliberately given 'consent'.

Some theorists of political obligation have now ceased to make any reference to 'consent' at all. They offer a different form of voluntarist argument that, like Locke's doctrine of tacit consent, looks not to activities that are part of universal citizenship (which, of course, did not exist in Locke's day) but to everyday life. Such arguments typically appeal to individuals' acceptance of benefits from the state, or their participation in liberal democratic institutions, as giving rise to obligations. This approach, like Locke's tacit consent, is neatly all-inclusive; indeed, it is a mere reinterpretation of 'tacit consent'. It is another way of inferring political obligation – yet apparently avoiding the difficulties associated with 'consent'. Locke's theory can be interpreted without reference to tacit consent and some commentators claim that this is the most appropriate reading.[14] Locke can be seen to argue that, having taken advantage of the social practice of inheritance, individuals (in fairness) have an obligation to play their part to keep the practice in being: or, having accepted the benefits of highways, they have an obligation to obey the government that builds and maintains them.

It is not clear that this approach does actually constitute an argument at all. It looks suspiciously like no more than an extended collection of conceptual truisms. The existence of an institution or practice necessarily implies that individuals are participating or co-operating within it; they 'benefit' because all do their share ('recognize their obligation') to keep the institution going. However, the 'benefits' cannot be independently specified apart from the participation, and the latter *is*, or constitutes, the practice itself. But even if this form of voluntarism is treated as a genuine argument, there are some basic objections to it.

It is not, for example, obvious how the obligations (if, indeed, there are such) consequent upon participation in the multiplicity of liberal-democratic institutions are related to *political* obligation. The equation of voting and consent does have the advantage that it focuses on a political activity. Moreover, because these arguments look to everyday life they are im-

14 For a recent example of this interpretation, see A.J. Simmons, 'Tacit Consent and Political Obligation', *Philosophy and Public Affairs*, 5 (1976), 274–91.

mediately open to the challenge that, if they show anything, it is that a differential political obligation exists. I have not found any attempts in the relevant literature to specify what counts as a 'benefit' but it seems clear that, taking liberal-democratic institutions in their entirety, some individuals 'benefit' a good deal more than others and the outcome of participation is very different for some individuals and groups than for others. This applies even if one takes the fundamental 'benefit' of liberal theory as an example; the protection of the property that individuals have in their persons. Empirical research shows that mortality rates differ between social classes;[15] that 'the poor do not receive the same treatment at the hands of the agents of law-enforcement as the well-to-do or middle class. This differential treatment is systematic and complete';[16] and that women are not afforded the same protection as men from sexual and other assaults by men[17] (and it can be added that men are widely believed to own the property that women have in their persons). Why, then, should most political theorists assume that the obligation held to be consequent upon participation in institutions, or acceptance of benefits, is an equal obligation for all citizens, whether rich or poor, working-class or middle-class, male or female?

Interestingly enough, Rawls concludes, on the basis of this form of voluntarist argument, that citizens are far from having an equal obligation – in fact, many citizens do not have a political *obligation* at all. It is only the 'better-placed members of society', who also take an active part in political life, who have a political obligation. The rest of the population have merely a *natural duty* to obey, which, 'requires no voluntary acts in order to apply'.[18] While Rawls has drawn a logical conclusion from arguments about participation and 'benefits', voluntarism and the ideal of social life as a 'voluntary scheme' have now been thrown aside for the bulk of the population.

This highlights the dilemmas facing theorists who wish both to retain voluntarism and to treat political obligation in the liberal-democratic state as unproblematic. An all-inclusive obligation can be inferred ('tacit consent'), but at the price of reducing the idea of self-assumed obligation to meaninglessness. Yet to admit that some individuals may have a lesser obligation than others, or that some have only a 'natural duty' of obedience, is either to shake liberal-democratic theory to its foundations or to move well

---

15 See, for example, A. Antonovsky, 'Class and the Chance for Life', in L. Rainwater ed., *Social Problems and Public Policy* (Chicago, 1974).

16 W.J. Chambliss and R.B. Seidman, *Law Order, and Power* (Boston, 1971), 475

17 See, for example, E. Pizzey, *Scream Quietly or the Neighbours Will Hear* (Penguin ed., 1974); B. Toner, *The Facts of Rape* (Arrow, 1977). See also the judgment of the Court of Appeal in *R. v. Holdsworth*, reported in *The Times*, 22 June 1977.

18 *A Theory of Justice*, 114, 116, 344

on the road to the abandonment of some basic liberal principles. And any attempt to give genuine content to the ideas of consent and self-assumed obligation immediately opens up all the critical questions about the liberal-democratic state that most contemporary theorists seem determined to avoid.

It is, perhaps, symptomatic of an unease about the present state of the argument about the relationship of the citizen to the liberal-democratic state that there is an increasing tendency for theorists to advance a rather startling argument. They argue that political obligation is owed primarily not to the state but to fellow citizens.[19] It must be added that they also assume that the state does have a justified claim on its citizens – but their own argument begins to cut the ground from under this assumption. The question cannot be avoided of why and on what grounds, if obligation is owed to fellow citizens, it must also be assumed that it is justifiably owed to the state.

It is not as surprising as it may appear at first sight that theorists have begun to argue in this way. The logic of the voluntarist arguments that look to everyday interactions of citizens, and to 'benefits' and 'participation', is that, if obligations are assumed in this way, they are owed to fellow members of institutions and fellow participants in social practices. I have already noted that this raises an important question about what counts as 'political' obligation. If 'political' obligation *is* owed to fellow citizens, then a sharp break must be made with liberal-democratic theory that insists that it is the state that is the locus of the political and the object of political obligation. The view of political obligation as owed to fellow citizens derives, as I have argued, from a perspective that takes seriously the idea of self-assumed obligation as a political ideal. This raises again the fundamental question of why, if self-assumed obligation is as important as three hundred years of liberal argument assures us it is, we should not assume *all* of our obligations for ourselves and organize our political life on that basis.

Theorists of the liberal state have only one convincing answer to that question. They can argue that participatory democracy is not empirically feasible; the liberal-democratic state is the best that we can do. If that answer is given – and it is implicit in many discussions of political obligation – the consequences need to be spelled out. The answer implies that voluntarism is irrelevant to political life. Although we are capable of assuming obligations in our everyday life, the activity has no place outside the private sphere. It is,

19 See, for example, M. Walzer, *Obligations* (New York, 1971); B. Zwiebach, *Civility and Disobedience* (Cambridge, 1975); K. Johnson, 'Political Obligation and the Voluntary Association Model of the State', *Ethics*, 86 (1975), 17–29; R.K. Dagger, 'What Is Political Obligation?' *American Political Science Review*, LXXI, 1 (1977), 86–94.

in short, to admit that the noble liberal ideal of individual freedom and equality and its corollaries of self-assumed obligation and the vision of social life as a 'voluntary scheme' can only be very partially realized.

Furthermore, if political theorists dismiss the possibility of participatory or self-managing democracy, they should stop pretending that the liberal-democratic state rests on a voluntarist basis of genuine commitments. That is, they should stop pretending that the freely created relationship of political *obligation* is involved, because this relationship is an integral part of a political ideal now admitted to be out of reach. Instead, they should argue directly that, given the empirical necessity of the liberal-democratic state and the advantages that it has over other existing forms of political system, there are good, but non-voluntarist, reasons for political *obedience*. Rawls' notion of a natural duty of political obedience, or a contemporary version of 'my political station and its duties', may commend themselves for this purpose. And there are, of course, political theorists who present a utilitarian account of the relationship between citizens and the liberal-democratic state. The reason why I have ignored this obvious competitor to voluntarism in my argument should now be clear. No matter how economical an argument utilitarianism can provide, or how appropriate it may appear, utilitarian arguments, despite the manner in which they are so often presented, are arguments for obedience, not obligation. However, theorists are unlikely to argue only in terms of 'obedience' instead of 'obligation' for this would strip the liberal-democratic state of a major portion of its ideological mantle. It would be to recognize that central liberal ideas, if taken seriously, lead beyond the liberal-democratic state.

Reading the *Social Contract*

Rousseau's writings have, from the day of the their first appearance, been subjected to every conceivable interpretation, both friendly and hostile. They were never ignored or read with indifference. One could indeed write an interesting monograph on the history of these readings. Most of them have been too crudely ideological to be of much intellectual worth in their own right, but they might well add up collectively to a chapter in the history of opinions. A more substantial group of interpretations traces the line of influences on Rousseau and those to which he, in turn, contributed. These efforts belong to a tradition of intellectual history that strives to remain as close as possible to the general study of the past, and so treats influences as a chain of causes and effects. Others have tried to put Rousseau in his age and place. They are preoccupied generally with social and economic history and so 'use' him. Psycho-historians have found Rousseau a natural subject. Political theory, in spite of all these efforts, is not, however, easily reducible to historical thinking. Literary and philosophical analysis also have claims on its attention. The archetypes, metaphors, and rhetoric of a given text and the structure of argument cannot be ignored. In fact they must precede any other work of understanding, for if we do not know the works we discuss, we simply do not know what we are talking about, or why it is worth doing so at all. Thus the line that has conventionally linked Rousseau to Kant, for example, may be a far from certain one, but we do want to know what it was about *Emile* that kept Kant glued to its pages. He was, of course, an extraordinary reader, but then he was not reading an ordinary book.

Emile is surely Rousseau's masterpiece, but the *Social Contract*, even if it is a far less accomplished work, has driven a wedge into every literate consciousness since the French Revolution. Why does it impinge so heavily on one's mind? There is probably no single satisfactory answer to the question. Perhaps there are as many reasons for the effect of the *Social Contract* as there are readers. A serious but puzzled reader may find that he is moved in two ways. Certainly he cannot help being stirred, one way or the other, by the pervasive tone of indignation that Rousseau made uniquely audible. Beyond that, however, he may find that each re-reading of the book reveals new meanings and different messages, and the exact character of Rousseau's intentions becomes problematical. The inherent unity of Rousseau's mind has often been shown. It is the complexity of his design that makes him fascinating. If, after several readings, one sees that the *Social Contract* is written in counterpoint one learns to read it both for the different lines of thought and feeling and for their ultimate relatedness. The trouble is that many listeners are not able or willing to follow fugues. They will listen selectively, so that only the very simplest tunes, the most obvious harmonies, will come through, and though they may well enjoy the music, they will never know the score.

To illustrate, though only partially, some of the voices that appear in the *Social Contract*, one may read it, book by book, chapter by chapter, to find egalitarian, democratic, and populist themes as well as one of dire tragedy. The first three can, for the sake of brevity, be grouped into one section, the last one is to be treated apart from them. That makes for only two readings, and they do not suffice, but only indicate how one might go about unravelling the whole text. There are surely other possibilities, but one must begin somewhere.

> What though on homely fare we dine,
> Wear hoddin gray, an' a' that,
> Gie fools their silks and knaves their wine,
> A man's a man for a' that!
>
> For a' that an' a' that,
> It's coming yet, for a' that,
> That man to man, the world o'er,
> Shall brothers be for a' that!

When speaking of egalitarian motifs in the following pages, a generally equal distribution of the burdens and advantages of society is meant. Democracy is taken to be a government in which the entire adult population takes part. Populism, the most elusive of these words, is used to refer to the demand for the social recognition of the common decencies and communal cohesion of simple people as the highest of human values, and therefore as worthy of the greatest respect. That there is a note of truculence in populism is inevitable, but that does not render it any less powerful a feeling. The best illustration of populist sentiment is Robert Burns' celebrated poem, from which a few lines are given above, but the whole should really be recalled for full effect – both for its resentments and its hopes.

What evidence is there in the *Social Contract* for arguments on behalf of these three political assertions? What is the case for this sort of Rousseau in the *Social Contract*? Even a very partial account, such as this one, shows that the case for treating the work as a charter for the claims of the common man is a powerful one, and that those who have read it thus were by no means mistaken. Whether it is the sole meaning is another question.

The topics of the four books of the *Social Contract* are relatively clear. Book one defines, describes, and explicates the social contract on which all societies rest; Book Two is about sovereignty, specifically that of the people; Book Three deals with forms of government; and Book Four discusses the mores which a republican polity requires.

The Introduction sets the question, whether a legitimate governance of civil society is possible. Given 'men as they are' and 'laws as they might be', can justice and utility be made one? That is, can the rules of society be made in such a way that both the moral and physical needs of those who are obliged to obey them are satisfied? We are then, in true populist vein, reminded that this is not what prevails and that everywhere men are in chains. The next call is, however, not one for shaking off the bonds, which would be acceptable only if force made right, in which case both the chaining and unchaining would be acts of superior power. We are, rather, to look for the social conventions that justify the chains (chap. 1). Nature is certainly not the source of this or any other social law. It only teaches self-preservation. The basis of every political order is therefore not to be found in nature, or even in the most natural of human associations, the family. Those who argue that it is, do so with evil intent. They picture men as a herd of sheep protected by a fatherly shepherd. This seductive picture mistakes the results of social practice for its origin. Slavery makes sheep-slaves, not nature. So much for Grotius, Hobbes, and Aristotle in their naturalistic paternalism or monarchism (chap. 2). The specifically Hobbesian form of legitimization as a prudential resort is dismissed as just another variant of the might-makes-right argument. It does not make for duty, only for calculation (chap. 3).

With nature eliminated, only art or agreement remains as the source of obligation. What can pass for agreement, however? Conquest, as Grotius had argued? Certainly not. The peace of the dungeon at the end of war is a dangerous fiction. Men are asked to renounce their responsibilities as men by reducing themselves to things, to slavery, to avoid wars. Wars, however, are not pre-social; only personal conflicts are that. War is over some object of possession, fought in order to appropriate something. And that itself requires the social institution of property, an artifice, in short. Above all, Grotius' theory defies all common sense. Conquest cannot yield anything like consent, for no one would accept a bargain as self-destructive as that of slavery. Even if he did, he could not impose this 'agreement' on his offspring (chap. 4). If one goes back far enough one does not find the degrading situation of herds, slaves, shepherds, and conquerors, but discrete individuals with no bonds to tie them into a people as yet, undefiled men as populism sees them, in short. To say that they make the body politic does not, however, mean that they may unmake it. That only follows from the might-is-right formula. On the contrary, as we now discover, the fundamental convention on which all things – good, bad and indifferent – are based, is indissoluble and is tacitly recognized everywhere. This is the agreement by which each one gives up all his rights and powers to society as a whole in exchange for social protection under conditions identical for all. Nothing could be more in keeping with equality (chap. 6).

Since all abide by the same rules and are equal parts of the whole, no one can have any interest in injuring the community as a whole. That would be a sort of self-injury. Of course, this says nothing about private hostilities nor does it prevent disobedience (chap. 7). The right of society to punish its delinquents is part of the contract and to the advantage of each and all. In deciding to punish murderers the original contractors agree to be punished if any one of them should commit that crime and in being punished one is merely 'forced to be free'. For the real meaning of the pooling of resources and submission to a single social will is that dependence of one person upon another is ended in favour of the subjection of all to the general will. The 'will' reminds us again that laws are made, not discovered (chap. 7). Impersonal though the general will is in its application, will remains a psychic function and as such a personal act. That is why society is a transforming experience. Each natural brute becomes a moral being. Only now does duty acquire any sense, intelligence any scope (chap. 8).

Civil liberty and property remake us. Because our own in a pre-social state is at worst mere possession by the strongest, at best the right of the first possessor, it is neither secure nor irrevocable. By making it all over to the sovereign whole we create a power capable of defending mine and thine, and moreover alter these into a public institution, property. For though property is a social right and a public trust, it brings with it defence against foreign aggressors and wrongful encroachments by one individual on another's right. What each one has, he has as a right, held as a grant from the sovereign, and he enjoys it in perfect security. In short, property is subordinate to the rights of the community and is not a private natural right, but it is held far more safely and equally. For social equality has now replaced the inequality of nature (chap. 9). The last sentence of Book One affirms the social equality of citizens under the law they have created by and for themselves in order to escape from the defects of the natural state. Equality is the only condition worth more than natural freedom. A footnote at the very end reminds us that it is bad governments that lead to gross inequality and that society is beneficial only when everyone has something and nobody has too much. The tone of resentment is as clear as that of the egalitarian arguments. Rousseau's anger is, moreover, directed against both the actual political order and its intellectual defenders.

Book Two. We have seen what the social contract should logically imply but never seems to mean in political practice. The common good, which is the common interest and the general will, tending to equality, cannot be alienated. In short, no one but the people, even if it does so tacitly, has the right to act as sovereign (chap. 1). However, only the original compact itself requires unanimous assent. Those who do not agree simply do not join the association. Thereafter majority decisions are binding. Everyone must be counted, whether for or against and no one may be excluded from the general will, if its universality is to be maintained. This is the meaning of indivisible sovereignty from which alone binding laws can issue. It is the task of men like Grotius to deny it, of course, because kings, and not the people, give out pensions and professorships. We note the populist and egalitarian emphasis (chap. 2).

The people's will, being the sole possible measure of right, must be allowed to express itself in such a way that the falsifications of dominating parties cannot overcome and mislead it. Voting must be entirely individual and factions must be prevented. If that is too much, let all groups at least be equal in strength. Otherwise some cabal is bound to become excessively powerful and certain to impose its own will. Individual wills cancel each other out, so that the public will emerges out of the rejected private wills. When groups vote that does not happen (chap. 3). The danger to be avoided at all cost is then usurpation of sovereignty by some special interest group. That does not mean that the community as a whole should absorb those goods and powers which are not needed for public purposes, but it is up to the sovereign to decide what is and what is not public. The private domain is set by a public decision. Since it is an agreement which binds all mutually to each other, there is no partiality in all this. What is done for the public is also done for oneself, as part of the community. As long as all public decisions are general, affecting all equally, no one can feel endangered (chap. 4). Justice can, indeed, come about in no other manner, for we are not able to know the word of God. When the people as a whole makes rules for the people as a whole, justice is created. Thus while the people may choose to institute privileges, the sovereign, which by definition only makes general rules, cannot favour or hinder specific individuals. That is the task of government, not of sovereignty (chap. 6).

It is possible for a people to achieve justice with the aid of an educative lawgiver or after a revolution when, like the Dutch, a society begins with a clean slate (chaps. 6, 7, 8). It is also necessary that states be small, because otherwise there is bound to be an impersonality in public life that drives people apart (chap. 9). Where unity prevails, shared objectives are before the eyes of all, and anyone can understand them. Finally, a just state must be wealthy enough for autonomy but not so rich as to attract hungry conquerors (chap. 10). Individually each one is interested in preserving his freedom from domination. To that end there must be equality. No one may be so rich as to be able to buy another, and no one so poor as to be forced to sell himself. To maintain this equality, the richer people must exercise moderation in their goods and influence, while the less well off must moderate their envy and avarice. It is likely to be a considerable moral task, but the laws can encourage men to attempt it (chap. 11). It is above all a matter of forming good habits, especially customary simplicity. Book Two then demonstrates the inescapability of popular sovereignty, once it is really understood that men enter society for their own benefit and should agree only to such laws as serve their interests as social beings and citizens. All laws, to be legitimate, must be such as any people would agree to, if they had only those ends in view which made them prefer society to nature in the first place. That implies the equal protection of the laws for each and all, and an equal obligation to obey them. Nothing is due to persons, only to the law. This supremacy of the law, which is what sovereignty means, originates in the people and falls on the entire people identically. The egalitarianism that is involved here is extensive and intense.

The nature of government comes next, in Book Three. The most important thing to remember is that government is not sovereignty. Governments are the mere agents of the sovereign and law-making people. Governors exist to execute the law, and can be recalled or recommissioned at any moment by the sovereign. There is obviously no contract involved here (chap. 1). Democracy can be either the rule of all or just majority rule, but in one respect it is always the best form of government. For those who make the law are sure to be its best interpreters (chaps. 3, 4). The case for democracy as good government is therefore a strong one, even if not all peoples are up to it, for only a small state with simple manners, equality of social rank, and above all no luxury can even try it. On the moral plane, there must be no vanity to make men slaves of opinion (chap. 4). Secondly, there are aristocracies that are all but democratic in form. There is the rule of the old which is natural and works very well among American Indians. Again, elective aristocracies, chosen for merit, are not to be despised. The trouble is that inequality does tend to increase and sooner or later aristocracies become hereditary, which is a disastrous form of government (chap. 5). Finally, nothing can really be said in favour of monarchy. Succession crises speak in favour of the hereditary principle, which gives young princes an education designed to produce bad kings (chap. 6). In view of all that, clearly a republic is bound to be better than a monarchy and a free state superior to a despotism. However, there is really no point in looking for the best form of government, since conditions differ (chap. 8). What is permanent is not the structure, but the purpose of government. Is the people well off or not? – that is the question. It is quite easy to tell. If they choose to have large families, they are content. A simple test applied to ordinary peasants is really all one has to look for; there is no need to be over-elaborate about forms of government. Nor should one look to stability as a standard. Wars, civil war, and the like do not affect most people very much. It is just the ruling classes that get involved. As for the arts and sciences, their baleful brilliance contributes nothing to good government; quite the opposite, in fact. Simple benefits for simple men, in short, are what one should look for in judging the success of governments (chap. 9).

If Rousseau can afford to sound almost like Pope about forms of government, it is because he had such a clear and democratic notion about the ends of administration and because the exercise of sovereignty is what really matters. It is the sovereign's task, after all, to see that the rules be maintained and enforced in keeping with their spirit and letter. The people must be frequently assembled to impose its sovereign supervision over the government. The latter is suspended as soon as such an assembly has gathered. Assemblies have only one function, to act as watchdogs, to see that the original law is preserved in every way by the government. The Romans had these assemblies and so did the primitive Frankish monarchies. At their best the citizens of a town act together for themselves. If there is more than one town, let the citizens of each town successively act for all; in that way you get no capitals (chaps. 12, 14). As in the case of civilization generally the tone here is as populist as it is democratic: no fancy values and no luxurious ways to outshine the honest citizen. That must be so, for otherwise the citizens will become indifferent to their civic existence: they will pay taxes with money, rather than by labour or in kind; they will prefer representation to direct participation, a feudal sham to self-government; and their freedom will be gone (chap. 15). Ultimately they will cease to keep a stern eye on the government. They may forget that they can dismiss, establish, and alter governments by simple law. When they do so they act as a simple democracy, thus closing the gap between the people, their laws, and their government (chaps. 16, 17). We have returned to the democratic voice.

Quite naturally Book Four moves into the mores that are capable of sustaining democratic polities. Clearly Rousseau has been considering democracy in two ways, as a form of political activity and as a social result. He concedes that the contentment of the common man is an adequate sign of good government. We are, however, also forced to conclude that, unless people assemble frequently to keep a sharp eye on their government, they are not likely to prosper. It is not the form of government, but its fidelity to the laws, that counts. That is why people if they are to exercise their sovereignty effectively must possess the appropriate republican *mores*, as we have already been told. So the last book of the *Social Contract* begins with that most democratic of all images, – solid peasants sitting under an oak, making their own political decisions. It is the greatest possible contrast to all ill-governed states. Here harmony prevails and magistrates can be chosen by lot, the most egalitarian of all elections, since office is a civic burden, not a privilege (chaps. 1, 2, 3). The evidence of history is not perhaps encouraging; not even Roman politics conformed to this happy vision. However, they did have censors and they do remind us that it is custom that rules a people's pleasures, not nature. And customs can be moulded by law (chap. 7). In sum, men do make themselves as they make their laws. Perhaps the group under the oak is not quite real, but republican virtue and a civil religion designed to support it are entirely thinkable. It is this set of beliefs that really matters. Without it majoritarianism makes no sense. Unanimity is required only for the original compact; for subsequent decisions a majority will do. It is sufficient because an assembly only has to assert the original laws and to ask whether the general will is being followed. If a few people differ, they are merely a mistaken minority, as long as republican virtue prevails. When it no longer does, then the majority may be in error, and then all is lost. When the majority is patriotic its rule can safely be accepted as correct and the minority can be tolerantly ignored as showing nothing but a human weakness. It is not numbers but its spirit that guarantees the sovereignty of the people and that gives a majority its weight in a republic. It has nothing to do with rights, social or natural. (chap. 2) For the great problem of an egalitarian, democratic, popular polity is not the rights and privileges of the few, but the well-being, both civic and personal, of the whole people or at least of the majority; that is, 'peace, unity, equality ... [the] enemies of political sophistication' (chap.1). It is a powerful case and no one who reads the *Social Contract* honestly can miss it. This is a book in defence of equality in all its aspects. That is not, however, its only significant message; it may not even be its major argument.

> Sing of human unsuccess
> In a rapture of distress.

The egalitarian and democratic aspects of the *Social Contract* are really the coherent working out of the implications of a single idea. Since convention, and not God or nature, is the origin of all societies, and since conventional rules are made, openly or tacitly, by all those who choose to join a society, the only justifiable political order is one that serves the interests of all, or at least of most of those who are thus associated. Democratic and populist government and *mores* follow from that. To be sure, it is perfectly clear throughout that actual institutions fail to meet these standards of legitimacy, and this provides Rousseau with frequent occasions for the expression of populist indignation. So far so good. The trouble is that men 'as they are' are quite obviously unable to live under laws 'that might be' and that the evidence of actuality proves men to be irremediably warped.

Mankind is simply a mistake. Human nature is fit only for solitude, but human needs make association a necessity. The two cannot be harmonized and the *Social Contract* demonstrates that even the most reasonable of legal orders can do nothing against the corrosive effects of self-oriented and inegalitarian human drives. The chains men bear cannot be rendered legitimate, because men are incapable of supporting a just yoke. Rousseau's theme is the tragic encounter between man's character and man's fate, between the self-absorbed ego and the co-operation that survival, even at its least elaborate, demands.

It is precisely because all social rules are made by men for men that the situation of social man is so hopeless. The master is no less enslaved than the slave, for both are locked into a mutual dependence from which neither one can free himself. Each has enchained himself (Book One, chap. 1). There is no one to blame. It may be true that slavery makes slaves and that nature does not create these abject herds, but it is men who enslave each other, and men who submit to it (chap. 2). The reason why men must alienate everything to the sovereign and endow it with such overwhelming power is that any vestige of extra-social freedom will be used by the strong to subject the weak to that condition of personal dependence from which association is supposed to save them. As we know it does not (chap. 6). That is why people have to be forced to be free. Their private self is always apt to be asocial (chap. 7). And while life under a contract may indeed transform that stupid animal into a moral being, the advantages to him are obscure. Justice may replace instinct, but not sufficiently to rule unchallenged (chap. 8). For while law may indeed treat all men as equals, bad governments do manage to make the rich richer and the poor poorer (chap. 9). Nature may be moulded by art, but it obviously cannot be destroyed, and a private will always remains to compete with the public will, not only on the political stage, but within each man. The message of Book One is, therefore, not unambiguous. It may be rousing to tell men that they can make their society such as it ought to be, in order to secure safety and justice. It is also true that one must face the realities of man's failure even to approach these goals.

Book Two begins with a simple statement, explaining the inescapable and destructive tension in political society. The general will tends to equality while the personal will moves men to inequality (chap. 1). Something else also begins to emerge. Some of the most basic political decisions cannot be left to the sovereign people. War and peace are questions of prudence and therefore fall into the sphere of government, not of sovereignty (chap. 2). Moreover, groups form spontaneously, and someone wiser than the people is needed to prevent faction. There is a need for wise men, and those named belong to myth, not to history, Lycurgus most of all (chap. 3). We are becoming aware that stupidity and incompetence are not to be discounted and presently the people is no longer nobly engaged in acts of social self-formation, but is openly called 'a blind multitude' that needs a law-giver (chap. 6). The figure of the law-giver is a study in despair, and for two reasons. He is a desperate device demanded by the incapacity of men to make rules for themselves; and he does not exist. His powers of mind and soul must be 'super-human', and that is all we need to know about him really. He is needed to de-nature men so that they can become citizens, and that is impossible. Even if it could be done, there is no human being capable of performing this miracle. Moreover, nothing can tell us more about Rousseau's opinion of the political talents of most men than the fact that they must be systematically and continually duped and mystified if they are to be shaped for social justice (chaps. 7, 8).

The self-cure of revolution is, moreover, only a qualified one. If it is a real founding it may succeed, but unless there really is a clean slate it is hopeless. Liberty cannot be regained (chap. 8). Revolutionary turmoil is no time for legislating in any case. Turbulent moments are exploited by tyrants, but not by true law-givers, who will act only in calm periods with docile people (chap. 10). The equality which the general will strives for is therefore only a hope, something men may long for; but the moral strength for it can be found neither among the people, who are stupid as well as egotistical, nor among legislators, who are usually bunglers like Peter the Great or tyrants. The great law-giver, like the just law and like equality, is a myth. Clearly also the psychological basis of participatory democracy and social equality cannot be found in nature or in art. Popular resentment alone would seem to survive.

If Book Two introduces the tragic theme, it is Book Three that develops the entire scenario. Government is absolutely necessary and it must be strong. It is the physical power that society needs to move at all. Because it must be strong, it is inevitable that government will aggrandize itself at the expense of the sovereign people. To this there is no simple solution. Any form of government has its weaknesses, and there is no best regime for all men at all times. Indeed, the relativism here is so strong that it amounts to saying that people have the governments they deserve (chap. 1).

The reason why governments must corrupt society is that they all have three wills, the general will, their own corporate will as a body of magistrates, and their private oligarchic wills. In theory the first will should rule; in practice it is the third. To be effective there must be specialized functions for governors, but special political skills lead to concentration of power. Governments must be bold and know how to act at the right moment. The fewer the members of a government the more likely they are to recognize their chances (chap. 2). That is fine if these 'chances' benefit society, but that is not usual. In sum, the victory of the clever and unscrupulous few over the dull multitude is inevitable.

Democracy is the name of the political escape from this treadmill; but it is only a name. For if men were able to govern themselves, they would not need governments at all. Therefore there are no true democracies among 'men as they are.' Even to try it is dangerous. For if the people in its capacity as government is, as it must be, corrupted, then the sovereign is also destroyed. There would be no reservoir of restraint left at all. The prevalence of civil war in such democracies as have been attempted proves as much (chap. 4). If true democracy makes excessive demands on the people, natural and elective aristocracy ask too much of rulers. The trend of inequality is toward its own enhancement and in due course aristocracies become hereditary (chap. 5). The movement of all governments is toward contraction and concentration of power and, in any case, few people are fit for freedom (chaps. 7, 8).

Science is helpless here, moreover, because one cannot measure the exact needs of a society for government. And so one cannot really expect to stop the well-known but irresistible slide into usurpation and general corruption (chap. 9). As old age creeps up on each individual, so does decay on societies. (chap. 10) Art is what makes polities, but it is not enough to brake the forces of nature. Medicine may prolong a life, but death cannot be averted. If Sparta and Rome perished, how can historical polities expect to survive? The claims of tradition are therefore very great. Antiquity is a proof of utility and one had better obey the oldest laws, since change is itself a sign of decay. The movement of societies is all in one direction – downhill (chap. 12). The final nail in the coffin of hope is in Rousseau's destruction of his own favourite myths. Sparta and Rome offer little ground for expectation; Rousseau never denied their largely imaginary character, but he wants finally to prove that even human fancy cannot devise a vision of perfection. The ancient republics, so virtous and free, were all grounded in slavery; the liberty of the few was paid for by the enslavement of the many. Slavery is, however, a wrong and a denial of a man's humanity. It cannot be justified and it proves that the past was no more perfect than the present. Only the forms of unfreedom differ (chap. 15). In conclusion we are reminded that all governments degenerate – as if we could by now have forgotten (chap. 18)!

The last Book reverts to some of the themes of the second one. Compared to the Third Book its tone is one of muted, rather than of outright, tragedy.

The opening image of simple men under their oak-tree is immediately followed by the reminder that, compared to that picture, Europe is indeed politically *in extremis*. The private will has now obliterated the general will (chap. 1). We are again reminded that there is no true democracy (chap. 3), and then we are shown what is at best possible, Severus' laws for Rome. This model of a possible law-giver dupes the people into a six-class division according to wealth. The Senate perpetuates the duplicity, and in the absence of luxury a sort of stable client-patron relationship keeps this wholly unequal society stable. To be sure, even this order degenerates (chaps. 4, 5). The art of politics, the conditioning of *mores*, is clearly the art of deception and, while it can hold nature at bay for a while, it is doomed to ultimate failure. Men 'being what they are' cannot be made to obey good laws that 'might be' invented. The reason why there is no legitimate political rule is quite simply that it is impossible. The tragedy is that we can imagine a world better than the one we can make. We are therefore in a position to judge actuality, but not to improve it.

When these two Rousseaus are placed next to each other by an impartial recorder rather than by a pair of competing advocates, the *Social Contract* does not seem incoherent. At no point does Rousseau look forward to a day when men 'shall brothers be for a' that'. He does not concern himself with the future at all, nor can it be said that he is telling his readers what to do or feel. He is not asking them to be hopeful. As Emile was told that political principles, such as those of the *Social Contract*, are to be used to judge the states he is about to visit, so the reader has been supplied with a yardstick. The system of measurement is egalitarian, democratic, and populist. The historical world falls short of every principle of justice against which it is measured. As a psychologist Rousseau was bound to ask himself why that should be so. Since he did not believe that one could remake men and indeed considered education overwhelmingly difficult even when only a single child was involved, he held out no prospects of reform. However, he did not preach resignation either. We emerge with a picture of social possibilities that mirrors the same confusion that appears in our hearts. We are capable of seeing the good, but we are too feeble and too stupid to act upon it. The result is self-deception and, like all good philosophers, Rousseau meant to rob us of our illusions.

Pre-political Movements in Modern Politics

My title does not imply that there was no politics before the era of industrial transformation, but rather that the structure, organizations, scope, objectives, and perhaps, above all, the language of politics changed fundamentally during this transformation, as both the nature of society and the nature of the units within which political action takes place were transformed. I shall take for granted the changes in social structure.

As for the state, it must be recalled that the territorially organized state, centrally administered, with a government which directly reaches down to every citizen and constantly determines his or her activities negatively or positively, is – at least for large geographical areas – a product of the era of capitalist development. It is not comparable in size to the units of face-to-face politics such as village communities or city states, or in structure to the pre-industrial monarchies. In the most powerful and effective of these, state power was either not centralized in the modern manner or it did not reach down below a certain level at all – e.g., civil or even criminal law was not directly the state's law or administered in the state's courts – or it reached down only selectively, for specific purposes or in a mediate form. As Wallerstein has pointed out, it tended to group its subjects not so much on a territorial as on an occupational or corporate basis. In other words, while the political activities in modern states must constantly seek to influence the central (territorial or national) government, in pre-industrial states of a large size this objective was rather exceptional. The widespread belief that the essentially just monarch would intervene to right the injustices done to his subjects if only he knew of them depends not only on the remoteness of central government but also on the rarity of its actual interventions in the everyday affairs of men and women.

This is a modified version of the paper given at a conference at Campinas, Brazil, in 1975.

'Modern' politics is based, not only on the transformation of the 'subject' into the 'citizen' (at least in theory) directly linked to the central government and involved in its activities actively or passively, but on the realistic assumption that political action must seek to change the government or its activities, and consequently on (national) forms of mobilization and organization. This 'nationalization' of politics goes hand in hand with the 'nationalization' of the economy, so that national organization, policy, and strategy become possible and perhaps necessary even for movements, such as labour unions, not aimed exclusively at influencing central government.

It is equally obvious, in the second place, that politics since the late eighteenth century also acquired a number of new devices – forms of organization, propaganda, campaigning, and procedures which were substantially new, even though they may have had their functional equivalents in earlier periods. The large literature about the origin and development of political *parties* proves the point. Some of these transformations were due to technical progress: to be effective even the newspaper required not only a certain degree of literacy and standardization of the national language, but also a certain degree of technology in mechanized communication. Others reflected changes in the social and political structure. The point need not be elaborated.

In the third place, both the objectives and the language of politics have been largely emancipated from ancient tradition and therefore revolutionized. The secularization of hegemonic ideas, and increasingly also of the ideas penetrating the masses, is as familiar as the transformation of monarchy, virtually the only form of government for large polities known for most of class society, into little more than a historical curiosity. Once again, the point does not require elaboration.

To distinguish thus between 'ancient' and 'modern' politics does not mean to reject 'pre-political' politics as necessarily backward, ineffective, or mistaken, i.e., as 'inferior' to modern politics. It may well be argued that 'ancient' politics was incapable of achieving certain results such as those envisaged by modern revolutionaries; this, however, was not because its ideas and instruments were inadequate as such, but because of the inability of *any* force to achieve objectives for which the historical conditions are not present. It would be absurd to argue that, if the Chinese rebels of the Taiping era had been clever enough to invent Mao's ideas, China would have become a People's Republic in the days of the youthful Queen Victoria. Moreover, within the limits of the historic context to which they were adapted and within the class societies which they could not abolish, pre-political politics was probably as effective as any other. Its limits were reached only when it attempted to cope with new problems which arose in the course of social transformations, which they had been designed neither to solve or even to recognize. The program of restoring the Ming dynasty, or any such analogous slogans were probably as effective a means as any of mobilizing popular revolution in China until the end of the nineteenth century. It is only in the twentieth century that such a program can be reasonably criticized as being inferior to, say, the Communist party as a device for overthrowing the old regime.

This paper thus asks what happens to such pre-political movements in the politics of the mid-twentieth century. It thus adds a footnote to my book *Primitive Rebels*, which attempted to establish the existence and the significance of such a phase of 'pre-political' popular politics during the early phases of the 'great transformation'.

Pure movements of the pre-political type, such as nativist movements, may occur during the period of transition to capitalist (or post-capitalist) society, but they are of negligible importance today when even the most backward countries possess at least the nominal equipment of modern politics, such as political parties, elections, and the like. The Saya San rebellion in Burma (1930–1), for example, which marked the beginning of Burmese national liberation, was purely pre-political; but it is extremely improbable today that so important a movement of such nation-wide significance would occur owing 'nothing to western political ideologies or institutions and (receiving) neither inspiration nor political techniques'[1] from modern movements. Indeed, except in some very remote corners of the world, we would not expect to find such movements at all. It must be remembered that even highly pre-political movements such as the Mexican Cristeros of the 1920s were not purely archaic. They were based on a systematic penetration of the countryside by the Catholic clergy, previously mainly an urban corps, in response to the liberalism and anticlericalism of the mid-nineteenth century, and they thus operated in a more 'modern' framework than similar movements would have done a century earlier. In short, most pre-political movements of political importance are today mixtures and combinations of the old and the new, and those which are not, though very interesting to the student, are of little practical significance. Moreover, even the most apparently 'archaic' phenomena of this kind may contain pre-political elements which are *not* traditionalist, which are formed of old materials but in a new context, and which consequently no longer have the same political implications or aims.[2]

1 Donald Eugene Smith, *Religion and Politics in Burma* (Princeton, 1965), 107
2 René Ribeiro, 'The Millennium That Never Came: The Story of a Brazilian Prophet', in Ronald H. Chilcote, ed., *Protest and Resistance in Angola and Brazil* (Berkeley, 1972), 181. Ribeiro points out the disturbing influence of modern pentecostalism on traditional millennial aspirations.

Nevertheless, prepolitical politics still remains important. The degree to which it does varies both within societies and between different geographical areas. Within any society its influence is clearly greatest among the strata whose pattern of life is least affected by the great transformation (characteristically parts of the peasantry) or whose pre-industrial activities are least changed by being transposed into a modern industrial-urban context (e.g., certain parts of the criminal subculture in old cities[3]). Its influence is least among those whose individual social mobility – in so far as it depends on success in learning the rules of a new 'social game' – is greatest (e.g., those entering the 'career open to talent' as defined in the new society) and among those most directly affected by the new ideologies, mainly through education (e.g., secular intellectuals). This does not imply either that middleclass intellectuals have totally sloughed off the pre-industrial traditions of their civilization or that, as theorists of modernization hold, the progress of modern politics is proportional to that of education. Still, it is clear, for example, that while the middle-class politics of Sri Lanka has long severed its original Buddhist roots,[4] the political behaviour of peasants remains more affected by Buddhist traditions. This contrast is perhaps most striking in the Islamic world.

Space does not permit a discussion of the factors which determine the extent to which the politics – or at least the popular politics – of a particular region remain imbued with pre-political elements; but it is clear that they are more prominent in Africa and Asia, and especially within the Islamic, Buddhist, and perhaps Hindu zones, than in Europe and the Western hemisphere. Thus the prevalence of Islam imposes powerful constraints on modern ideology and politics, as is shown by the tendencies to 'reislamization' of even deliberately secular revolutionary regimes, such as Algeria.[5] A number of reasons may be suggested for this: the strongly activist and militant tradition of this religious ideology, often linked in the past with conquering empires; its political (i.e., antiracial and egalitarian) component; the considerable success of Islam in resisting western physical and ideological penetration; and not least the combination of ecumenical cohesion and solidarity with a highly decentralized structure – i.e., its reliance on a local base of grass-roots activists rather than a hierarchic and institutionalized

---

3 For the highly traditional Japanese gangster subculture, see Koji Kata, *Japanese Yakusa* (Tokyo, 1964); Kazuo Taoka, *Yamaguchi-Gumi, Third Generation* (Tokyo, 1973); and Florence Rome, *The Tattooed Men* (New York, 1975).

4 Kumari Jaywardene, *The Rise of the Labor Movement in Ceylon* (Durham NC, 1972)

5 Irene Gendzier, *Frantz Fanon: A Critical Study* (New York, 1973), 259

'church'[6]; and perhaps its ancient character as both an urban and a rural religion.

If the significant pre-political movements of the present are fusions of the old and the new, so are all modern movements, particularly in the Third World. Men and women do not break totally with their past, least of all in the field of ideas, which are expressed in language, the product of numberless pre-industrial generations, and especially not in the field of politics, where human aspirations remain unchanged, though the hopes and methods of achieving them may alter. 'Liberty, equality, fraternity' changed their meaning and political role once these words had become the slogan and program of the French Revolution, but they themselves had political connotations before then, and these no doubt (especially in the case of 'fraternity') echoed in people's minds. Moreover, the concepts were familiar though perhaps in a different terminology. It is almost inevitable that masses of men and women who come to modern movements as first-generation immigrants from the great territories of traditional ways of life will translate new terms into old, or that their experience will colour their adoption of the new ones.

In so far as the new ideas and methods are clearly dominant, the pre-political elements in such movements may not appear clearly, though we know that there is often a great difference between what, say, national or even local leaders of socialist and communist movements say and what their rural followers understand them to mean. However, even the 'new ideas' themselves may be coloured by the old experience. Thus the passion, militancy, and ruthlessness of nineteenth- and twentieth- century anti-clericalism in Christian countries has tended to be directly proportionate to the strength and dominance of the religious institutions it combated. The stronger the shackles of the old world, the greater the effort needed to break free from them. British working-class atheists in the nineteenth century characteristically came from very pious households, and it was Jewish anarchists from the most orthodox backgrounds rather than emancipated middle-class German Jews who insisted on demonstratively eating ham in public on the Sabbath. Mexican anticlericalism was an anti-crusade of fire and blood, because it was, more often than not, an offensive of government, urban middle classes, and workers — the standard-bearers of modernity —

6 This may be measured by the scale of the annual pilgrimage to Mecca in some Islamic countries, which has been intensified by modern communications. For instance, the annual average number of pilgrims from Indonesia increased from around 6,000 in 1900 to about 30,000 by 1930 (Fred R. von der Mehden, *Religion and Nationalism in South East Asia* (Madison, 1963), 117); by 1960 the total annual pilgrimage to Mecca numbered about half a million; and in the late 1970s about a million and a half.

against the stifling conservatism of the countryside. Probably the history of the USSR and China will show that the most determined adversaries of the old ways in the village were less the intellectual cadres, so often with a soft spot for the peasantry, than sons of peasants converted to the virtues of the new ways, perhaps through army service,[7] and perhaps drawn from the rebellious young. The continued insistence in the USSR today on militant anti-religious propaganda, as well as in China on anti-Confucian campaigns, remains impressive.[8]

However, quite apart from adding a special tinge to modern politics, pre-political ideas may influence them directly. First, in so far as modern politics are genuinely electoral – i.e., based on a wide suffrage with competing candidates – they must in some ways reflect the opinions and feelings of bodies of voters, many of whom are pre-political in our sense. Candidates who fail to pay at least lip-service to them do not get elected, at least in honest elections. Hence, paradoxically, there is more scope for the expression of pre-political views in parliamentary democracies than under the restricted electoral systems of nineteenth-century Europe or Latin America or, naturally, than under dictatorial systems. Thus the extension of the vote to women almost automatically strengthened the role of parties associated with traditional religion, at least for a period, thus reinforcing the already strong male chauvinism of, say, the French Radical Socialists. In Italy in 1953 more than half of all women, but only just over one quarter of all men, voted for the Christian Democrats.[9] However wide the gap between the promises of politicians and their performance, and however reluctant the leadership of a movement may be to make concessions to the 'backwardness' of its followers, some account of their pre-political ways has to be taken. This creates particularly serious problems for anti-traditional movements which are often torn between the desire to attack traditional views and the expediency of compromising with them.[10]

7 Teodor Shanin, *The Awkward Class: Political Sociology of Peasantry in a Developing Society: Russia 1910–1925* (Oxford, 1972), 192, observes that in 1925–6 70 per cent of the chairmen of *volost* (sub-district) executive committees in rural Russia were ex-soldiers.

8 We are here considering atheist anticlericalism only. The anticlericalism of minority religious communities against state churches, such as that of protestant sects in nineteenth-century England, is another matter.

9 For various data supporting this, see S.M. Lipset, *Political Man* (New York 1963), 260; Maurice Duverger, *La participation des forces à la vie politique* (Paris, 1955); Herbert Tingsten, *Political Behavior: Studies in Election Statistics* (Stockholm, 1937), chap. 1; Ricardo Cruz Coke, *Geografía electoral de Chile* (Santiago, 1952), 128–9; and Eduardo Zalduendo, *Geografía electoral de la Argentina* (Buenos Aires, 1958).

10 See Maria Antonietta Macchiocchi, *Lettere dell'interno del P.C.I. a Louis Althus-*

Second, the appeal to pre-political ideas is not only a reflection of these ideas among the masses, but it can also be used to formulate programs and modes of political cohesion which are characteristic of modern politics and may indeed have been inconceivable in the pre-political era: nationalism, populism, and various mass movements of the radical right (fascism, etc.). That such movements utilize ancient sentiments such as xenophobia (against foreigners, immigrants, and other out-groups), the appeal of group religion (Catholicism among the Irish, Islam from Morocco to the Philippines), or that they claim to aspire to a pre-industrial utopia of peasants and artisans (as on the wilder fringes of Nazism), should not mislead us into regarding them as traditionalist.[11] They may indeed represent the very opposite in developed countries: the attempt to create fictitious versions of traditional solidarities and utopias by those permanently severed by history from the real ones. However, if nationalist, populist, and other similar movements must be considered as essentially modern in origin, historical function, and context, their use of archaic material reflects local pre-political tradition. William II's German Empire, as part of its attempt to establish a tradition for itself, put up a statue to William I on the Kyffhäuser Mountain, in which by ancient belief the dead Emperor Frederick Barbarossa sits, waiting to be reborn.

Conversely, most pre-political movements are combined with, or come to terms with, some sort of modern one, either by imbuing them with their content, by selecting between them, or in other ways. Thus it is clear that many African political parties, whatever their nominal ideology and program, are largely held together by tribal solidarities.[12] A more complex situation is that in which support for modern movements such as the Communist party consists of different elements, some of them traditional and sometimes incompatible with each other. Thus in Indonesia the appeal of the Communist party appears to have been partly revolutionary in the secular class sense, partly by mobilizing the traditional ideology which stressed the oneness of the common people and the agrarian revolutionism summed up in the combination of 'millennarianism, messianism, nativism and belief in the Holy War',[13] partly by stressing the (non-Islamic) glories of

ser (Milan, 1969), on the conflict between the demand to propagate birth control and the traditional value of numerous children.
11 Thus in the membership of the Nazi party in 1933 peasants were more heavily under-represented, relative to their proportion in the population, than any other social group. Women, heavily over-represented in the electorate of 'traditionalist' conservative or religious parties, formed a lower proportion of the Nazi electorate as late as 1930 than they did in any other party except the Communists. Tingsten, Political Behavior, 43
12 Thomas Hodgkin, African Political Parties (Penguin Books, 1961), 65–7
13 Sartono Kartodirdjo, 'Agrarian Radicalism in Java: Its Setting and Development', in Claire Holt, ed., Culture and Politics in Indonesia (Ithaca, 1972), 83–4

the Indonesian past and thus gaining the support of the non-Islamized regions and elements, but partly also by an alliance with traditional (anti-Islamic) local interest groups. They 'juggle[d] their efforts at combining the old and the new' – as it turned out unsuccessfully.[14] From the point of view of the pre-political population, joining a modern movement or party may be combined with activities which seem irrelevant to that party, but not to the members, e.g., joining an evangelical sect. This is like combining the revolutionary consciousness of Lenin's era with that of Martin Luther.[15]

At first sight one might suppose that pre-political movements find it easier to combine with – or rather to be absorbed by – modern traditionalist movements rather than by militantly anti-traditionalist movements, since the former speak a pre-political language at least in part. Nineteenth-century conservative politicians assumed that this was so, and therefore hoped for the support of peasant voters against godless socialist workers. The fact that precisely the most traditional peasants have in the twentieth century often turned out to be not merely objectively revolutionary, but subjectively supporters of anti-traditional parties such as Marxist ones, proves that matters are not so simple.[16] This is not to underestimate the significance of such factors preserving traditional modes of thought as physical or social isolation and illiteracy.[17] Moreover, other things being equal, it is clearly easier to communicate with people in political terms they already understand than in terms whose meaning must first be explained to them.[18]

But other things are not equal. In the first place the familiar traditional pre-political ideology does not conceal social realities. Neither church nor

14 Rex Mortimer, 'Traditional Modes and Communist Movements: Change and Protest in Indonesia', in John Wilson Lewis ed., *Peasant Rebellion and Communist Revolution in Asia* (Stanford, 1974), 14

15 For combinations of religious sectarianism and modern movements, see my *Primitive Rebels* (Manchester, 1959), chap. IV; A. Moscato and M.N. Pierini, *Rivolta religiosa nelle campagne* (Rome, 1965), 130–2 on Lazzarettists; Wesley Craig, 'The Peasant Movement of La Convención', in Henry Landsberger ed., *Latin American Peasant Movements* (Ithaca, 1969), 286; and Oscar Lewis, *Pedro Martínez* (New York, 1964).

16 See Eric Wolf, *Peasant Wars of the Twentieth Century* (London, 1971), and Hemza Alavi, 'Peasants and Revolution' in R. Miliband and J. Saville eds., *The Socialist Register* (London, 1965)

17 Donald Zagoria, 'Asian Tenancy Systems and Communist Mobilization of the Peasantry', in Lewis ed., *Peasant Rebellion and Communist Revolution in Asia*, 42, 59–60

18 Outsiders seeking to mobilize the peasantry have long attempted to do so consciously, from the German poet Büchner's experiment in using the language of Lutheranism for revolutionary propaganda in 1830 ('Der hessische Landbote') to Francisco Julião.

king can mobilize peasants unless peasants think that both correspond to their interest as peasants – or in their own terminology, that they are a 'true church', a true' or 'just' king, or an emperor who enjoys the mandate of heaven. The most familiar cases of persistently militant traditionalist peasants, mobilized by conservatives, are free peasant proprietors enjoying considerable autonomy and privileges, like the Tyrolese, the Basques and Navarrese, and the original Swiss cantons – i.e., peasants who can in a sense be said to be defending victories won in earlier struggles. Conversely, mere traditionalism did not prevent, say, the peasants of Extremadura or Alentejo from supporting the left, if it appeared to correspond to their interests.[19]

In the second place, the mere classification of an ideology as traditionalist or modern is not enough. What we must know is how relevant the parts which are communicated to the peasants, appear to be *to them*. They may reject anti-traditionalist ideologies like Marxism, not because they are 'godless', but because, coming from townsmen who do not understand the rural world, they are beside the point. Thus townsmen may think that the simple slogan 'expropriate the landlords' *must* appeal to landless or land-poor peasants, but it may be, more often than not, meaningless to them unless translated into concrete terms of the particular land they know, or into the terms of what may be called 'peasant jurisprudence' which defines who has a right to what land under what circumstances.[20] For similar reasons the appeal to collectivize the land (on the mistaken ground that peasant communities like those of Tsarist Russia or Andean America were already a sort of collective farm) may miss the point. Alternatively, the political demands of an urban-based socialist movement may largely neglect the actual agrarian demands of the peasantry, however sympathetic it might otherwise be to the socialists.[21] On the other hand, if the propaganda of the non-traditional left appears to make sense to the peasants, the obstacles in its way may be easily surmounted. Thus in the Italy of the 1950s the tendency of women to believe that political opinions also imply actual membership of a political party was notably *greater* in the backward South than in the North. The reason given for this unexpected and highly untraditional behaviour is that 'in the South

19 For an interesting comparison between neighbouring peasant communities with very different histories and political alignments, see John W. Cole and Eric Wolf, *The Hidden Frontier: Ecology and Ethnicity in an Alpine Valley* (New York, 1974).

20 For this complex problem, see for example Shanin, *The Awkward Class*, appendix B; my 'Peasant Land Occupations' in *Past & Present* 62 (1974); and my 'Peasants and Rural Migrants in Politics' in Claudio Veliz ed., *The Politics of Conformity in Latin America* (Oxford, 1967), 50.

21 For a good example of this lack of contact, see the Italian land occupation movement of 1919 described in Luisa Levi Accati, 'Lotta rivoluzionaria dei contadini siciliani e pugliesi nel 1919–1920', *Il Ponte*, 10 Oct. 1970.

membership of a party has the significance of a decisive step towards the emancipation of women'.[22]

In the third place, the actual modalities of politics may have a hidden ideological content, which must not be overlooked. Thus a classical bourgeois type of party, appealing for parliamentary votes, may – however traditionalist its language – have little meaning as such to peasants, both because they may, not unrealistically, suppose that electing a party majority for a national parliament has little to do with how peasants best defend their interests, and also because the actual principle of bourgeois election (e.g., voting by arithmetical head-counting) appears incomprehensible or even harmful.[23] Many therefore assimilate the new and irrelevant mechanism of elections to some old and relevant one, e.g., either to the maintenance of community solidarity by voting *en bloc* as a community (for instance by dividing Colombia into a patchwork of solidly Conservative or Liberal *veredas*[24]) or, more usually, to the familiar exchange of service for favours of old-style patronage systems. Traditionalist voting may therefore not be ideological voting for the traditional way of life, but the insertion of pre-political reasoning into a framework of modern politics. Conversely they may understand a modern movement whose activities seem sensible to peasants – e.g., because it organizes the construction of village schools[25] better than a party whose parliamentary activities are remote from theirs.

Nevertheless, the integration of pre-political activities and movements into suitable modern ones, whatever their ideology, must overcome one major obstacle. While their political ideals and aims can normally be translated with little difficulty into modern terminology where this is apposite, the methods and *mechanisms* of modern politics are, as we have seen, generally quite different from those of pre-political politics. It is thus, paradoxically, easier for a pre-political revolutionary to join a modern revolutionary movement, or possibly for pre-political group solidarities and

22 Elio Caranti, *Sociologia e statistica delle elezioni italiane nel dopoguerra* (Rome, 1954)
23 This may be so also for the pre-political urban poor. See *Primitive Rebels*, chap. VII, and P.A. Allum, *Politics and Society in Postwar Naples* (Cambridge, 1973), *passim*, but esp. 58ff.
24 Orlando Fals Borda, *Peasant Society in the Colombian Andes: A Sociological Study of Baucio* (Gainesville, 1962), 43; Robert H. Dix, *Colombia: The Political Dimensions of Change* (New Haven, 1967), 214
25 For the importance of such grass-roots school construction in peasant politics, see Jorge Dandler, *El sindicalismo en Bolivia* (Mexico City, 1969), chap. 3, and Julio Alfaro and Teresa Ore, *El desarrollo del capitalismo en La Convención y los nuevos movimientos politicos de campesinos con tierra 1963–1973* (Lima, 1974) part II, 23.

hatreds to turn into modern nationalism,[26] than for pre-political reformists to turn into modern reformists. There is no real pre-political equivalent to the modern state-sponsored arrangements to guarantee farm prices and buy up farm surpluses, and consequently no equivalent to the political campaigns to achieve such guarantees. There is a pre-political equivalent to the control of the urban cost of living (the food riot or *taxation populaire*[27]), but it is clearly remote from most modern ways of demanding or achieving it. There is no pre-political equivalent at all for changing the policy of central governments other than by prayer or insurrection; and in modern states all major policy changes imply exerting influence upon the central government. Admittedly certain localized methods (mainly derived from city experience) can be adapted to serve on a national scale; for example, the techniques of journeymen craftsmen (trade societies) can turn, as in England in the nineteenth century, into trade unions, though not always.[28] But on the whole most political activities, including most of the political activities of even the most revolutionary movements when there is no actual revolution, are quite different from the pre-political activities designed to ensure analogous results.

A number of pre-political phenomena or movements are therefore either doomed to disappear entirely or to change their social function. Moreover, a number of pre-political activities must also disappear with the context which made them apparently rational.

Among those for which, even in peripheral areas of the modern world, there is increasingly little place are, it may be suggested, social banditry and the urban 'mob'.[29] I have discussed the problem of banditry at length elsewhere.[30]

As for the urban mob, it seems likely that its political role and activities are on the decline, though a number of classical urban insurrections of the old type are still recorded – e.g., Naples in 1943, Bogotá in 1948, and Santo Domingo in 1965.[31] There are both social, ecological, and political reasons

26 Doubt arises on this point because we know very little about the relation of the nationalist ideology formulated by intellectuals and politicians to the actual beliefs of their followers, for example among peasants.
27 E.P. Thompson, 'The Moral Economy of the English Crowd', *Past & Present* 50 (1971)
28 There is no continuity between the declining *compagnonnages* of France and the new labour unions of the nineteenth century.
29 See *Primitive Rebels*, chaps. II and VII.
30 My *Bandits* (London, 1969; Penguin Books, 1971)
31 The 'Cordobazos' of 1969 and 1971 in Argentina clearly belong to a modern phase of urban insurrection, though in 1971 the role of elements socially similar to

for this: the decline of the *Gemeinschaft* of the old slums before the *Gesellschaft* or modern market and consumer-oriented society;[32] heterogeneous mass immigrations; the enormous physical spread of cities with their widely scattered *favelas* or *barriadas*; the decline of local power centres before those in the national capitals; and so on. The strength of the classic urban riot or insurrection rested upon *a/* the concentration and intermingling of the centres of power, the residences of the rich and the poor being in the same quarters, which maximized sensitiveness to mass action; *b/* the ideological unity of all groups, which gave riots under certain circumstances an accepted legitimacy and hence effectiveness; *c/* the likelihood of wild market fluctuations in the cost of living; and *d/* the virtual absence of any mechanism other than direct action for communicating mass demands. These circumstances are now increasingly rare, especially in combination, though within much more restricted environments (such as university cities and precincts) they may still be found.

The classic situation of the urban mob must not be confused with that of the squatter settlements (*favelas, barriadas*, etc.). The location of the mob is the old city centre, but *barriadas* tend to be increasingly peripheral or distributed over a large city area. The mob consists largely of natives of the city; the *barriada* is essentially inhabited – though as time goes on perhaps to a diminishing extent – by immigrants. Unlike other city poor, the squatter owns his own dwelling, or at least does not pay rent.[33] Research has demonstrated that the dwellers in squatter settlements are neither the poorest nor the least integrated into the modern society into which they have chosen to enter. As country people who maintain contacts with their kin and friends in the country, they are rooted in a partly pre-political world, and the familiar reaction of immigrant cultural self-defence in the city reinforces some of the old ways.[34] But the political behaviour of squatters is not so much an archaic survival, like that of Neapolitan slum-dwellers,[35] but

those in pre-political urban risings seems to have been quite large. B. Balve, M. Murmis, *et al.*, *Lucha de calles, lucha de clases: elemento para su analisis (Cordoba 1969–1971)* (Buenos Aires, 1973)

32 Rather than isolating the 'culture of poverty' along the lines of Oscar Lewis, it may be more useful to distinguish 'cultures of poverty' based on what Allum calls 'the rural aspects of slum society in Naples' (*Politics and Society*, 59) from those which seem clearly more anomic, as in some black ghettoes in the United States.

33 According to Jaime Gianella, *Marginalidad en Lima metropolitana* (Lima, 1970), in 1967 68.5 per cent of the residents of the old city of Lima paid rent, but only 16.5 per cent of those in *barriadas* did so.

34 See William Mangin, ed., *Peasants in Cities: Readings in the Anthropology of Urbanization* (Boston, 1970).

35 See Allum, *Politics and Society*, esp. chap. 4, 'Political World Pictures'.

modern; where necessary they are adapting ancient methods rationally to new situations.

This may indeed be essential, if only because the very process of collective squatting in cities (unlike that of rural land invasion, with which it often has great similarity) brings the squatters into the centre of a modern political situation. As soon as the urban invasion has been recognized by the authorities (as normally happens sooner or later) the major problem is to secure public services; the recognition and the services imply direct dealings with the municipal or government authorities and provide the basis for political bargaining through urban or national political machines.[36] This may take the familiar form of clientelist politics, dominated by a hierarchy of patrons, but this is not necessarily pre-political. (In any case the demand for *personal* favours – jobs, permits, welfare assistance, etc. – must not be confused with the demand for *collective* favours such as the supply of electricity or transport for a settlement.) Squatter settlements are inevitably to some extent integrated into the political system, though in other respects they may remain both physically peripheral and socially outcast or at least underprivileged. Their politics are determined both by the desirability of keeping in with the authorities, who alone can provide favours and services, and the opposition, which appeals to their dissatisfaction. Hence perhaps the appeal to them of demagogic *caudillo* figures, preferably those who have been or are likely to be presidents. In 1970 no less than 84 per cent of the inhabitants of squatter settlements (*tugurios*) in Bogotá voted for the populist presidential candidate, the former dictator Rojas Pinilla.[37]

Among the pre-political activities which must inevitably disappear are all those connected with the characteristic pre-political method of governing large territories, namely monarchy. The revolutionary attempt to replace the (false and just) pretender have increasingly little scope, and even the dream of a millennial or revolutionary return to some golden dynastic era of the past – the Incas or the Ming – is clearly on the way out, if it has not already disappeared. The tradition of a possible return to the Inca empire has a long history in the Andes, and the propagandist rhetoric of innovators even today is not unmindful of it (cf. the Tupamaros and the appeal to Tupac Amaru in Peru since 1968[38]; but in fact there is no sign any longer of a *significant* appeal to the Inca myth in the Peruvian peasant movements.

36 See K.L. Karsh, M.L. and A.V. Schwartz, *The Evolution of Law in the Barrios of Caracas* (Los Angeles, 1973).
37 *Informe al Congreso, 1970,* 181. The electoral appeal of the former presidents Odría and Pérez Jímenez in Lima and Caracas is known.
38 See my 'Peasant Land Occupations', 149, for references, and also Juan M. Ossío ed., *Ideología mesiánica del mundo Andino* (Lima, 1973). The Bolivian Indian

Though a rising to restore the Ming dynasty allegedly occurred in China as late as 1952, it may be doubted whether there will be another.[39] This change is due not merely to the actual disappearance of monarchies, but clearly also to transformations in political and ideological experience, not least perhaps to the discovery of (irreversible) historical change in real life.[40] Ancient myths cannot survive the destruction of the historical context which allows them to have a specific meaning.

This does not mean the disappearance of the pre-political attitude to the supreme political ruler, the apex of the social structure and source of justice who may be counterposed to the injustice perpetrated by inferior authorities. It may be transferred to the president.[41] The tendency for modern mass movements and new regimes to turn leaders of government into semi-mythical (charismatic) figures, godlike or father-like, is marked, not only in the 'iconization' of Stalin or Mao, but also in developed countries (cf. F.D. Roosevelt) even when not encouraged by official policy. The identification of 'the time of justice which will come' with the return of a lost leader is familiar, as is Argentina (Peron – *justicialismo*); and, as the survival of Peronism after the actual death of Peron suggests, it is even today interpreted in part metaphorically rather than literally. However, though such pre-political attitudes persist, and are perhaps integrated into more modern ones, the classic pattern of pre-political action based on them cannot normally so persist.

Some of these attitudes may therefore disappear or be pushed back on the

---

leader of 1899, Zarate, is said to have claimed Inca descent. Ramiro Condarco Morales, *Zarate: El 'Temible' Willka* (La Paz, 1965)

39 Jean Chesneaux, *Les sociétés secrètes en Chine* (Paris, 1965), 267

40 The belief in the return of the golden age – for example, by the re-awakening of the Emperor Frederick Barbarossa from his cave in the Kyffhäuser Mountain or by the coming together again of the severed head and body of *Inkarri* in the Peruvian myth – is not a belief about the chronological future, since the modern sense of history is absent among those who have it. See my 'The Social Function of the Past', *Past & Present* 55 (1972). For those whom life forces into the experience of modern historical change, it becomes increasingly difficult to maintain a symbolic or mythical theory of revolution ('the world is turned upside down – one day it must and will be turned the right way up') in the shape of a specific succession of historical events linked with the past ('the world was turned upside down by the conquest of the Spaniards – one day it will be restored by the return of the Inca empire'). As soon as the return of the Incas becomes a question of actual chronology, even those who believe the myth in general are then bound to deny it. 'Creo que ya no volvería ahora el tiempo de Inkariy. Como podría volver ahora? ... No el tiempo del Inkariy ya no puede volver. O quizas talves pues. Tupa Amaru es otra persona. Posiblemente era el también Inka. Creo que no.' Ossío, *Ideología mesiánica*, 309, 352

41 Ossío, *Ideología mesiánica*, 453

outer margins of politics. Others, however, survive with changed functions, especially when – it may be suggested – they exist in organized or institutional form independent of purely local community structures.[42] This is the case with certain religious institutions and what may be loosely called corporations and societies. Here the formal continuity of the institution actually encourages flexibility and adaptability, the less specific or specialized their original function. Thus guilds disappear with the decline of the urban artisan economy or are transformed (like the London livery companies) into primarily social clubs, unless, like the trade societies of journeymen (wage-earning) artisans in the nineteenth century, they can discover an equivalent function in modern industrial society and transform themselves into trade unions. On the other hand, religious organizations can more easily adapt to a changed environment (so long as any kind of traditional religion maintains its hold), because, however closely identified with a specific social order, their function is not confined to activities within it. The Roman Catholic Church, though plainly feudal in the middle ages, survived the fall of feudalism.

Among examples of such flexibility the so-called popular 'secret societies' may be mentioned. The adaptation of the Sicilian Mafia (in so far as the term 'society' is apposite[43]) to changes in Sicily and the world is familiar. Little is known about the fortunes of the ancient Chinese secret societies in China since 1949, but these bodies, which appear to have functioned in imperial China as self-defence organizations for their members, as a sort of parallel society or counter-culture within the Confucian framework, and as nuclei of political opposition and rebellion, still function outside China from Singapore to San Francisco, probably with declining political and increased racketeering functions. A useful example of flexibility is that of the Abakuà, a male ritual society imported by slaves from the Niger delta and established in Cuba by the late 1830s, and better known as the ñañigos. It seems to have acted first as a pro-African and anti-assimilationist force among the slaves, later as a body of fighters in the contests of Havana barrios against each other, as a criminal racket, and as a body establishing control over the port-workers, therefore becoming active in labour unions and also establishing its value to politicians. Its 'black consciousness' appears to have made it

42 Practices and institutions too identified with a particular local community – for example, local saints and fiestas – may find it hard to survive the transformation of these communities. It might be useful to investigate the fortunes of local patron saints in the twentieth century as distinct from those whose appeal is far wider, such as the Virgin of Guadalupe in Mexico.

43 See Henner Hess, Mafia: zentrale Herrschaft und lokal Gegenmacht (Tübingen, 1970); Anton Blok, The Mafia of a Sicilian Village 1860–1960 (Oxford, 1974); Testo integrale della relazione della commissione parlamentare d'inchiesta sul fenomeno della Mafia, 3 vols. (Rome, 1973); Donald Cressey, Theft of a Nation (New York, 1969).

sympathetic to Fidel Castro, but though it still flourishes its post-revolutionary development is obscure.[44]

We have already referred to the persistence of the role of traditional religion, both as ideology and organization. It is probably the most powerful surviving pre-political element in modern politics, as witness the activity of confessionally based parties (e.g., Christian Democrats) even in Europe since the war. This may be affected in future, however, as there are signs of disintegration within the traditional Christian churches.

Finally, there are pre-political forms of activity which may persist because they are the same as activities within modern politics, though their ideological formulation and justification may differ. That old pensioner from Pozzuoli near Naples who, as late as 1970, identified political patrons and patron saints,[45] sounds unusually pre-political, even for Naples; but there is nothing inevitably pre-political in clientelist politics as such.

Most of the pre-political phenomena with which students of modern politics are concerned, are combinations and fusions of the old and the new, or more exactly infusions of old elements into a new political and ideological framework. Nevertheless, there are certain significant movements in which the pre-political elements are dominant rather than recessive. We may, in conclusion, attempt – with the utmost caution – to suggest why they sometimes occur. Two situations favourable to such 'archaism' may be suggested.

The first is the obvious case of straight resistance to modernization. The Mexican Cristeros fought everything the twentieth century seemed to bring to them from the godless cities. The Saudi Arabian prince who attacked the new television station in Riyadh by force of arms resisted everything that disrupted the ancient order of Koranic society. It may be suggested that such traditionalist movements to hold up progress are today more likely to take a conservative rather than a traditionalist-revolutionary form, except perhaps when identified with xenophobia, because movements for social justice and liberation have by now been closely associated with certain characteristically

44 Lydia Cabrera, *La sociedad secreta Abakuà* (Havana, 1958); Rafael L. Lopez Valdes, 'La sociedad secreta "Abacuá" en un grupo de obreros portuarios', *Etnología y Folklore* (Havana) 2 (1966); Pedro Deschamps Chapeaux, 'Margarito Blanco "Ocongo de Ultan"', *Bol. Inst. de Hist. y del Archivo Nacional* (Havana), July–Dec. 1964

45 Allum, *Politics and Society*, 99: 'Instead of [our] San Proculo we need someone like San Silvio Gava, or San Giancinto Bosco, but they come from other zones and don't care about us ... The trouble is, we have always chosen the wrong saint, always ... I remember when I was young and a personality like De Nicola presented himself here to become deputy, we preferred a leftwinger, whose name I can't even remember.' De Nicola was a leading southern politician.

modern ideologies (e.g., those of the left), which are strongly modernist, and with activists and leaders who come from the modern zones of life – cities, universities, military service, etc. It may also be suggested that the growing penetration of most parts of the world by modern commercial society, consumer goods, and the like undermines this type of movement. However, the Iranian revolution of 1978–79 demonstrates the mass appeal of traditionalism.

The second situation may be the one identified by McLane in his study of the Vietnamese 'political sects' – the Cao Dai, Hoa Hao, and Binh Xuen.[46] The success of these 'archaic' movements in the 1940s and 1950s, he suggests, is due to a failure of the Viet-Minh revolution to spread sufficiently rapidly in South Vietnam; there was hiatus between the breakdown of rural society and administrative institutions and the post-war attempts of the Viet-Minh, the French, the Bao Dai and Diem governments to bring the peasantry into a single political system. During this hiatus the archaic sects spread among the pre-political peasantry, developed independent bases of military and political power, and partially preempted modern political organizations. The Cao Dai and Hoa Hao, founded respectively as syncretic and neo-Buddhist religious organizations without any clear political purpose, and the Binh Xuen, originally a criminal racket based on a bandit area near Saigon, had only the vaguest political and social program, and 'the ideas of their leaders' – largely, it seems, socially similar to *mafiosi* – 'were largely irrelevant to the problem of how society should be structured and how political power should be distributed when the French rule ended.' Nevertheless, in the confused and complex situation of war and post-war, they developed as powerful mafias and filled a political vacuum created largely by the unusual weakness of nationalists and communists in the southern villages. Until suppressed by Diem in 1955 they may have controlled as many peasants as the Viet Minh, though probably in the manner of war-lord militias rather than by means of any specific social appeal. In short, they were the product of an incomplete or partially unsuccessful revolution, and their main effect was to delay the completion of that revolution.[47]

Probably such phenomena are most likely to occur for a time during analogous situations when state power is temporarily in abeyance or during prolonged revolutionary transitions or crises of breakdown in pre-industrial societies. However, the vacuum will be partly filled by archaic 'parallel systems' emerging spontaneously only when alternatives are not available, e.g., modern political parties and movements or more orthodox local

46 John R. McLane, 'Archaic Movements and Revolution in Southern Vietnam', in M. Miller and R. Aya eds., *National Liberation: Revolution in the Third World* (New York, 1971)
47 *Ibid.*, 69, 71, 86–7

power-systems such as war-lords. The lengthy revolutionary civil wars of the twentieth century, such as the Mexican, Russian, Chinese, and Vietnamese, or possibly on a smaller scale the Colombian, might repay study in this respect. It should be borne in mind that the crises in which such pre-political movements may emerge are *political* as well as social, i.e., they probably imply a temporary disappearance of the state's framework. India contains more than enough material for pre-political revivals, but its politics have consistently remained within the framework of a modern state and its political system includes parties of the modern type, whether reactionary, revolutionary, or otherwise. Whether the Sicilian Mafia would have emerged as a semi-independent power-centre if Sicily had separated from Italy (as seemed briefly possible in 1943–4), we do not know; but since Sicily did not, it has continued to remain in the shadows, operating through such political parties, organizations, and institutions as are accessible to its pressures.

There is little doubt that, in general, the pre-political element is today significant not in itself but through the ways in which it colours and influences the institutions of modern politics. For a new socio-economic structure in the end implies a new political structure and this in turn a new politics. Let me conclude with a quotation from W.F. Wertheim, an expert on the movements of South East Asia:

> The next stage in the emancipation movement was to adopt a new principle from the Western world: the usefulness of modern organization. The impossibility of attaining their ends by individual achievement ... compelled the southeast Asians, whose main asset vis-à-vis the colonial powers was their number, to discover the meaning of collective action. The history of the emancipation movement can be written largely in terms of the activities of all kinds of organizations. Trade unions multiplied to emancipate the urban laborer and the plantation coolie ... ; traders' organizations tried to break through the monopoly of foreign groups, among whom the traditional 'sworn brotherhood' type of organization also gave way to more modern ones; farmers' unions fought the oppressive power of the landlords; women's organizations aspired to emancipation from traditional male domination; youth organizations fought traditional authority.[48]

It is the discovery that modern organization is better suited to the struggle in a modern society, rather than the discovery of modern ideology, which accounts for the decline of pre-political movements in the modern world.

48 W.F. Wertheim, *Dawning of an Asian Dream: Selected Articles on Modernization and Emancipation* (Amsterdam, 1973)

The New Jerusalem of Moses Hess

Moses Hess was one of the first people to acknowledge Marx's intellectual stature and his future impact on history. In a letter written as early as 1841, he says:

> You may expect to meet the greatest, perhaps the only living philosopher: he will shortly have all the eyes of Germany centered upon him when he will appear in public, in his writings as well as at the university ... He transcends not only Strauss, but Feuerbach as well ...
>
> Dr Marx (for this is the name of my idol) is at most 24 years old: he will deal the death blow to all medieval philosophy and politics; he combines the deepest philosophical profundity with a cutting wit. Can you imagine Rousseau, Voltaire, Holbach, Lessing, Heine and Hegel all integrated – not just thrown together – into one person? This is Dr Marx.[1]

Yet many years after his death, Theodor Herzl, the founder of political Zionism, said that if he had read Moses Hess' *Rome and Jerusalem*, he would not have written his own *The Jewish State*.

Hess thus stands at the crossroads of more than one political and ideological movement: he is revered today as one of the forerunners of socialism as well as of Zionism. In the attempt to broaden the philosophical base of Marxism, Hess' writings have now been published in a number of communist countries, and in Israel his writings have been edited by Martin Buber for the Zionist Library.[2] The Central Zionist Archives in Jerusalem as

---

1 Hess to Berthold Auerbach, 2 Sept. 1841, in Moses Hess, *Briefwechsel*, ed. E. Silberner (The Hague, 1959), 79–80

2 E.g., Moses Hess, *Philosophische und sozialistische Schriften*, eds. Auguste Cornu & Wolfgang Mönke (Berlin-DDR, 1969); Moses Hess, *Pisma filozoficzne 1841–1850*, ed. J. Garewicz (Warszawa, 1963); Buber's 2-volume Hebrew edition of Hess' Selected Works was published in Jerusalem in 1954–56, under the title *Ktavim Klaliyim* and *Ktavim Zioniyim ve-Yehudiyim*.

well as the Institute for Marxism-Leninism of the Central Committee of the CPSU each proudly possess and display some of his manuscripts. Upon his death in 1875, the German socialists added the inscription *Vater der deutschen Sozialdemokratie* to his tombstone; and after the creation of Israel, its government, then led by the Israel Labour Party, arranged for his remains to be transferred to the cemetery at Kinnereth, on Lake Tiberias. There, in the graveyard of the first Israeli kibbutz, he now lies interred next to the other founders of socialist Zionism – Dov Borochov, Nachman Syrkin, and Berl Katznelson.

Hess' contribution to both socialism and Zionism is thus generally acknowledged.[3] Yet he still figures as hardly more than a footnote in both histories of socialist and Zionist thought, though the recent interest in the Young Hegelians has drawn more attention to his writings than before.[4] But what has rarely been spelt out is the theoretical link between his communist philosophy and his attachment to a Jewish national renaissance. To orthodox Marxists in particular, this poses a vexing problem, and his proto-Zionism is sometimes dismissed as a mere aberration of an aging thinker, 'obviously utterly incompatible with Marx's materialist theory of history.'[5]

It is my intention to show how there exists an immanent link between Hess' socialist criticism of bourgeois society and his preoccupation with matters Jewish; that the same criticism which draws him to communism draws him to seek a national solution to the Jewish problem; that in seeking such a solution, he gives a socialist reinterpretation to the predicaments and problems of the modern, secularized Jew; and that, in his attempt to integrate the national element into his philosophy of history, he may be in-

3 We now possess the comprehensive biography by Edmund Silberner, *Moses Hess: Geschichte seines Lebens* (Leiden, 1966). For an earlier and most influential biography, see Theodor Zlocisti, *Moses Hess*, 2nd ed. (Berlin, 1921). See also the brilliant essay by Isaiah Berlin, 'The Life and Opinions of Moses Hess', now reprinted in Philip Rieff ed., *On Intellectuals* (Garden City, 1970), 137–82. Georg Lukács' essay on 'Moses Hess and the Problem of Idealist Dialects' (1926) is now also available in English translation (*Telos*, no. 10, Winter 1971, 3–34). A recent addition to the Hess literature is Bruno Frei, *Im Schatten von Karl Marx – Moses Hess, Hundert Jahre nach seinem Tod* (Wien-Köln-Graz, 1977). A full bibliography of Hess' writings was compiled some years ago by Edmund Silberner, 'Zur Hess Bibliographie', in *Archiv fur Sozialphilosophie*, Bd. VI–VII (1966–67), 241–314.
4 See Sidney Hook, *From Hegel to Marx*, new ed. (Ann Arbor, 1962), 186–204; David McLellan, *The Young Hegelians and Karl Marx* (London, 1969), 137–60; Horst Stuke, *Philosophie der Tat* (Stuttgart, 1963), 189–244; Karl Löwith, ed., *Die Hegelsche Linke* (Stuttgart-Bad Canstatt, 1962), 47–62; Jürgen Gebhardt, *Politik und Eschatologie* (Munchen, 1963).
5 So, for example, Mönke and Cornu in their otherwise judicious Introduction to *Philosophische und sozialistische Schriften*, lxvii.

strumental in filling a gap left in Marxian socialism. Seen in this light, his *Rome and Jerusalem*, while being a turn-about compared to his earlier assimilationist views, addresses itself to questions which figured earlier in his thinking and is therefore to be viewed as an integral part of his thought and of his quest for a transformative philosophy which may be a solution to a number of facets of modern society – and which may solve his own identity problem as well.

Hess' first book, published in 1837, was *The Holy History of Mankind*. The work appeared anonymously, its author hiding behind the designation 'A Young Spinozist'.[6] As we shall see, the association with Spinoza is significant. From its theoretical aspect this work combines a Young Hegelian historiosophy with a social *Weltanschauung* derived in part from the Saint-Simonists. The basic thesis of this work is that human history is characterized by periods in which subject and object are alternately united and disunited. In Saint-Simonian terms, history is an intermittently alternating succession of organic and unorganic periods, i.e., periods of subject-object unity are 'organic' periods, and those in which there is a breach and alienation between subject and object are 'unorganic' periods. After having surveyed, with some obvious over-simplification, the sequence of these periods in human history, Hess arrives at the threshold of the modern age. The industrial period is depicted as a new alienation between subject and object: but out of the disruption (*Zerrissenheit*) of the industrial age there grows the vision of a new, harmonious future, based on the abolition of the contradictions between the individual and society, a social humanism premised on the abolition of private property.

Yet despite its universal theme, this work reveals the beginnings of Hess' struggle with the Jewish question. It is obvious that in a historiosophical work of this kind Hess had to consider the contribution Judaism had made to history. This is essentially formulated in Hegelian language. The main contribution of the Jews was in giving monotheism to the world and in introducing the spiritual dimension into religious consciousness. The climax of this spiritualization of the world by Judaism was embodied in the appearance of Jesus, but since Jesus' appearance – and especially since his rejection by the Jews – Judaism's contribution to history had come to an end.[7] As Hess

---

6 *Die heilige Geschichte der Menschheit*, von einem Jünger Spinozas (Stuttgart, 1837). The future-oriented direction of Hess' thought, already evident in this work, was much reinforced some time later by the publication of August von Cieszkowski's *Prolegomena zur Historiosophie* (Berlin, 1838); Hess' later *Philosophie der Tat* (1843) bears witness to this impact. For an English translation of the latter work, see Albert Fried and Ronald Sanders eds., *Socialist Thought* (Garden City, 1964), 249–75.

7 *Philosophische une sozialistische Schriften*, 71–2

expresses it in this book, there are two peoples in history whose past contribution to history was considerable but who have no future: one of these are the Jews who today are a spirit without a body, and the other are the Chinese who are a body without a spirit. Both these peoples have no future whatsoever.

To the extent that, according to Hess, Jews do have a future in modern times, it is as individuals and not as a collective entity; as individuals the Jews should merge into the general universalism. This is why Hess considers Spinoza to be the classic example of the modern Jew, the first to have breached the walls of Jewish exclusiveness, to have left his tribe and been excommunicated by it, thus becoming a world citizen; such is the path to be followed by the modern Jew (i.e., by Hess himself); hence the significance of the concluding chapter of the book named 'The New Jerusalem' which deals with the new society that is to come into being.[8] Hess emphasizes that it is 'here, in the heart of Europe, that New Jerusalem will be built'.[9] Here, in the heart of Europe and not in Palestine.

We find a parallel in a manuscript from the same period (1840) called *Poles and Jews*.[10] Here too, Hess deals with two peoples having a distinguished past history whose present position is problematic. In the main, this essay draws a distinction between the Poles and the Jews concerning their chance of attaining national existence in the modern period. While the Poles, according to Hess, have a future because they never resigned themselves to the partition of Poland and the disappearance of their polity, he does not consider the Jews to have the social power necessary for attaining national expression. The Jews suffer from an absolute lack of national consciousness (*Mangel an Nationalsinn*), and the example which Hess gives for this lack is the way the Jews reacted to the Damascus Blood Libel. In spite of all the protests and reaction on the part of Western Jewry, the upheaval caused by the Damascus affair did not lead to the emergence of a general Jewish national consciousness.

What is significant in this connection is not only that Hess deals with Jewish subjects also during the period of his universalistic socialistic vision, but that in these writings his attitude to Judaism is not merely as to a religion. *His yardstick concerning the future of Judaism is not whether Judaism has a future as a religion, but whether it has a future as a nation.* True, the answer is negative; but it is important that even during his period

8 Ibid., 66–74
9 Ibid., 65. In 1840, Hess wrote an introduction to a work he never completed, called 'Die ideale Grundlagen des Neuen Jerusalem' ('The Ideal Foundations of the New Jerusalem'); a copy is in the Zionist Central Archives.
10 Copy in the Zionist Central Archives; see also Silberner, *Moses Hess*, 62.

of absolute negation of Judaism, Hess' criterion for his evaluation of Judaism is national and not religious. In *Rome and Jerusalem* the answer to the future of Judaism as a nation is positive, and in this lies its novelty. However, his view of Judaism in national terms is already rooted in the period in which Hess denied Jewry's ability of regeneration, and from this point of view it is interesting to note that Hess was one of the first in the modern era to see Judaism in national terms even while denying it a future.

At the same time, it must be noted that at this period Hess wrote one of the harshest statements which has ever been made about Judaism by a Jew. It is connected with Marx's essay on the Jewish question. Marx wrote his essay, *On the Jewish Question,* in 1843 and it appeared in 1844.[11] In the year 1845 there appeared Hess' essay, *On Capital,* which contains very severe pronouncements regarding the Jews in the spirit of identifying Judaism with capitalism.[12] Only recently has it been shown that Hess' work preceded that of Marx: Hess wrote his essay in 1843 and sent it to Marx for publication; this, however, did not work out and Hess' work was only published a year and a half later. Hence, Hess' work was known to Marx while he wrote his essay, *On the Jewish Question,* and most of the images which appear in Marx's works are borrowed from Hess.[13] More than that, Hess' work, *On Capital,* contains material which is much more extreme than anything used by Marx; and it is to Marx's credit that he did not include this material in his work. For example, Hess writes that originally the Children of Israel were idolators and that their principal god was Moloch who demanded blood sacrifices. Hess, who knew Hebrew from his childhood *Heder,* used this knowledge in his essay: in the course of time, so he says, a sublimation occurred and the Jews passed from blood (*dam*) sacrifices to money (*damim*) sacrifices, this being the origin of the Jewish money cult, as money took the place of Moloch. Throughout the essay Hess calls the God of Israel 'Moloch-Jehova', and it is difficult to find a parallel to such a collective blood libel in even the most virulent anti-Semitic literature. These expressions of Hess are less well known than Marx's essay, *On the Jewish Question,* but they are much more drastic and ironically even served Marx as a source of information when he wrote his essay.

But on the whole it should be stressed that in contrast to Marx who did not struggle – at least explicitly – over the problem of his Jewish identity (he was, after all, born to a family which had converted to Christianity), Hess' universalistic postulate was for him not merely a theoretical speculation, but also represented no doubt a solution to the problem of his personal existence

11 See Karl Marx, *Early Writings*, trans. T.B. Bottomore (London, 1963), 1–40.
12 'Über das Geldwesen', in *Philosophische und sozialistische Schriften*, 329–48
13 See Silberner, *Moses Hess*, 184–5.

and his own identity. Since he tried hard from the outset to find a solution to this problem, one can understand that the failure of the Emancipation had far-reaching repercussions on his world view.

Hess' book, *Rome and Jerusalem*, appeared in 1862. It is subtitled 'The Last National Problem'. The work made little impact at the time of publication and was soon forgotten. His socialist friends considered this work a personal idiosyncrasy and did not take it seriously; Reform rabbis criticized it violently and Orthodox rabbis could not but approach it with a great deal of scepticism.

The Rome of the title is neither Imperial Rome nor Papal Rome, but *Roma terza* of Mazzini and Italian nationalism. As Hess put it in his Introduction:

> With the liberation of the Eternal City on the Tiber begins the liberation of the Eternal City on Mount Moriah; with the resurrection of Italy begins the resurrection of Judea. The orphaned children of Jerusalem will too be permitted to participate in the great renaissance of the nations ... [14]

The autobiographical details with which the book opens impress one as revealing something of the agonies of a person discovering his own people after struggling through the purgatory of an undifferentiated universalism:

> Here do I stand once more, after twenty years of estrangement, in the midst of my own people, sharing their festivities and their days of sorrow, their memories and their hopes, their spiritual struggles in their own house and with the cultures within which they live and with whom they cannot fuse organically despite two thousand years of cohabitation and effort.
>
> A thought which I believed I had repressed for ever has come to life once more: the thought of my nation, inseparable from the heritage of my ancestors, from the Holy Land and the Eternal City, where the belief in the divine unity of life and the future Brotherhood of Man was born. [15]

The main thrust of the work is its conception of Judaism as a nation and its perception of the Jewish problem as a national problem and not as a mere problem of equal rights and the emancipation of a religious minority. The uniqueness and novelty of Hess do not lie only in the fact that the Zionist solution put forward in this work directs the Jewish people to the Land of Israel, but that Hess' conceptual system views the Jews in the terms of nineteenth-century national liberation movements. This distinguishes him from some other proto-Zionist thinkers who preceded him, such as Rabbi Judah Hai Alkalai and Rabbi Zvi Hirsch Kalischer, whose vision was confined

14 *Rom und Jerusalem –Die letzte Nationalitätenfrage*, new ed. (Tel Aviv, 1935), 5
15 Ibid., 12

by Jewish traditionalism and hence was unable to relate their perception of the Jewish problem of universalistic terms.[16]

It is clear that from the moment Hess views Judaism in national terms he can no longer consider Emancipation as a solution: only if Judaism is kept within the confines of a religious sect can Emancipation solve its problems. Moreover, according to Hess' ideas, Emancipation only creates new tensions between the modern Jew and the national society surrounding him, which does not and cannot see in him an integral part of its national culture. Emancipation is based on the universalist doctrines of the French Revolution, but it functions in a world whose basic doctrine is the rise of national movements; hence it is ridden with insuperable internal contradictions.

Hess was consequently also more aware of the rise of anti-Jewish nationalist racialism, particularly in Germany.[17] Precisely because Hess' point of departure is that of the secular world, he was one of the first to recognize that during the period of Emancipation and secularization there occurred a transition from the old Christian anti-Jewishness to a new national racial anti-Jewishness – to modern anti-Semitism. In spite of the fact that these things were only in their beginnings, Hess was perceptive enough to see already in 1862 the dangers of this new anti-Semitism in Germany, and his utterances on this subject are chillingly prophetic.

Viewing the Jewish problem in national terms led Hess to his criticism of German Jewry's Reform movement. His main argument is simple enough: Reform ignored the fact the Jews were a nation and saw Judaism in religious terms only. It wished to make Judaism into a kind of protestantism with a Jewish colouring, thus distorting the historical essence of Judaism. Hess was not merely concerned with religious matters and his argument against Reform is not on the level of religious liberalization. It refers to the disruption of the Jewish people's historical consciousness which the Reform Movement puts into a Procrustean bed based on the experience of Christianity; a large part of *Rome and Jerusalem* is devoted to demonstrating the immanent lack of hope of a solution based on the principle of religious emancipation within a situation of rising national movements.[18]

16 See Arthur Hertzberg, ed., *The Zionist Idea* (New York, 1969), 101–15.
17 See esp. *Rom und Jerusalem*, 23–6, 36–9.
18 Ibid., 57–70. Very indicative of the changes in Hess' self-awareness is the way he related to his given name, Moses. During the years preceding the publication of *Rome and Jerusalem*, Hess tried to push that name with its obvious Jewish connotation into the background: he published under the names M. Hess, Moritz Hess, and (after he moved to Paris) Maurice Hess. With the publication of *Rome and Jerusalem*, he readopted the original 'Moses', and in the book itself he mentions how proud he is to be able to resume his real name again, adding that he would have been even happier if his name were 'Itzig' (ibid., 56).

Hess' solution is to set up a Jewish socialist commonwealth in Palestine. It should be emphasized that this was to be a *socialist* commonwealth, because some of the literature on Hess, especially in communist writings, frequently presents Hess as though in the later national, Jewish phase of his public activity, he cut himself off from the socialist past and, as it were, changed from a socialist to a Jewish nationalist. This is incorrect, for Hess' socialist assumptions still exist, except that in *Rome and Jerusalem* Hess combines his support of revolutionary Mazzinic nationalism with his socialist vision.

As far as Hess is concerned, the Jews cannot remedy their position unless the Jewish proletariat can be rooted within the framework of a national Jewish society. This is why Hess is aware that the Jews who will emigrate to Palestine will not come from the middle classes of Western Jewry. It would not be the Jewish bourgeoisie of Central and Western Europe which would constitute the social infrastructure of Jewish socialist society in the land of Israel.[19] Rather, the Jewish commonwealth will constitute an answer to the plight of the Jewish masses in Eastern Europe and the Muslim world.[20] Hess' awareness that these two large communities – i.e., Eastern European Jewry and Oriental Jewry – would form the basis for the Jewish state is of central importance for our understanding of the way Hess visualized the Jewish national society which was to arise in the land of Israel.

The foundations of the Jewish socialist commonwealth would be based on public ownership of the land and of the means of production: production would be organized on co-operative and collective lines. One of the interesting elements in Hess' book is his attempt, which occasionally borders on forcing the evidence, at reading into the history of the Jewish people quasi-socialist concepts, a trait which became common practice in the Zionist Labour Movement later on, though Hess was the first to do so. Thus Hess sees in the traditional Jewish social ethos a proto-socialist element: Christianity, according to Hess, is individualistic and this is why it was Christian society which produced capitalism (how far Hess has come from *On Capital*!); Judaism on the other hand, is based on the family, i.e., *on a unit already characterized by elements of social solidarity*. Furthermore, in gentile society, both pagan and Christian, the central image is that of the male, while in Judaism it is that of the woman and mother. Thus, if the principal characteristics extolled in gentile society are the aggressive ones, focused in the image of the man or the father, the specifically Jewish characteristics are those of love, suffering, willingness to help, and understanding one's fellow-being – characteristics connected with the Jewish

19 Ibid., 127–31
20 Ibid., 135–6

mother. In a most interesting mixture of metaphors Hess states that every 'Jewish mother is a *mater dolorosa*.'[21]

All the Biblical laws connected with the Sabbath, the fallow year, and the Jubilee, Hess interprets in socialist terms, and he goes so far as to designate the Mosaic Code as 'social democratic'. He goes beyond the literary meaning of the verse in the *Sayings of the Fathers*, 'He who says, what is mine is mine and what is thine is thine, is a mediocre character: some say, this is a character like that of Sodom'. Hess claims that this saying shows that the Jewish ethos always harboured a suspicion of individualism based on private property.[22]

In *Rome and Jerusalem* there is a note about Hassidism which makes an interesting marginal comment. His attitude to Hassidism is characteristic of his state of mind as a whole, for he presents it as an organic experience as opposed to the opportunistic individualism of the German Reform movement. Hess argues that, even though a whole system of what he calls superstitions developed in Hassidism, yet the internal cohesion of the Hassidic community, the fact that it does not live an individualistic but a communal life, is further evidence for the social ethos of Jewish society, and may well constitute the basis for a future integration, based on socialistic premises. Thus Hess is able to combine secular criticism of some customs of the Jewish religious tradition with a realization of its contribution to the social context of general Jewish national existence.[23]

As a whole, Hess' conception of the subject of nationalism follows Mazzini's harmonistic approach which combined national particularity with a universal vision. As Mazzini said, by being a member of a nation, I am also a member of the human race, and the only way of belonging to humanity is by belonging to a specific nation. Nationalism and universalism are not mutually exclusive, but complement one another.

This approach of Hess' to the national problem has some connection with a central aspect of Hegel's thought which has been overlooked by Marx; attention should be drawn to it, because it focuses on what appears to me to be Hess' specific contribution to socialist thought.

In Hegel's political philosophy, three modes of trans-subjective social relations are posited – the family, civil society, and the state – human beings being able to relate to one another in one of the following three ways: particular altruism, universal egoism, and universal altruism.[24]

21 Ibid., 13
22 Ibid., 221
23 Ibid., 219ff
24 G.W.F. Hegel, *Philosophy of Right*, trans. T.M. Knox (Oxford, 1942), para. 157ff. See my *Hegel's Theory of the Modern State* (Cambridge, 1972), 132–47.

The family is a set of relationships based on particular altruism. Within its framework a person is prepared to perform – and does perform – actions for the sake of others – not from self-interest, but from a feeling of obligation towards the other person. I support my parents, educate my children, etc., not because I expect to receive anything in exchange, but from considerations deriving from the way in which I understand the meaning of the nexus created by my being a son or daughter, parent or spouse. When this feeling no longer exists and as a result my relationship to these people no longer derives from the nature of my family link with them, then we say that the family is breaking up. At the same time, this altruism, this readiness to do something for others, is limited to a certain group of people having a biological or marriage linkage. As a particularistic relationship it does not embrace everyone and is hence immanently limited.

Against this particularistic altruism there arises the possibility of a relationship to other people based on universal egoism. In this case my attitude to other people is ordered and determined by my self-interest, and this is, of course, the specific area of economic life, i.e., civil society (*bürgerliche Gesellschaft*). I engage in trade neither to supply the needs of others nor to prevent people from starving, but because the hunger of others is the means by which I seek to ensure the supply of my own needs. This is the universal egoism at the root of civil society, which is founded on self-interest.

Hegel argues that the traditional political philosophies from Hobbes to Montesquieu perceive the state as if it were no more than an agreement based on mutual, universal benefit. According to Hobbes and Locke, human beings constitute themselves into political societies for the purpose of defending their interests. According to Hegel these considerations are characteristics of a civil society and cannot form the basis of a state. If these were the foundations of a state, Hegel argues, how can one justify the tax system, or even more, how can one legitimize a situation in which the state imposes on its citizens the duty of military service, and with it the possibility of being killed? If the state exists, to quote Locke, in order to defend my 'life, liberty and estate,' how are these defended if I am killed on the battlefield? If the state were really founded on such egoistic considerations, how could we blame anyone for smuggling his money into a foreign country, sending his wife and children there, finally joining them, the moment any danger threatened his country? The fact that we condemn such conduct (which would certainly not be condemned were it the case of a bank or of some business and not of a state) proves, according to Hegel, that we wish to see in the state something beyond a purely rational protection of our self-interest. Just as in a family one is prepared to do things for others, even at the expense of renouncing or sacrificing something, so it is with the state: the individual's partnership in it is not in the nature of a quasi-business agreement which one can join or leave at will; it is rather a readiness based on the citizen's relationship with other people for whom he is prepared to bear sacrifices and from whom he also expects sacrifices for his sake. The moment this willingness disappears, as Hegel perceived in the Greek polis at the time of its decline, the political relationship disintegrates, precisely as the family relationship disintegrates when this willingness disappears within the more restricted framework of the family. The state is therefore a system of an altruistic universal relationship.

These considerations had to be clarified as an introduction to the following argument. From a certain aspect it can be said that the substance of Marx's socialism does not essentially differ from the substance of the universal altruism which Hegel attributes to the state. But while Hegel bases his universal altruism on its growth out of the dialectical relationship of the family and civil society, for Marx the universal altruism of future society is not based on any prior mediation: it is unmediated and therefore not dialectic. One might perhaps say that at a time of class-war proletarian solidarity constitutes that same dialectic by means of which universal altruism comes into effect. But in the post-revolutionary society, class-consciousness disappears and what remains is an abstract, universal altruism, without mediation and without roots in the concrete social existence of human beings. It has been said of Marx that his dialectic approach only refers to an analysis of the past and present while the image of his society of the future is, to a considerable extent, undifferentiated and one-dimensional. It seems to me that also in this matter of the disappearance of the intermediate strata between the individual and the universal commonalty there is some short-cut in the dialectic dimension of Marx's thinking.

As against this, the interlinking of socialism and nationalism which Hess suggests for the Jewish people in *Rome and Jerusalem*, and which he naturally views as universal, contains something of an answer to the problem of the abstractness and the absence of mediation by which Marx's vision of the society of the future falls short.

For in the case of Hess, nationalism constitutes a mediating factor, analogous to the family, between the individual and the universal commonalty. In a nation the individual learns to move beyond his individuality, to consider himself interwoven into society, to be firmly tied to other people and to act on the basis of this relationship. By acting together within the framework of a nation, people already prove their willingness to do something for others; by it they admit the existence of mutual relations which are not a function of interests, but are an expression of solidarity and a quest for the common life. In such a view, nationalism is not antagonistic to socialism, but represents a small-scale laboratory socialism, since nationalism educates a person to act out of solidarity with other people.

Thus Hess' view enables us to transcend the non-dialectical one-dimensionality appearing in Marx; this also points to a theoretical link between nationalism and socialism as a matter of principle and not just as a concession to historical reality. There is no doubt that one of the theoretical weaknesses of the socialist movement in Europe was its lack of awareness of the problem of nationalism. This is particularly noticeable with Marx, and here he continues the Hegelian tradition of under-estimating the societal force and significance of nationalism. This accounted for the purely instrumental attitude of most of the Social Democratic parties to nationalism. Even with regard to that branch of European social democracy, Austro-Marxism, which tried to come to grips with the complexities of the national problem in the intricacies of the multinational realities of the Habsburg empire, matters rarely moved beyond an instrumental and tactical attitude. Similarly, in the debates on the national question between Lenin and Rosa Luxemburg, the subject was discussed purely from an angle of revolutionary strategy and tactics.

Hess is unique in the early socialist movement in that he saw the theoretical relationship between nationalism and socialism, considering them both as two modes of a trans-individualistic relationship, both thus becoming two different aspects of the solution to the problem of atomization and alienation of modern man in contemporary bourgeois society. Similarly, Hess arrived at his socialism and his Zionism through the same criteria by which he criticized his contemporary civil society. From this aspect Hess should be seen not only as an interesting biographical case of a Jew who came a long way from assimilationist socialism to Socialist Zionism, but also as a thinker whose theoretical contribution towards an understanding of the relations between socialism and nationalism is of universal significance.

Marx and Macpherson: Needs, Utilities, and Self-development

Man is distinguished from all other animals
by the limitless and flexible nature of his needs.
MARX [1]

The contributors to a recent collection of essays, *Human Needs and Politics*, differ sharply about whether or not the concept of human needs has a rightful place in social and political theory. Some see this concept as a necessary ingredient in any humanistic political theory, while others regard the notion itself as the mark of an invidious distinction (needs *versus* wants) that inevitably has unacceptable theoretical and practical consequences. What unites most of them, however, is the belief that the most important feature of the concept of needs is its intrinsic orientation to some mode of political action.

Thus the staunchest advocate of this orientation, Christian Bay, describes his intention as 'developing certain conceptions of human needs which in my view will be most likely to be optimally useful toward facilitating liberating political education'. At the opposite end of the spectrum is Antony Flew, who maintains that 'an emphasis upon needs, as opposed to wants, gives purchase to those who see themselves as experts, qualified both to determine what the needs of others are, and to prescribe and enforce the means appropriate to the satisfaction of those needs'. Somewhere in between stands Ross Fitzgerald, who is disturbed by the wide currency of 'talk about needs' but who also finds it necessary to account for the fact. He argues that we should regard it as evidence that the notion of need has primarily a rhetorical function (its rhetorical power being rooted in its very ambiguity), i.e., it is essentially a disguised imperative or call to action. Our seeming inability to construct

---

1 'Results of the Immediate Process of Production' (1863–66), in *Capital*, I, trans. Ben Fowkes (London, 1976), 1068

social theories without such ambiguous concepts is for him 'an emblem of the dilemma of contemporary political theory as a whole'.[2]

I agree with those who have called attention to the problematic character of the needs/wants distinction (or the distinction between true and false needs) and of the explicit or implicit practical consequences which those who make the distinction deduce from it. A critical theory of needs – that is, a theory located in the Marxian tradition of the critique of capitalist society – is not necessarily based on it. As C.B. Macpherson has noted,[3] Marx's own theory of needs – a powerful and challenging theory which has not yet received the attention it deserves – does not depend on this distinction.

Until now the theory of needs has been a neglected aspect of critical theory, overshadowed for the most part by analyses of production, imperialism, and economic crisis. This neglect is fast being repaired. Agnes Heller's book on Marx's theory of needs was published in English in 1976. Herbert Marcuse's new book asserts that the basic change of consciousness now presupposed in socialist theory is one which 'aims at a new "system of needs"'. And in two recent articles C.B. Macpherson has assigned the theory of needs a central place in social and political theory.[4]

There is a notion of how human needs develop under capitalism in Marx's work, but it is not set out neatly and must be reconstructed from scattered passages. Marx sees the development of needs in capitalist society as having both positive and negative features which in part reciprocally influence each other. On the positive side is capitalism's destruction of what Marx calls the limited forms of satisfaction characteristic of earlier cultures: needs are free to exhibit a richness and diversity not previously known, and human individuality can blossom in this freedom. On the negative side is capitalism's own limiting condition, represented both by the commodity form of need-satisfaction and capital's over-riding need for profit. As capitalism matures the latter increasingly becomes a fetter on the former, a fetter that will be broken in the coming of socialism and communism.

Macpherson has formulated an original variation on this theme, initially drawn from his critical reading of liberal political theory, but in its later expressions more directly tied to Marx's version. This is his well-known opposition between two 'models of man', man as an infinite consumer of

2 Ross Fitzgerald ed., *Human Needs and Politics* (New York, 1977). The quotations are from 1, 213, 212, respectively.

3 C.B. Macpherson, 'Needs and Wants: An Ontological or Historical Problem?' in ibid., 32–4

4 Agnes Heller, *The Theory of Need in Marx* (London, 1976); Herbert Marcuse, *The Aesthetic Dimension* (Boston, 1978), 36; C.B. Macpherson, 'Do We Need a Theory of the State?' *Archives européennes de sociologie*, XVIII, 2 (1977), 243; 'Needs and Wants: An Ontological or Historical Problem?'

utilities *versus* man as exerter and enjoyer of his capacities. There is less explicit testimony in his writings that he sees capitalism as a necessary stage for the actualization of this opposition's positive side, but it is implicit at times. Especially in his more recent essays Macpherson speaks of a 'contradiction' between the two models – and the real modes of behaviour for which they stand as ideal types – that is rooted in the capitalist mode of production. Resolution of the contradiction involves not a complete overcoming of utility-maximizing by self-developmental activity, but a considerable 'downgrading' of the former and expansion of the latter.

What both versions have in common is the idea of an inherent, developing tension between contrasting modes of behaviour with a common source. They avoid the naive celebration of economic progress and purely quantitative indicators of well-being. But they also avoid using a pre-established, abstract model of the 'good society' in their critique of capitalism. This idea of an internal tension is the source of both the strengths and the weaknesses in Marx's and Macpherson's social theory.

Marx's notion of what happens to human needs under capitalism appears first in his early writings and later undergoes substantial modifications. *The Economic and Philosophic Manuscripts* present a one-sided attack on capitalist society, asserting that it denies all 'human' needs or – what is apparently the same idea – reduces needs to a 'crude' level: 'Just as industry speculates on the refinement of needs, so also it speculates upon their *crudeness*, and upon their artificially produced *crudeness* whose true spirit therefore is *self-stupefaction*, the *illusory* satisfaction of needs, a civilization *within* the crude barbarism of needs.'[5] Marx describes the growth of needs under the regime of private property and wage labour as an exercise in mutual fraud, where the new desires elicited by production for exchange are an 'alien compulsion' that dominates the individual. Marx contrasts this state, where persons are mere means for each other, with an ideal state where persons produce 'as human beings' and in so doing affirm their true human nature.[6]

There is no internal tension in this conception. Capitalist society based on private property and wage labour dehumanizes man and his needs necessarily and completely. This purely negative condition is contrasted with a positive alternative that is its ideal opposite: everything lacking in the former

5 *Frühe Schriften*, I (Stuttgart, 1962), 608–16; quotation on 615–16 / *Economic and Philosophic Manuscripts of 1844* trans. T.B. Bottomore, in Erich Fromm, *Marx's Concept of Man* (New York, 1961), 140–8; quotation (amended) on 147–8
6 'Excerpt-Notes of 1844', in L.D. Easton and K.H. Guddat eds., *Writings of the Young Marx on Philosophy and Society* (Garden City, NY, 1967), 275–81

is fulfilled in the latter. The tone is one of damnation and salvation, or the loss and recovery of mankind's essence as a species.

Marx's later conception is a significant departure from his earlier one. It drops the invidious distinction between natural and artificially imposed conditions and is therefore able to set out a dialectical theory of opposed positive and negative forces at work within the institutions of capitalist society.[7] The idea of a dialectic of needs is developed most fully in the *Grundrisse*.

The one-sided representation of capitalism in the *Manuscripts* has been transcended. Capitalism now appears as a necessary presupposition for the emergence of human individuality and freedom. This positive aspect of its historical mission is explicitly cast in terms of the theory of needs:

> The discovery, creation and satisfaction of new needs arising from society itself; the cultivation of all the qualities of the social human being, production of the same in a form as rich as possible in needs, because rich in qualities and relations – production of this being as the most total and universal possible social product, for, in order to take gratification in a many-sided way, he must be capable of many pleasures, hence cultured to a high degree – is likewise a condition of production founded on capital.

Part of the 'civilizing influence' of capital, Marx continues, is to break down 'all traditional, confined, complacent, encrusted satisfactions of present needs'.[8] He believed that geographical barriers as well as static modes of production limited the expression of needs in earlier societies, and this constricted the human capacity for enjoyment and thus human development itself.

Marx relates the liberating and civilizing mission of capitalism to a key concept which links his thought with John Stuart Mill's: individuality. In the passage quoted above and in others, he interprets individuality as 'universal-

---

7 Macpherson claims that Marx's theory of need as a whole 'makes no use of the natural/artificial distinction' ('Needs and Wants' 34); this is too strong an assertion as far as the 1843–4 writings are concerned, but it is correct with respect to Marx's later theory. In her careful discussion of this point Agnes Heller remarks that the concept of 'artificial need' is ambiguous in Marx, and she argues that there is a significant shift of emphasis in Marx's theory from the *Manuscripts* to the *Grundrisse* (*Need in Marx*, 50–4). My own reading of Marx is consonant with Heller's. Thus I cannot agree with Patricia Springborg's recent interpretation, which sees the true needs/false needs, artificial/natural distinction as fundamental to Marx's thought ('Karl Marx on Human Needs,' in *Human Needs and Politics*, 157–73); for example, the imputation (164) of the concept of artificial needs to the *Grundrisse* finds no support in Marx's text.
8 *Grundrisse der Kritik der politischen Ökonomie* (Berlin, 1953), 312–3 / *Grundrisse*, trans. Martin Nicolaus (London, 1973), 409–10

ity', i.e., as a social situation which nurtures the full range of potential human capacities for creativity and enjoyment. According to Marx, capitalism teaches mankind to be dissatisfied with the satisfaction of needs at the level of 'mere subsistence' and creates a *need* to strive beyond it.[9] The greater complexity of needs and the production that makes possible their satisfaction are equally the result of capital's inner dynamism. In another passage the concepts of individuality and universality are explicitly joined; here Marx relates them both to the market exchange economy brought by capitalism, and again he insists that this was a necessary stage in history:

Universally developed individuals, whose social (*gesellschaftlich*) relations, as their own communal (*gemeinschaftlich*) relations, are hence also subordinated to their own communal control, are no product of nature, but of history. The degree and the universality of the development of wealth where *this* individuality becomes possible supposes production on the basis of exchange values as a prior condition, whose universality produces not only the alienation of the individual from himself and from others, but also the universality and the comprehensiveness of his relations and capacities.[10]

These passages give us a clear idea of the positive moment in the dialectic of needs under capitalism. The main points may be summarized as follows: 1/ precapitalist societies imposed severe limits on the development of human creative capacities; 2/ the new needs emerging under capitalism are – at least in some important respects – an expression of a fuller human personality and its capacity for enjoyment; 3/ the particular needs thus emerging are manifestations of a new 'general' need (of indeterminate scope and qualities) for production and consumption beyond the point of simple subsistence; 4/ a 'richness in needs' is an essential aspect of individuality and human freedom; 5/ individuality is the comprehensive development of human capacities, and this presupposes an era of history in which universal exchange relations – a market society – can flourish.

What is the negative moment in this process? While permitting the qualitative and quantitative expansion of needs, the mode of production, characterized by the control over the means of production by capital, the commodity form, and wage labour, imposes its own limit and barrier. The

---

9 Ibid., 231 / Nicolaus trans., 325. This theme reappears in *Capital*: the capitalist 'spurs on the development of society's productive forces, and the creation of those material conditions which alone can form the real basis of a higher form of society, a society in which the full and free development of every individual forms the ruling principle'. *Das Kapital*, in *Karl Marx: Ökonomische Schriften* (Stuttgart, 1962), I, 704 / *Capital*, I, 739

10 *Grundrisse*, 79 / Nicolaus trans., 162; see also 73–6 / 156–8.

tension between the two opposing moments will be resolved when the results of capitalism's positive work – associated individuals rich in new needs and capacities – discover that their new attributes cannot be fulfilled within capitalism's institutional forms.

Marx describes those obstacles as limits 'to production founded on capital'. And of course the limits to production are also – looked at from another angle – the limits to individuals' enjoyment of what is produced for their needs. By combining what Marx says in different passages we arrive at the following list of the limits to needs and their satisfaction in capitalist society: 1/ 'necessary labour as limit on the exchange value of living labour capacity'; 2/ surplus value as 'barrier to the development of the forces of production'; 3/ individuals limited in appropriating social wealth by their alienation.[11]

The limit referred to in the first point is capitalism's failure to achieve the levels of capital investment of which it is capable, thus to reduce necessary labour time without reducing workers' incomes, because of the anarchy of the market-place. The third is well known: labour creates the property of others which appears as 'alien wealth' (fremdes Reichtum) outside its control. The second point is, I believe, the key one. Marx says that the idea of surplus value as a barrier means that wealth can only be expressed in the form of exchange value; this limit is the 'restriction of the production of use values by exchange value; ... real wealth has to take on a specific form distinct from itself, a form not absolutely identical with it, in order to become an object of production at all'.

The first limit does not appear to be as serious a problem as Marx thought it was. Needs change and expand under capitalism, as Marx himself emphasized, thus changing the meaning of the phrase 'socially necessary labour time'. The expansion of needs under capitalism converts what were once 'luxury' needs into 'necessary' needs, because by the latter Marx understands not what is required for mere biological survival, but rather the normal or average 'habits and expectations' (Gewohnheiten und Lebensansprüchen) among the population.[12] At the very least, therefore, one would have to call this a 'moving limit', and in view of the general rise in real income and consumption levels in advanced capitalist societies, this does not seem to be a significant barrier to increasing production.

The second point is a curious one: it is not clear what kind of barrier is presented by alienation, for Marx does not explain how the alienated form in which wealth is created (as private property) affects the possibilities of its further increase. (In the Grundrisse Marx does not emphasize the themes of dehumanization and domination so prominent in the passages on alienation

11 Ibid., 318–25, 438–40 / 415–23, 539–42. The specific passages cited in the following paragraph are from 324, 440, and 319 / 422, 541, and 416.
12 Das Kapital, 1, 169–70 / Capital, 1, 275. Cf. Heller, Need in Marx, 29–39.

in the *Manuscripts*.) In any case Marx adds immediately the cryptic and unexplained comment that this form 'is itself fleeting and produces the real conditions of its own transcendence'.[13] Thus of the three 'barriers' it is the necessity for producing wealth as exchange value that is the fundamental and most enduring limit which capital erects to the expansion of productive forces. What is produced is determined by what can be profitably produced: the 'needs of capital for valorization' (*Verwertungsbedürfnisse*) stand opposed to and rule over the 'needs of workers for development' (*Entwicklungsbedürfnisse*).[14]

The kinds of use values that are created – the material and cultural basis for the unfolding of needs and for their satisfaction – are determined in general by capital's need to shape them as exchange values. The appearance of goods as commodities is thus the specific form of wealth which, Marx says, is distinct from (or not 'absolutely identical with') real wealth itself. Since this is clearly a necessary condition for the existence of capitalist society, it is important for us to understand just what kind of limit it represents.

If the imperative for profitable production leads to economic crisis and manifest deprivation (malnutrition, inadequate housing and health care, and so on), and if existing productive resources are under-utilized despite this deprivation, we could say that there is a conflict between capital's needs and those of individuals. Or even if there is in general an adequate level of subsistence, and yet large numbers of individuals experience needs that cannot be met through the commodity form of production (the need for the creation of 'direct' use values, such as free public transportation), we could also speak of a conflict between the two kinds of needs. But if neither of these conditions obtains, would any such conflict exist?

The question must be raised because Marx does *not* suggest in his later theory that the new needs emerging under capitalism are themselves distorted, 'false', or manipulated by virtue of being restricted through the commodity form or exchange value.[15] The critique advanced in the 1843–4

13 *Grundrisse*, 440 / Nicolaus trans. here amended, 541–2
14 *Das Kapital*, I, 744 / *Capital*, I, 772
15 I am mostly in agreement with Agnes Heller's interpretation of Marx, but not on this point. She contends (51–2) that Marx 'discovered the problem of the manipulation of needs,' for example in the following form: 'Individual freedom is therefore mere appearance: the individual chooses the objects of his needs and moulds his personal needs in a way that conforms not with his personality, but with their [*sic*] position in the division of labour.' This may be a reasonable interpretation of the *Manuscripts*, but I do not think that it holds for the *Grundrisse*. At one point in the latter (325 / 422), Marx writes of capital that 'while it has the tendency to heighten the productive forces boundlessly, it also and equally makes one-sided, limits, etc. the main force of production, the human being himself, and has the tendency in general to restrict the forces of production'. Marx does not further explain what this one-sided character of human development is.

writings – the cultivation of 'imaginary cravings', the predominance of 'having' (possessing) over 'being', and the mutual fraud by which individuals achieve an alien compulsion over each other's needs – is muted in the *Grundrisse* and *Capital*. In other words, the new needs themselves are on the whole unproblematic. One could go further: Marx represents them generally in a positive light, as the expression of new capacities for the self-development and enjoyment of the human personality.

In his later theory, Marx's critique is founded on the barriers to expanding production (and thus to expanding the satisfaction of needs) represented by capital's need for extracting surplus value and profit. I believe that Marx thought of this primarily as a quantitative rather than a qualitative problem. In other words, he considered the main issue to be, not the *types* of needs elicited by exchange relations, but the actual limitations on the material and cultural means of enjoyment imposed by low wages. The primary emphasis here is on the barriers to the full development of the productive resources organized by industrial capitalism, whose chronic economic crises prevent society from extracting more than a fraction of their potential productivity.

There is, to be sure, one principal subsidiary theme in the later theory, namely the connection between exchange and alienation. In a passage quoted earlier Marx argues that the universality of capitalist exchange relations has a dual effect: on the positive side, it is responsible for eliciting the full range of human capacities; on the negative side, it causes a pervasive alienation of the individual from himself and from other persons. If I understand correctly Marx's point, I think he suggests that this dual effect is the result of exchange relations themselves, when they extend throughout an entire system of social interactions. And the negative aspect can only be overcome by abolishing exchange relations (what might be called the 'market principle') and founding an economic order on the production of 'direct' use values. The scope of alienation in modern society is a function of the scope of the market principle in the satisfaction of needs.

Thus the dialectic of needs in Marx's later writings is essentially the dialectic of alienated exchange. Universalized exchange relationships broke down the 'herd-like' conformity in precapitalist cultures and allowed human individuality, with its full range of capacities for enjoyment, to show itself.[16] This is its positive side. Its negative side is alienation, loss of control by individuals over the product of their labour. Socially created wealth as the basis of enjoyment is thus an 'alien wealth', and the range of potential use values is determined by exchange value, i.e., what can be profitably produced. The needs of individuals for development are subordinated to the needs of capital for the realization of exchange value.

16 *Grundrisse*, 395–6 / 496

C.B. Macpherson's thought is related to Marx's in at least two important respects: 1 / the tension between two opposing models of man found throughout his writings is analogous to the opposing sides in Marx's theory of needs; and 2 / individual self-development of human capacities as the social ideal is common to both. This second point joins both Marx and Macpherson to J.S. Mill and his concept of individuality.

Macpherson's idea of a tension between two opposed concepts of man has been phrased in a number of ways: as different models of human behaviour, as different presuppositions of liberal-democratic theory, and as different self-images held by many individuals in bourgeois society. These are for Macpherson various forms in which the same tendencies are expressed. Like Marx he sees them as having positive and negative dimensions. In conceptual terms the negative side is represented best by Bentham's utilitarianism, and the positive side by J.S. Mill's concept of democracy. Yet this is not a purely ideological matter, for these theories both express actual and potential aspects of social development and also themselves partially shape that development by their influence on the way we see the world and on the goals we set for ourselves. Thus, although Macpherson usually refers to them as theories about man and human behaviour, he also sees them as 'representing' or describing real patterns of social action and as actually having influenced (and as still influencing) the course of modern history. In this sense we may be entitled to call them ideal types.

Envisioning the essence of man as infinite appropriator and infinite consumer of utilities originates with Hobbes and culminates in Bentham's work. This view involves a series of propositions. First, its key concept, utility, 'defined as a quantity of pleasure minus pain, was taken as the sole criterion of individual and social good'. Second, social good was defined as 'the maximization of the aggregate of individual utilities'. Third, the goal of the state was to erect a proper framework for the pursuit of utility-maximizing interests, consisting of freedom of individual movement and security for life and property. Fourth, the primary purpose of this political framework was to permit the market-place to determine the allocation of resources and thus the actual creation of material utilities for individual satisfaction.[17]

Under ideal conditions there should result the maximum amount of freedom for individuals to maximize the utilities they choose for themselves. But this is blocked by the ownership of property and the separation of labour from the means of labour. This occasions a continuous 'transfer of powers' from non-owners to owners of the means of labour, where power refers to a person's 'ability to use his own capacities productively'; and this transfer,

17 C.B. Macpherson, *Democratic Theory: Essays in Retrieval* (New York, 1973), 173

representing a diminution in the non-owner's powers, has three aspects. The first is the loss of value added to a product by labour over and above what is paid for in wages, which is a familiar idea from Marxian theory. But there are two other aspects that bear directly on the failure to maximize satisfactions. The one is the diminution of a person's productive powers, defined as the capacity to produce material goods, to the extent to which the person cannot determine for himself or herself the choice of activities on which to exercise those powers. The other is a diminution in a person's extra-productive powers, 'that is, his ability to engage in all sorts of activities beyond those devoted to the production of goods for consumption, to engage in activities which are simply a direct satisfaction to him as a doer, as an exerter (and enjoyer of the exertion of) his human capacities, and not a means to other (consumer) satisfactions'. The connection between the two is stated as follows: 'For the presumption is that the way one's capacities are used in the process of production will have some effect on one's ability to use and develop one's capacities outside the process of production. A man whose productive labour is out of his own control, whose work is in that sense mindless, may be expected to be somewhat mindless in the rest of his activities.'[18]

Macpherson names this ability to command the labour of others 'extractive power'; it represents a diminution in the 'developmental power' of those who must sell their labour power. Thus in practice the social goal of maximizing utilities results – by virtue of the continuous transfer of powers – in the inhibiting of the exercise of potential capacities for self-development among the majority of persons. But it is also an unworthy goal in itself, quite apart from its outcome in practice. Macpherson sees a strong tendency in bourgeois society to define 'utility' primarily as 'material utility'; thus the maximization of utility becomes a kind of vulgar materialism. This social system encourages individuals to assign too high a value to materially oriented concerns.

The fact that for Macpherson utility-maximizing behaviour in this sense is not an acceptable goal – or, to put it another way, that this is not an acceptable account of the human essence – is best illustrated by what he chooses to contrast with it. The ideal of maximizing utilities is the negative side of modern social theory and practice; its positive side is the ideal of full development of the individual's capacities for both creative labour and enjoyment. This ideal is based

> on a view of man's essence not as a consumer of utilities but as a doer, a creator, an enjoyer of his human attributes. These attributes may be variously listed and assessed: they may be taken to include the capacity for rational understanding, for moral judgment and action, for aesthetic

18 Ibid., 64–7

creation or contemplation, for the emotional activities of friendship and love, and, sometimes, for religious experience. Whatever the uniquely human attributes are taken to be, in this view of man their exertion and development are seen as ends in themselves, a satisfaction in themselves, not simply a means to consumer satisfactions. It is better to travel than to arrive. Man is not a bundle of appetites seeking satisfaction but a bundle of conscious energies seeking to be exerted.[19]

Macpherson says that this view has its roots in ancient and medieval political thought and was resurrected in different forms in the nineteenth century by such diverse thinkers as Carlyle, Nietzsche, Ruskin, and Marx; but it owes its prominence as a competing ideal in liberal-democratic theory to John Stuart Mill and his followers.

Notwithstanding the transfer-of-powers argument, it is unclear at first glance why these two ideals and behaviour patterns are opposed to each other. Why could the creation of utilities not serve as a means for the realization of individual capacities? Macpherson has noted this objection and formulated a reply to it. He maintains that the two are not logically contradictory 'in the abstract' but that they are in fact incompatible – in two respects. 'First, what is opposed to the maximization of individual human powers is not the maximization of utilities as such, but a certain way of maximizing utilities, namely, a system of market incentives and market morality including the right of unlimited individual appropriation.' The capitalist market-place causes the production of utilities to constrict developmental powers. This leads to the second point: It is also the capitalist market-place which disguises the right of unlimited appropriation of labour's means of production – held as the private property of a minority and distributed unequally – as the equal right of every individual to pursue the unlimited consumption of utilities.[20] Thus it is the specific social context in which the new behaviour pattern and the new image of the human essence (man as infinite consumer) arose that sets the two in permanent opposition.

Macpherson's recent book, *The Life and Times of Liberal Democracy*, presents in sharper focus the main elements of the outlook held throughout all his writings. It opens by presenting the positive and negative currents as a tension within liberal-democratic theory: 'For "liberal" can mean freedom of the stronger to do down the weaker by following market rules; or it can mean equal effective freedom of all to use and develop their capacities. The

19 Ibid., 4–5. Elsewhere (54) the list is extended, but basically along the same lines; there, however, an important point is added: 'And of course the capacity for transforming Nature is presupposed in this view of men [sic] as essentially a doer, a creator, an exerter of energy, an actor; this is broader than, but includes, the capacity for materially productive labour.'
20 Ibid., 34–5

latter freedom is inconsistent with the former.' It immediately goes on to assert that resolving the tension is a matter affecting the future of liberal democracy in the world of actual politics. Finally, it locates the root causes of that tension in the economic system, and puts the point in language indistinguishable from Marx's. Macpherson now speaks of 'the contradiction between capitalist relations of production as such and the democratic ideal of equal possibility of individual self-development' or, more succinctly, of 'a contradiction between capitalist relations of production as such and the developmental ideal'.[21]

Although in this book Macpherson states his own view more explicitly in terms of Marxian theory, his theory of social change is closest to one of its specific variants, whose best-known representative is Herbert Marcuse. For Macpherson the possibilities of progressive social change are a function of potential changes in popular consciousness. The move towards an adequate political framework for the democratic ideal (participatory democracy) remains blocked by a preference for 'affluence' over 'community' and a belief that the market society can guarantee affluence. Participatory democracy is predicated on a 'downgrading or abandonment of market assumptions about the nature of man and society', a reduction of social and economic inequality, and 'a change in people's consciousness (or unconsciousness), from seeing themselves and acting as essentially consumers to seeing themselves and acting as exerters and enjoyers of the exertion and development of their own capacities'.[22]

Macpherson's critique of bourgeois society parallels Marx's in obvious ways. It also diverges from Marx's in some respects, and represents one of the most interesting and important variations of that critique to appear in this century. With respect to the aspects of their work discussed in this essay, the chief similarities are: 1 / the idea of an internal tension between contrasting tendencies in capitalist social relations, and 2 / the idea that market-related activities are the main source for regressive or negative influences on behaviour and popular consciousness. The chief dissimilarities are: 1 / Macpherson's inclination to see the democratic ideal as an ethical principle rooted in Western political thought as a whole, and thus in a sense standing outside the dialectic of the labour process in capitalism, as opposed to Marx's greater emphasis on the emergence of demands for popular democracy out of the labour process itself; 2 / as a corollary to the first, Macpherson's implicit concession of greater autonomy to the political sphere and his firm commit-

21 *The Life and Times of Liberal Democracy* (New York, 1977), 1, 2, 62, 70
22 Ibid., 91–2, 99, 102, 115. The reduction of social and economic inequality is, of course, mainly a matter of institutional change, but achieving it would again depend on its being made a serious demand by a committed majority of citizens, and thus it would depend also on changes in popular consciousness.

ment to the appreciation and preservation of liberal democratic values, as opposed to the relatively stronger emphasis on the subordination of the political to the economic sphere, and the inadequate attention devoted to political (as opposed to economic) processes, in Marx's thought and in Marxism generally.[23]

Macpherson's work has infused new life into the radical critique of bourgeois society. In so doing he has opened up some key issues for contemporary social theory.

1 / The relation between two spheres of activity (consumption of utilities *versus* development of capacities) is sometimes stated by Macpherson as a simple opposition or contradiction, and sometimes as super- and subordination. In both formulations a 'material' sphere is opposed or subordinated to a non-material one; the latter includes rational thought, aesthetic activity, moral or ethical behaviour, friendship, and love. This is clearly a hierarchy of 'higher' and 'lower' forms of human activity with the production of material utilities relegated to the latter category.[24] This conception stems from both ancient Greek political philosophy and Christian thought, and on it was based an analogy between different types or classes of persons and different attributes of the human organism; the rational element was to rule over the others in both society and personality. I wonder whether it is applicable in the context of the modern market society. Universalized exchange relationships tend to break down divisions between spheres of activity; thus most of the 'developmental' attributes listed above are bound in some way to the production of utilities. This is not to say that we cannot discriminate between more worthy and less worthy pursuits, using some reasoned criterion to say how we think human beings ought to act. But it is not clear that the separation and gradation of activity in terms of material and non-material spheres can provide an adequate criterion. For 'utility' is not merely (or even primarily) constituted by the physical properties of material goods, but rather it is a culturally determined mode of satisfaction in which both material and symbolic or non-material dimensions interact.[25]

Two different contrasts overlap in Macpherson's writings: *a* / the distinction between material and non-material spheres of activity; *b* / the produc-

---

23 I reiterate the point that the difference is one of emphasis; I am not suggesting that the political sphere and democratic values are totally neglected by Marx or by various traditions of Marxism. For Macpherson's own views on this see his essay, 'Do We Need a Theory of the State?'

24 Yet Macpherson rejects the idea of a hierarchy of needs. 'Need and Wants', 35

25 I follow Marshall Sahlins in seeing 'utility' as itself constituted by symbolic determinations (which would include Macpherson's developmental attributes). See his *Culture and Practical Reason* (Chicago, 1976) for a full discussion of the idea of the symbolic constitution of utility.

tion of utilities as determined by market relations *versus* utilities as they might be produced in some unspecified non-market context (or in a less intensely market-oriented context). When the market-place is the primary force in the creation of utilities, the attributes of man as a consumer of utilities block the fuller emergence of man's developmental attributes. What remains to be clarified further in this theory is the relation between the production and consumption of utilities, understood as the means to other ends, and the exertion and enjoyment of human capacities, understood as activities undertaken for their intrinsic worth. The kind of non-market context that would be preferable to the market context for this means-ends relation also requires clarification.

2 / Macpherson's concept of an opposition between two kinds of activity (utility-maximizing *versus* developmental) has a dual character: it ranges back and forth between the way we think (problems of ideology) and the way we act (patterns of behaviour). Modern political theory thus is read not just as postulating various definitions of the human essence, but also as saying something true about the actual make-up of bourgeois society. This is a source of strength in his thought, because it remains faithful to the intentions of the theorists whose writings he has examined, most of whom regarded their own work as contributions to the struggle to achieve the social changes they viewed as desirable. To employ Macpherson's own terminology, one would say that these opposed models of man are both descriptive and justificatory.

Yet there is, of course, a gap between ideology and behaviour: one usually precedes or lags behind the other, and furthermore behaviour patterns rarely exhibit the symmetry and order of sophisticated intellectual systems. For example, Macpherson interprets Bentham's work as the *locus classicus* for the view that man is essentially an infinite consumer of utilities, and he also suggests that the majority of citizens in capitalist societies today actually understand their own activity and expectations in terms of this model. Further, J.S. Mill's model is seen as contrasting sharply with Bentham's and indeed as being incompatible with it; and so by analogy the consumption of utilities in our market society is incompatible with the exertion and enjoyment of capacities. This opposition is dependent, as I have noted above, on an idea of utility as an exclusively 'material' sphere. But if 'utility' in market society is in fact an interrelated material-symbolic dimension, then the ideological opposition developed in liberal political theory might be quite different from the actual tensions in the behaviour patterns – and in people's understanding of those patterns – in capitalist societies today.

3 / The opposing models described by Macpherson are meant to be considered, I believe, as developing in a dynamic interplay throughout modern history. But there are formulations which also give a different

impression, so that the relation between them appears to be a static confrontation of mutually exclusive presuppositions. The latter impression is reinforced by the frequent use of terms such as incompatible, inconsistent, and contradictory. The former is implicit in passages such as the following: 'I shall suggest that the continuance of anything that can properly be called liberal democracy depends on a downgrading of the market assumptions and an upgrading of the equal right to self-development.'[26] This seems to make the issue one of relative priority rather than of substituting one for another as complete systems. If one speaks of a contradiction between them, then one must believe that the realization of the democratic ideal means the overcoming not only of capitalist relations of production but of any residue of market relations in whatever form (such as Yugoslavia's market socialism). But if one speaks of downgrading and upgrading, then one can envision a whole series of 'mixed' social systems in which effective democratic control over market relations could be sought through various institutional means, resulting in more or less radical transformations in current forms of work, consumption, bureaucracy, ownership of enterprises, and the distribution of income and wealth.

4 / It is unclear to what extent Macpherson regards the opposed behaviour patterns as rooted equally in the dialectic of capitalist social relations. Writing of the two senses of 'liberal' in liberal-democratic theory, the freedom of the stronger to benefit unequally from market rules *versus* the equal freedom of all to develop their capacities, Macpherson states that the latter 'has outgrown its capitalist market envelope and can now live as well or better without it.'[27] This remark is consonant with Marx's theory of needs, which holds that both progressive and regressive tendencies emerge simultaneously under capitalism. Macpherson suggests here that the capitalist 'envelope' nurtured the fledgling network of expanded capacities until it was ready to stand on its own, whereupon it found its progenitor's domain too confining.

There is also another, different strain in Macpherson's thought. In it the model of man as infinite consumer and appropriator is seen as a rebellion against an older (and better) tradition in political thought, a rebellion that succeeded only temporarily and that is challenged by the nineteenth-century resurrection of the older tradition. He views this new model as in any case ethically or morally repugnant, on the theoretical level, and on the practical level as inconsistent with any democratic theory worthy of our commitment. In this strain the social and economic institutions of bourgeois society are confronted from outside, so to speak, by a demand for a political order which

26 *The Life and Times of Liberal Democracy*, 2
27 Ibid.

that society cannot grant in principle. This demand is grounded in the same ethical viewpoint from which is derived the notion of a hierarchy of activities discussed earlier. A case can indeed be made for it in philosophical terms. What has not been elucidated sufficiently are the reasons why the realization of this demand, originating outside the institutional evolution of bourgeois society, can now be regarded as a practical possibility for society as a whole, which was never the case in the precapitalist period. In Marx's theory of needs, where both positive and negative aspects represent a rejection of precapitalist ways, this problem does not arise.

The differences between Marx and Macpherson in this respect are over-shadowed by a larger commonality of outlook. Both hold (along with J.S. Mill) individuality as a supreme value; unlike Mill, both regard the overcoming of market relations as ultimately necessary for the realization of individuality.

Macpherson's discussion of John Stuart Mill in his *Life and Times of Liberal Democracy* shows how much the latter's work influenced Macpherson's positive model of man as exerter and enjoyer of his capacities. At the same time he criticizes Mill for failing to understand that capitalist social relations are and will remain the chief obstacle to the realization of the democratic ideal of equal self-development. Commenting on Mill's belief that a network of producer's co-operatives would ensure the fairness of market relations, he notes: 'A system which requires men to see themselves, and to act, as consumers and appropriators, gives little scope for most of them to see themselves and act as exerters and developers of their capacities.' The implicit judgment about market relations here is similar to Marx's recommendation for the abolition of exchange in the second stage of socialism or in communism.[28] Two important points remain unclear: 1/ Why are the two kinds of activity mutually exclusive? 2/ What kinds of real alternatives are possible?

Capitalist social relations are indeed inconsistent with the democratic ideal in a number of specific historical contexts. Among them are the holding of wages at or near minimal subsistence levels, imperialist domination of national economies, authoritarian control over management decisions, the manipulation of political processes in favour of propertied interests, and gross inequalities in the distribution of income and wealth. All of them are still with us to varying degrees and in different places today. Yet many of

28 Ibid., 61. A careful discussion of Marx's position is being developed in Stanley Moore's forthcoming book, *An Obscured Alternative: Marx on Socialism and Communism.*

these evils have also been mitigated in varying degrees in the evolution of capitalist societies, and it is not unreasonable to suppose that further progress in this regard can occur. At the same time, different forms of the same evils have been institutionalized in the state-socialist regimes which came to power in an ideological crusade against capitalism. Let us suppose there is widespread agreement in our own society on the desirability of reducing the extent of such practices, and perhaps of eliminating at least some of them. The key question remains: Are market relations the principal fount of those evils, and is this where the attack on them must be focused?

I have argued that both Marx and Macpherson see the rule of the 'market principle' over the satisfaction of needs in capitalist society as the chief obstacle to social progress. I believe that their critique lacks sufficient precision on this point, and as a result, their theories reach a limit in terms of their own development. This limit prevents them from being able to deal adequately with the contemporary stage of capitalist society.

So far as Marx's theory is concerned, whereas his first model (in his *Manuscripts*) was one-sided in its rejection of capitalism, his second model (in his *Grundrisse*) was – ironically – too one-sided in its positive conception of the expansion of human needs in capitalist society. The basic flaw in the second model is his assumptions that the new needs are themselves unproblematic and that the root of the social problem lies only in the 'form' of their satisfaction, namely, the ubiquitous exchange form inherent in capitalist market relations. These assumptions forced him to accept as the only viable alternative a conception of need-satisfaction that is routed through the production of direct use values.

The 'overcoming of scarcity' that is presupposed in this conception is defeated by the relentless expansion of needs. For what Marx's second model misses basically is the fact that needs themselves change, in terms of their 'form', (i.e., the ways in which they are articulated), in response to the major change in the form of satisfaction noted above. The needs experienced by the majority of the population in advanced industrial societies today are shaped and moulded in their innermost structure by market relations, and there is as yet no evidence that would lead us to expect any wholesale popular rejection of this process of need-formation and need-satisfaction in the future.

Macpherson's theory requires a further refinement in the concept of utility-maximizing behaviour that grounds his ethical objection to possessive individualism. Earlier I suggested that his hierarchical ordering of non-material *versus* material activity is an inappropriate basis for a critique of contemporary society. The inadequacy in this dichotomy is its restricted notion of 'utility' itself. I do not believe that it is possible to separate what I have called elsewhere the 'material and symbolic correlates of needing', or to ignore what Marshall Sahlins terms the 'symbolic constitution of utility' that is always present in man's 'material' activity.[29] From this standpoint utility is regarded, not as either the purely material or purely individualized expression of need, but rather a socialized form of need-articulation that is governed by cultural values and interpersonal experience. There are indeed many vulgar-materialist forms of possessive individualism, but it is not certain that they are bound inherently to market and exchange relations, or that they would be abolished by eliminating those relations.

I think it may be unwise and possibly self-defeating to centre the critique of capitalist society in an ideological crusade against market relations as such. It is certainly true that the actual evolution of capitalist market relations institutionalized class domination and the maldistribution of income and wealth; yet many other social systems did (and do) so as well, including centralized economic planning under state socialism. What will be required for *any* modern economy are decision-making forums for allocating productive resources effectively in response to a very complex array of needs and wants. If a society is committed to the steady extension of the democratic ideal, it will have to ensure that those forums are responsive to popular control and that they encourage reasoned discussions about the worthiness of particular felt needs and goals. A system of market relations that is limited in its range by social policy regulations and welfare considerations can have a role to play in allocating resources to meet the great complexity of needs expressed in contemporary industrial societies.

Making this suggestion does not necessarily place one in the camp of those who regard market relations as a paradise of human freedom and who urge that our best course is to allow them the widest possible scope in our lives. It means simply that they should be held as one of our options for matching means and ends at the level of social and economic policy. They have no privileged status in the range of options; but they should not be seen as the *bête noire* for the democratic ideal.

There is another alternative, a familiar one in utopian social theory, where exchange and market relations are minimal: a society organized around small-scale, largely self-sufficient producers' co-operatives. When each group produces most or all of the requirements for its own needs, it is producing direct use values that never appear in the market place. There can still be specialization and the division of labour, and so long as exchanges take place on the basis of reciprocity, for example, without a medium of exchange, no market relations are involved. It is obvious that size limitations for the

29 W. Leiss, *The Limits to Satisfaction*, rev. ed. (Toronto, 1979), 63–7; Sahlins, *Culture and Practical Reason*.

social units are essential, for there are practical limits to the physical range wherein reciprocal exchanges can be made to work. In most utopian visions of this sort, handicraft production is emphasized as a virtue as well as a necessity.

Macpherson has objected to J.S. Mill's notion of producers' co-operatives that have market relations because it would require persons 'to see themselves, and to act, as consumers and appropriators', and because it would still give 'little scope for most of them to see themselves and to act as exerters and developers of their capacities'. The opposition between the two kinds of activity appears to be so fundamental that only a society organized as a loose association of autonomous, self-sufficient co-operatives could realize the self-developmental ideal. If I am correct in supposing that a complex, large-scale industrial system could not be run on the basis of producing direct use values, or (what I take to be an equivalent proposition) on the principle of 'to each according to his or her needs', then the same requirement would apply to Marx's vision of communism.

Would this be an appropriate social context for nurturing, and for allowing free rein to, human individuality? For both Marx and Macpherson, I believe, hold the fullest development of the individual's exertion and enjoyment of his and her capacities to be the supreme value. And in so doing, while also stipulating an absence of market relations, they present us with a dilemma. The small-scale, autonomous co-operatives would tend, I suspect, to exact the high degree of conformity in personal behaviour that seems to be characteristic of small communities everywhere. Social relations in such communities have their own worthy ideals, but the concept of individuality and the self-developmental ideal championed by Marx, Mill, and Macpherson are not normally among them. The social context that would meet the conditions for a better society laid down by these thinkers has not yet been presented adequately.

Macpherson asks: 'Is it too much to suggest that this awareness of quality [of life issues] is a first step away from being satisfied with quantity, and so a first step away from seeing ourselves as infinite consumers, towards valuing our ability to exert our energies and capacities in a decent environment?'[30] I believe he is correct in seeing quality-of-life issues as important evidence of a newly emerging dimension in the political economy of contemporary capitalist societies. But it need not be interpreted as a rejection of one behaviour pattern in favour of its supposed opposite. These issues emerge directly out of antagonistic elements within the system of production and consumption of utilities. They represent a growing understanding of the fact that the pursuit of material and psychological well-being primarily through

30 *The Life and Times of Liberal Democracy*, 102

market relations is self-contradictory. The unintended consequences or 'negative externalities' resulting therefrom – environmental pollution, health hazards (including widespread abuse of alcohol and tranquillizers), lack of outlets for creativity in occupations, a sense of powerlessness in the face of social complexity – detract sharply from the degree of satisfaction derived from work, play, and consumption. In addition, there is the widespread feeling of being 'no better off' than before despite dramatic rises in real incomes.[31]

To varying degrees the citizens in today's capitalist societies have already declared their support for public policies that restrict the play of market forces in many areas of their lives. It is easy to denigrate the accomplishments of the welfare state, for the imperfections of what might be called 'bureaucratic humanism' are all too evident. But it is also easy to underestimate the distance we have travelled from its ruthless nineteenth-century predecessor, and not all that difficult to imagine how it might be improved with the means currently at our disposal.

By comparison with the not-so-distant past there has been a considerable downgrading – but not abandonment– of market assumptions among the population as a whole in capitalist societies, and likewise a considerable upgrading of those essential preconditions for the development of a fuller range of individual capacities. Much more remains to be done. When it has been achieved, the beneficiaries will, I trust, realize how much they owe to those like Marx and Macpherson, who insisted that an unjust society held the promise of far better things than even its most ardent admirers had imagined.

31 This point is explored well in Tibor Scitovsky, *The Joyless Economy* (New York, 1976), and Fred Hirsch, *Social Limits to Growth* (Cambridge, MA, 1976).

STEVEN LUKES

The Real and Ideal Worlds
of Democracy

Brough Macpherson's democratic theory strikes a distinctive note. Resolutely Anglo-Saxon in its range of reference and its crisp, clear, analytic style, it unites a Marxist-inspired critique of 'capitalist market society with its class-division'[1] and of the underlying market assumptions of the justifying theory of liberal democracy with the constructive 'liberal' aim of 'retrieving' from that theory the 'notion of a democratic society as one that provides equally for the self-development of all the members of a political community'.[2] His motivating animus is against possessive individualism – 'this perverse, artificial, and temporary concept of man', inherited from 'classical liberal individualism', as 'essentially a consumer of utilities, an infinite desirer and infinite appropriator' whose over-riding motivation is 'to maximise the flow of satisfactions, or utilities, to himself from society'.[3] His positive commitment, by contrast, is to a 'co-operative and creative individualism' which rescues 'the humanist side of Mill's liberalism (the side based on his idea of man as essentially an exerter and developer of his human capacities) from the possessive individualist side (based on the Benthamite concept of man as essentially consumer and appropriator)'.[4] Thus he places himself among 'those who accept and would promote the normative values that were read into the liberal-democratic society and state by J.S. Mill and the nineteenth and twentieth century idealist theorists, but who reject the

1 *The Life and Times of Liberal Democracy* (Oxford, 1977), 21
2 'The False Roots of Western Democracy' in Fred R. Dallmayr ed., *From Contract to Community: Political Theory at the Crossroads* (New York and Basel, 1978), 26
3 *Democratic Theory: Essays in Retrieval* (Oxford, 1973), 20, 63, 24; *Life and Times*, 43
4 'Individualist Socialism? A Reply to Levine and MacIntyre', *Canadian Journal of Philosophy*, VI, 2 (June 1976), 198

present liberal-democratic society and state as having failed to live up to those values, or as being incapable of realising them'.[5]

Macpherson's project, therefore, has four main components. First, to identify the origins of market assumptions in the political theories of the seventeenth century and to trace their history from Locke through the classical economists to Bentham and James Mill and thence down to the present. Second, to trace the distinctive features of liberal democracy in 'the real world of democracy', in contradistinction to the communist and the populist or 'underdeveloped' variants. The 'life and times of liberal democracy' is portrayed as the historical amalgamation of possessive market ideas and ethical humanist claims that, in the nineteenth-century economy of scarcity, were, rightly, seen as necessarily linked together: the only way to free all individuals 'to use and develop their human capacities fully' was 'through the productivity of free-enterprise capitalism'.[6] The third component, therefore, is an argument to show that actual or prospective technological developments make possible a post-scarcity form of liberal democracy in which there is 'a possibility of our discarding the market concept of the essence of man, and replacing it by a morally preferable concept, in a way that was not possible when previous generations of liberal-democratic thinkers, from John Stuart Mill on, attempted it'.[7] Hence, the fourth component of Macpherson's project: to inquire into 'a possible future model of liberal democracy' which is based on 'the equal right to self-development',[8] being a model of 'participatory democracy, combining 'a pyramidal council structure with a competitive party system',[9] involving 'a stronger sense of community than now prevails'[10] and new and expanded conceptions of liberty,[11] property,[12] and human rights.[13]

This project is subject to various criticisms. Two are worth singling out, both of which deny the feasibility of a democratic theory's discarding one side of liberalism while building on the other. From a Marxist perspective, its attempt to preserve continuity with liberalism (or one side of it) and 'bourgeois political practice' may be judged to be 'reformist'. On this view, there is no 'possibility of "retrieving" the old order, while doing away with

5 'Do We Need a Theory of the State?', *Archives européennes de sociologie / European Journal of Sociology*, XVIII, 2, (1977), 224
6 *Life and Times*, 21–2
7 *Democratic Theory*, 37
8 *Life and Times*, 21–2
9 Ibid., 112
10 Ibid., 100
11 See *Democratic Theory*, chap. V.
12 See ibid., chap. VI.
13 See ibid., chap. XIII, section 5.

its defining characteristic: a market in labour and goods': what is required is a 'shift of terrain ... a shift in politics, a changed political practice, a changing of sides in the class struggle'. Macpherson's position is social democratic, a form of left-wing liberalism, an effort to 'reform or manage' capitalism, mitigating its worst features while obscuring its essential traits, and resting 'its faith on the development of productive capacities and the progressive and continuous evolution of political forms'. [14]

From an oddly parallel liberal standpoint, Macpherson's project of breaking with liberalism's market assumptions while retrieving its ethical core may be judged to be unrealistic, on the argument either that the former are ineliminable, applying to all advanced or all non-stagnant, growth-oriented societies, or that the former are inseparable from the latter or that there is, indeed, no conflict between them, since 'self-development' is compatible with, indeed may essentially require, market incentives and competitive striving. Thus many contemporary liberal thinkers, among them John Rawls and Robert Nozick, argue (in different ways) for *both* a market system based on incentives and a Humboldtian/Millian vision of the maximal development of human individuality. [15] At issue here, between Macpherson and such thinkers, may be an account of what constitutes human fulfilment, or of the conditions under which it may be approximated, or both.

Neither of these criticisms of Macpherson's project seems compelling to me. On the contrary, I take it to be a project that is of the greatest interest and importance, above all at a time when the advanced capitalist states are undergoing a cumulative 'legitimation crisis', [16] and the issues of the limits of the state's intervention in the economy, of the costs of growth and of market morality, and of forms of widening democratic participation are on the agenda of public debate. [17] Indeed, it is especially relevant to the Mediterranean liberal democracies where 'Eurocommunism' has raised in a new form the whole issue of continuity with liberal democracy in the transition to socialism. [18]

So while endorsing Macpherson's project, I shall rather address a number of problems arising out of his execution of it. I shall say nothing about its first

14 Andrew Levine, 'The Political Theory of Social Democracy', *Canadian Journal of Philosophy*, VI, 2 (June 1976), esp. 191–3
15 See J. Rawls, *A Theory of Justice* (Oxford, 1972), 523–5; R. Nozick, *Anarchy, State and Utopia* (Oxford, 1974), part III.
16 See J. Habermas, *Legitimation Crisis* (London, 1976); James O'Connor, *The Fiscal Crisis of the State* (New York, 1973), and the writings of Claus Offe.
17 See Michael Best and William Connolly, *The Politicized Economy* (Lexington, 1976) and William Connolly, *The Public Interest* (Washington, DC, 1977).
18 See, e.g., S. Carrillo, *Eurocommunism and the State* (London, 1977); F. Claudin, *Eurocommunism and Socialism* (London, 1978); and N. Poulantzas, *L'Etat, le pouvoir, le socialisme* (Paris, 1978).

component. Here his achievement has been the most considerable and the most effective, especially his brilliant interpretation of the seventeenth-century roots of market theory. Of course, all kinds of questions can be, and have been, raised with respect to his controversial interpretations of Hobbes, Locke, the Levellers, Bentham, the Mills, and so on, but I shall not be concerned with such questions here.

As for the second component, his view of the 'real world of democracy' does raise a number of problems, chief among them the following. His account is in terms of the 'justifying theories' of liberal, communist, and third-world democracy, seen as ideological contenders on the world stage – 'three concepts of democracy actively at work in the world today', none of which can realistically be claimed to be 'the only true democracy' and each of which is claimed by its adherents to be superior.[19] But he does not attempt, in relation to the latter two kinds, any analysis of the relation between theory and practice, concept and reality. Thus liberal democracy gets bad marks for failing to live up to its values, being tied to 'an inherently unequal market economy',[20] but the other two are not marked at all, but treated rather as alternative concepts 'prevailing' elsewhere,[21] as though theory adequately described reality. Not only does this approach ignore the extent to which societies of these kinds fail by their own standards (and the structural reasons for this) but it also precludes consideration of the extent to which there are shared common standards by which all three systems may be judged.

It is, perhaps, for this reason that Macpherson can say of communist states that they could plausibly claim to be democratic in the 'broader sense' that contains 'an ideal of human equality' which 'could only be fully realised in a society where no class was able to dominate or live at the expense of others', since although there is an 'absence or severe restriction of civil and political liberties', there is, according to the 'socialist model' [sic], no 'trans-

---

19 *The Real World of Democracy* (New York and Oxford, 1966), 58, 35, 36–7.
  Macpherson does not come clean as to how much of a moral/political relativist he is. Are these concepts incommensurable, such that there are no common standards to which they appeal; or are they competitors in the same race? He suggests the latter when he describes them as sharing 'the same ultimate moral end' – 'to provide the conditions for the full and free development of the essential human capacities of all the members of society' – but differing 'as to what conditions are needed, and as to how they must move to achieve those conditions' (37). But this argument would be undercut if the contending concepts of democracy involved different accounts of what *constitutes* 'the full and free development of the essential human capacities'. Macpherson appears to believe that there is one and only one correct account, but he offers no argument to support this belief.
20 'The False Roots', 19
21 E.g., *Real World*, 35–6

fer of powers from some men to others for the benefit of the others'.[22] And perhaps it is for the same reason that he can characterize 'newly independent underdeveloped countries' (in the mid 1960s) as examples of a single type, whose democratic doctrine invokes 'the will of an undifferentiated people as the only legitimate source of political power' and in which 'there are few or no exploitative class divisions once the foreign rule has been ended', since, with a few exceptions (such as the Congo and Vietnam) 'the independence movement has expelled the foreigners decisively enough that the class analysis is inapplicable'.[23]

These judgments are, to say the very least, not very persuasive and accordingly they have the effect of weakening an analysis that purports to be of 'the real world'. According to that analysis, 'societies that have rejected the capitalist system' (the communist and newly independent underdeveloped countries) have the (inherent) 'moral advantage' of not diminishing 'any man's satisfaction by a compulsive transfer of part of his powers to others for the benefit of others' and the (temporary) 'moral disadvantage' of not providing the same civil and political liberties – which, however, they 'have every reason to introduce ... as soon as they can afford them'[24] (their non-introduction presumably being explained by low productivity). Such a balance-sheet could only begin to be convincing after a full description of the actual moral record of the societies in question, an attempt to explain their failures (indicating to what extent these are structural and inherent), and a clear statement of the standards against which they are being judged.

On the other hand, Macpherson does give us a highly suggestive sketch of this kind with respect to liberal democracy, from which he concludes that it has a poor record when measured against its own ethical and humanist ideals by virtue of its class division and in particular of 'scarcity and the extractive market situation that have made people behave atomistically'.[25] To the extent to which these features are removed, he argues, a non-market and egalitarian form of liberal democracy becomes possible.

This raises the central problem of the third component of Macpherson's project: what socialists traditionally call 'the problem of the transition'. This is, of course, not just Macpherson's problem. But his formulations raise a number of specific problems to which I shall merely allude here. Does 'the

22 Ibid., 22; *Democratic Theory*, 14–15
23 *Real World*, 23, 29, 31, 32. Macpherson here appears to deny the reality of 'neo-colonialism', 'dependency', 'unequal development', the role of 'national bourgeoisies', etc., on which there is by now a vast literature.
24 Ibid., 66
25 'Individualist Socialism?', 199

prospective conquest of scarcity',[26] which is the precondition for the transition, imply a no-growth society? If so, is it realistic in the context of the contemporary international economy, and, if it is, does not ideal democracy then become the privilege of the affluent in a highly unequal world? What, in the transition, is the role of class-based politics and class struggle? Which social or political forces are progressive and democratic, in Macpherson's sense of moving towards the abandonment of the (capitalist?) market?

More generally, what, in the transition, is the relation between a change in consciousness and political action? In 1965, Macpherson argued, with respect to communist societies, that '[p]eople who have been debased by their society cannot be morally regenerated except by the society being reformed, and this requires political power ... there is no use relying on the free votes of everybody to bring about a fully human society. If it is not done by a vanguard it will not be done at all.'[27] In 1977, with respect to liberal democracies, he wrote of a kind of dialectic between changes in consciousness and increasing democratic participation – finding the possible 'loopholes' in the 'vicious circle' which links consumer consciousness, social inequality, and low participation (such weak points including the increasing awareness of the costs of economic growth, and of the costs of political apathy, in local communities and at the workplace, and increasing doubts about the ability of corporate capitalism to meet consumer expectations while reproducing inequality).[28] A crucial question, to which we need an answer, is why the 1965 answer should not apply to liberal democracies (especially since Macpherson holds that in them individuals are 'culturally conditioned to think of themselves as infinite consumers'[29] and are thus, presumably, 'debased by their society') or, for that matter, why the 1977 answer, or some version of it, should not apply to non-liberal democracies. Needless to say, such questions are of the greatest contemporary moment, and it is a virtue of Macpherson's work that it raises them in an acute form.

It is with Macpherson's attempt at the fourth component of his grand project – to develop a 'non-market theory' of liberal democracy – that the remainder of this essay will be concerned. To anticipate, my argument will be that this attempt is successful in separating out the developmental from the possessive elements of liberal individualism but that it fails in so far as it does not carry the argument through to the criticism of that very individualism itself.

It is probable, Macpherson argues, that 'the continuance of Western societies combining individual liberties and democratic rights depends on

26 Democratic Theory, 22–3
27 Real World, 19–20
28 See Life and Times, 106.
29 Democratic Theory, 62

those societies providing their members with an equal right to realise their essence as exerters, enjoyers and developers of their individual human capacities'.[30] Thus his theory of ideal democracy invokes an 'ontological' view of man's 'essence', and, in particular, the supersession of one such view by another:[31] 'the postulate of man as essentially consumer and appropriator' must be superseded by the 'concept of man as essentially an exerter and enjoyer of his own powers'.[32] Or, in another formulation, it must be realized that 'man's essence is not maximisation of his utilities but maximisation of his human powers'.[33] How, then, does Macpherson conceive of these powers and how are they to be maximized?

In earlier formulations, he writes of the 'ethical' concept of a man's powers as signifying 'a potential for realising some human end' and necessarily including 'not only his natural capacities (his energy and skill) but also his *ability* to exert them'.[34] In a later, and clearer, formulation, he speaks rather of the 'developmental concept of power' (in the singular) as signifying 'a man's ability to use and develop his capacities'.[35] The amount of a man's power 'always depends on his access to the means of exerting his actual capacities' and is to be 'measured in terms of the *absence of impediments* to his using his human capacities'. In short, 'a man's power, defined as the quantity of his ability to use and develop his human capacities, is measured by the quantity of external impediments to that ability'. The amount of a man's abilities, he writes, 'depends on present external impediments'; the amount of his capacities 'on innate endowment and past external impediments'.[36]

Thus 'ability' is seen as the absence of 'external' impediments (and might, therefore, more naturally be called 'opportunity'; we will, however, stick to Macpherson's usage). 'Capacities', by contrast, appear to signify an 'inner' potential, which may or may not be externally blocked. This distinction between 'external' and 'internal' is problematic: how it is drawn depends on how the 'individual' is conceptualized, where the boundaries of the agent's self are taken to lie, what he may be taken, and take himself, to have internalized.[37] For example, are moral or legal obligations, or the require-

---

30 Ibid., 36
31 Ibid., chap. II
32 Ibid., 37, 32
33 Ibid., 32
34 Ibid., 9
35 Ibid., 42
36 Ibid., 40, 58, 71, 52
37 See the essay 'Power and Structure' in my *Essays in Social Theory* (London, 1977), and also J. Feinberg, *Social Philosophy* (Englewood Cliffs, NJ, 1973), chap. 1, esp. 12–13.

ments of loyalty, say, to an individual or a group or an institution, or the cultural imperatives of the 'success ethic' to be counted as 'external' or 'internal'? It is true that, in one lonely paragraph, Macpherson acknowledges that 'society' is not 'only an impeding agent' but also 'a positive agent in the development of capacities', a 'medium' and a 'necessary condition' of their development.[38] But this acknowledgment does not extend to his seeing social relations as in part constitutive of the identity of the individual, which is, accordingly, transformed as those relations change. It is just because, on the contrary, he sees the individual ('man') abstractly as an atom whose nature ('capacities') is independent of the relations in which he is involved, that he can suppose his capacities and his ability to be separately identifiable (indeed measurable) and independently generated. If, however, the nature and identity of the individual is, even partly, determined by his social relations, then these will also play a role in determining both his potentialities and the impediments to their realization.

We have seen that Macpherson, in explication of his central concept of 'developmental power', whose maximization is to be the touchstone of a future liberal democratic system, uses three interrelated notions: *ability*, *impediments*, and *capacities*. Let us look at them more closely.

Let us begin with 'capacities'. These are described variously as 'natural', 'human', and – most often – 'essentially human'. At one point, they are classified as 'rational, moral, aesthetic, emotional, and productive in the broadest sense'.[39] Somewhat more specifically, he writes that they may 'be taken to include the capacity for rational understanding, for moral judgment and action, for aesthetic creation or contemplation, for the emotional activities of friendship and love, and, sometimes, for religious experience', and also 'for transforming what is given by Nature' (in a sense broader than 'the capacity for materially productive labour'), 'for wonder or curiosity', 'for laughter' and 'for controlled physical/mental/aesthetic activity, as expressed for instance in making music and in playing games of skill'.[40]

While acknowledging that the essentially human capacities 'might be variously listed', and that 'such a list could be extended and rearranged in many ways', and whether they are 'attributed to divine creation, or to some evolutionary development of more complex organisms', he takes their existence to be a 'basic postulate' which is both 'empirical', verifiable in a broad way by observation', and 'a value postulate, in the sense that rights and obligations can be derived from it without any additional value premise, since the very structure of our thought and language puts an evaluative content

38 *Democratic Theory*, 57
39 Ibid., 61–2
40 Ibid., 4, 54

into our descriptive statements about "man"'.[41] That postulate is, as we have seen, the 'view of man's essence not as a consumer of utilities but as a doer, a creator, an enjoyer of his human attributes'[42] – such attributes consisting in the capacities listed above.

Various perplexing problems arise here. Take, in the first place, the capacities listed. To suppose that, as characterized, they are sufficiently determinate for their degree of realization, and thus their maximization, to be specified is to beg a set of crucial questions. For people widely disagree about what *constitutes* 'rational understanding', 'moral judgment and action', 'aesthetic creation and contemplation', true 'religious experience', and so on. (Thus liberals and Marxists disagree with one another, and among themselves, about how rationally to explain their social world; utilitarians, contractarians, intuitionists, and perfectionists give conflicting accounts of morality; proponents of high and low culture disagree about the nature of art; adherents of different religions notoriously disagree about the nature of religion, etc.) To label human capacities by reference to their achievement is either to leave their nature indeterminate or to suppose such contested questions resolved in one way rather than another, which, to say the least, requires argument, and is question-begging, since alternative answers may be tied to alternative theories of human nature. Furthermore, history, especially recent history, gives some chilling lessons concerning the dangers to a liberal society, let alone liberal democracy, of a society's supposing such questions to be authoritatively resolved.

In the second place, one may ask, why *this* list? What, for example, of the human capacities for consumption and acquisition, for emulation and competition, for status-ranking, for domination and subjection, for the infliction and the acceptance of suffering, or indeed for malevolence, cunning, degradation, destructiveness, and brutality of all conceivable kinds? What principles govern the selection of Macpherson's (admittedly vaguely specified) list? Is his argument not really a way of endorsing certain forms of life by dignifying them, without warrant, as uniquely realizing 'essentially human capacities'?

This question cannot be resolved, as Macpherson suggests, empirically ('by observation') since the capacities I have mentioned, and doubtless many others, are indubitably characteristic of humans, even 'essential' to them – and not obviously less in evidence than those on Macpherson's list. Moreover, they are often held to justify forms of social and political life that he would reject, and some of which he would abhor. Nor will it resolve the question to appeal to 'the very structure of our thought and language', since

41 Ibid., 53–4
42 Ibid., 4

'we' differ about human nature and what is essential to it, and some – from Plato and St Augustine to de Maistre, Nietzsche, and Dostoevsky's Grand Inquisitor, not to mention Locke and Bentham – have asserted very different basic postulates and drawn very different social and political conclusions. Furthermore they have, in general, assumed that the social and political problem is not to maximize human capacities but rather to minimize the harmful consequences of their exercise.

This difficulty, of establishing a determinate set of 'essentially human capacities' as the basis for a justificatory theory of democracy, is only rendered more acute by a further assumption Macpherson makes, which he admits to be 'at first sight ... a staggering one': namely, the 'postulate of the non-opposition of essentially human capacities'.[43] The case for a democratic society, he argues, fails without this assumption. A 'fully democratic society is only possible when both genuine and contrived scarcity have been overcome'; then 'the essential human capacities may all be used and developed without hindering the use and development of all the rest'.[44] But surely this assumption is pretty staggering at second and third sight too. For why should we suppose that there ever could be a society in which 'rational, moral, aesthetic, emotional and productive' activities and relations would not be subject to regulation, limitation, and mutual adjustment, in the light of principles of justice, rendered necessary by conflicting claims and interests? To reply, as Macpherson might, that such regulation and limitation could never constitute a diminution of human capacities, if it were just – according, perhaps, to rules 'that can be rationally demonstrated to be necessary to society, and so to [man's] humanity'[45] – is, once more, to beg the question. For such a reply would, once more, build a particular moral vision into the notion of 'essentially human capacities''.

What we have so far shown is that Macpherson's 'essentially human capacities', with respect both to their content and their selection, presuppose, rather than ground, a particular moral theory. In the absence of any transcendental or quasi-transcendental argument to the contrary (à la Kant or Rawls or Habermas) such a conclusion is inescapable. And indeed, of course, Macpherson appeals to such a moral theory – which, he claims, derives from 'Western humanist and Christian traditions that go back to the Greeks and to medieval natural law' and which he invokes by speaking of 'the *equal* right of every man to make the best of himself'.[46] This is basically a form of individual moral perfectionism. For Macpherson's argument to stick, such a theory must play the role of specifying ideal possibilities whose realization is

43 Ibid., 55
44 Ibid., 55, 54
45 Ibid., 56
46 Ibid., 32, 21

blocked by actual social and political arrangements and to whose realization social and political action is to be directed. But, unfortunately, Macpherson says very little about how such possibilities *are* to be specified – what constitutes human excellence and, most importantly, what forms of social life or what sorts of social, cultural, and institutional activities and relationships would enable it to flourish, indeed *constitute* its flourishing. In the absence of such specification, we simply have the promise of an abstract, anti-utilitarian, individualistic moral perfectionism, formulated in the language of man's essentially human capacities.

To all this, Macpherson might reply that one must start at the other end: we 'must start', he writes, 'from the hindrances' or 'impediments' to the realization of such counterfactual, ideal possibilities.[47] Thus his analysis 'concentrates on the hindrances in modern market societies ... because this is what requires most analysis if we are to find a way through from a liberal market society to a fully democratic society'. A 'social and political theory car only be concerned with impediments that are socially variable', as opposed to 'physical impediments which cannot be altered by any action of society'; moreover, he focuses on *external* rather than 'internalised' impediments on the arguments, first, that the latter were external before they were internalized, and, second, that they are 'analytically more manageable'; besides, they interact with internal ones, each reciprocally reinforcing the other, but, conversely, a rational analysis of external impediments may contribute 'to the breakthrough of consciousness, and so to a cumulative reciprocal reduction of both kinds of impediment, and a cumulative realisation of democracy'.[48] Accordingly, the following impediments are 'deduced from the human condition': 'lack of adequate means of life', 'lack of access to the means of labour', and 'lack of protection against invasion by others'.[49]

The great virtue of this position is that, under the first two headings, it considers constraints or restrictions on liberty which most liberal theorists systematically ignore, and in particular the restrictions upon choice implicit in the manipulation of demand and in the consequences of material inequality, especially of the ownership of property. However, once one leaves the more obvious forms of deprivation (e.g., poverty or unemployment), the specification of 'impediments' becomes more problematic. Macpherson's key idea is that non-ownership of – or the lack of free access to – 'materials to work on or work with' (land and, more particularly, capital) constitutes such an impediment, diminishing non-owners' powers since they have to 'pay for the access with a transfer of part of their powers'.[50]

47 Ibid., 57
48 Ibid., 57, 59, 76
49 Ibid., 59–60ff
50 Ibid., 64

This argument will only really carry conviction when supplemented by a specification of the precluded possibilities that non-ownership impedes (which would, I believe, show that non-ownership is not the only way of denying access to the means of labour). Only then can a satisfactory argument be mounted against those who claim that the market and private property are not impediments to but rather conditions of the liberation of human possibilities. What is missing, in other words, is a detailed demonstration of what desirable and possible forms of relationship and activity are blocked by the central institutions of capitalism. In its place we have an abstract argument, purporting to show that, because these institutions involve 'a continuous transfer of power' between 'non-owners and owners of the means of labour',[51] they impede the maximization of (abstract) individuals' (unspecified) powers.

This, however, points to a deeper difficulty still. The 'maximization of powers' is the maximization of individuals' 'ability' to use and develop their human capacities, as measured by the impediments to their doing so. It therefore amounts, formally speaking, to a set of counterfactuals which specify what individuals could attain but for specified present preventing causes. But how are these counterfactuals to be specified?[52] How distant is the possible world we must imagine from the actual world? (Of course, the more distant it is, the greater the scope and complexity of the impediments or preventing causes.) In other words, how much of the actual world are we to take as given in setting up the counterfactuals? Or, in yet other words, what do we hold constant in comparing the actual with the possible? In particular, do we hold the very individuals, the maximization of whose abilities (power) is in question, to be constant, or themselves subject to transformation, and, if so, to what extent? *Which* individuals' powers are to be maximized: present, actual individuals or future, 'morally regenerated' ones?

Sometimes, Macpherson speaks of the counterfactual 'standard by which the theory must judge the democratic quality of any society' as 'the presently attainable maximum (i.e., the maximum level of abilities to use and develop human capacities given the presently possible human command over external Nature)' and of those capacities as being 'actual capacities'.[53] Elsewhere, however, he stresses that it is not enough 'to claim only to maximize the use of each man's present capacities': to maximize men's powers is 'to maximize the future development, as well as the present use, of each man's capacities', including 'those whose capacities had been stunted by external impedi-

---

51 Ibid., 65
52 On this problem, see the recent brilliant book by Jon Elster, *Logic and Society: Contradictions and Possible Worlds* (Chichester and New York, 1978), and my 'Power and Structure'.
53 *Democratic Theory*, 58, 40

ments'.[54] Such fully developed capacities can be conceived as a quantity, being 'the *amount* of [a man's] combined and co-ordinated mental, physical and psychic equipment, whether as it actually exists at a given time or as it might exist at some later time or under certain different conditions.'[55] But the whole problem lies here. For what *are* these different conditions? Do they include the 'regeneration' of the individuals concerned, their reshaping or 're-education', and, if so, to what degree? How is the line to be drawn between developing an individual's capacities and changing that individual?

What I hope to have shown is that Macpherson's account of human powers raises the following crucial and difficult questions. First, the 'essentially human capacities' rely for their specification upon an abstract, individualist ethical perfectionism, not yet spelled out. Second, the impediments to their use and development remain indeterminate, as long as those capacities and the forms of social life which both enable and constitute their realization remain unspecified. And third, the ability to realize them, whose maximization is the criterion of liberal democracy, is therefore indeterminate for these reasons, and for the further decisive reason that the (abstract) individuals, whose powers are to be maximized, are likewise indeterminate.

The great merit of Macpherson's liberal democratic theory is that it brings back into prominence the critical developmental perspective of the ethical and humanist side of liberalism and that it brings, from Marxist theory, a sharp awareness of the structural and institutional obstacles, within capitalism, to human emancipation. It has nothing to say about the nature of such obstacles in non-capitalist societies and it is (understandably) indecisive concerning the possible mode of transition from a capitalist to a post-capitalist form of liberal democracy.

However, it remains at an inappropriate level of abstraction and thereby bears the stamp of the liberal individualism it so acutely criticizes. Individuals and their powers and capacities are conceived in abstraction from the social relations and forms of community which, on the one hand, impede and, on the other, facilitate and constitute their further development. By reasoning exclusively in terms of man and the individual, Macpherson retains too much of the abstract humanism for which Marx criticized Feuerbach.[56] Social relations structure human activities and potentialities, which

54 Ibid., 57
55 Ibid., 56. Thus, he even writes that 'the full development of human capacities, as envisioned in the liberal-democratic concept of man – at least in its more optimistic version – is infinitely great. No inherent limit is seen to the extent to which men's human capacities may be enlarged' (62).
56 As Marx wrote in his sixth thesis on Feuerbach, 'the essence of *man* is no abstraction inherent in each separate individual. In its reality it is the *ensemble* of social relations'.

cannot be conceived independently of them, and this applies both to actual and to possible societies. Any fully developed democratic theory must get into the detailed business of comparing the actual and possible structures of living which are implicit in contemporary political struggle and debate. In short, for Macpherson's great project of retrieving liberal-democratic theory from the possessive individualism of the liberal tradition to be carried through to its conclusion, his penetrating critique of its possessiveness must be completed by an abandonment of its individualism.

The Dialectics of Domination: An Interpretation of Friedrich Dürrenmatt's *The Visit*

No citizen shall ever be wealthy enough to buy another,
and none poor enough to be forced to sell himself.
JEAN-JACQUES ROUSSEAU

Heroes and gods, ancient kingdoms and mythical lands – these are absent
from Dürrenmatt's tragi-comedy. It depicts a world of ordinary mortals – a
human world in a specific historical formation. Here are no divine mysteries,
no magic, no accidents.

It is a modern narrative. Its episodes unfold in the familiar structure of
contemporary industrial market society. They reflect the nature of such
society, not some primordial human essence.

It is the story of a small town whose people are confronted with horrifying
and tempting circumstances. What appears to them as extraordinary are,
however, only the hidden, secret logicalities of their ordinary world. The
familiar is accentuated, magnified, brought to its logical conclusion. The
structure of their historical existence, submerged until now, surfaces with an
intensity that appears alien and monstrous. In grotesque, absurdist, comic,
and solemn exaggeration they are permitted to gaze at the bitter truth of the
inner reality of their world: freedom denied and consciousness deformed.
But they only perceive their precious world turned upside down. Diligently
and swiftly they restore and improve it. They pass from one dark region of
historical existence to another. We witness the self-delusion which such a
passage entails.

The play is a powerful, haunting parable – the masterpiece of a brilliant
artist. Different from and superior to his *Romulus the Great, An Angel
Comes to Babylon*, and *The Physicists, The Visit*[1] stands alone.

1 Friedrich Dürrenmatt, *The Visit*, trans. Patrick Bowles (London; (1962, 1973);
original German title; *Der Besuch der Alten Dame* (Zürich, 1956)

The episodes of the play, in their symbolism, disclose the historicity of two distinct but interconnected modes of dehumanization: poverty and opulence. They reveal the hell of poverty and the false paradise of wealth. Dürrenmatt's is a philosophic tale of the pernicious interdependence of poverty and wealth and the dialectics of their apogee – domination.

The plot of the play, in summary, is this: a severely impoverished and steadily deteriorating town is preparing to receive its special visitor, Claire Zachanassian, the wealthiest woman in the world,[2] a native born. The leaders of the town seize the occasion to solicit her financial assistance. This crucial and delicate task is performed by Ill, the owner of the general store, who had a love affair with her when both were in their youth. At a ceremony in her honour she offers one million – one half for the town and the other half to be shared among each family – upon one condition: that Ill be killed. This is to rectify a past injustice: in a paternity claim against Ill, he secured, through bribery, false testimony against her; she left town and became a prostitute; the child died. A millionaire found her in a brothel and married her, thus initiating her financial empire.

The townspeople initially reject the offer with moral indignation. But soon after we find them purchasing goods on credit at an accelerating rate. Ill senses the impending danger; he solicits the support of the leaders of the community, but in vain. Zachanassian informs the schoolmaster and the doctor that she is responsible for the financial ruin of the town. She had purchased secretly the entire town and had all the factories and every business shut down. Finally, the town meets Zachanassian's condition; ritualistically they transvaluate the meaning of their action. The town delivers the body and she pays the money.

The story takes place in a small European town in the year 1955.[3] There is nothing monumental or memorable in these particulars; Dürrenmatt is not celebrating the mundane and insignificant. What he is stressing is the fact that the particularity of appearances veils what is truly fundamental: the nature of a society and the spirit of an age, the dynamics which condition the quality of human interaction. The true home of this drama is the global dominion of capital. Within the boundaries of this dominion all places and all moments are identical. Nothing is unique. Differences belong only to appearances; particularities are deceptive masks. An iron uniformity prevails.

2 In the postscript she is referred to as 'the richest woman in the world'. However, the story suggests opulence unrivalled by anyone, female or male.
3 In the postscript we are told that the town is 'somewhere in Central Europe'. No specific country is named. The action of the story takes place 'in the present'. I arrive at the year 1955 as follows: Claire left Guellen in 1910 after her unsuccessful paternity claim. Forty-five years have lapsed since, according to the mayor's and the ex-Chief Justice's account.

We must dispel the illusion that we could have qualitatively different lives if only we could change mere chronology and geography.

In the dominion of capital there is one eternal present, the universality of which negates all topographic variations. Capital knows no national boundaries; it is cosmopolitan. Zachanassian can, as long as the world is under the jurisdiction of capital, impoverish *any* human habitation. This small town represents all the towns of the world.

Her wealth and power are immense. Heads of government, royalty, dignitaries, celebrities, all gravitate towards her.[4] She is more powerful and influential than any office-holder or political leader. Her power is total; she is the economic base of society. It is this grotesque, extreme power that Dürrenmatt wishes us to visualize. It is not simply a question of the enormous amounts of money with which she can lure, bribe, and corrupt.[5] Rather, her money, as capital, controls the inner workings, the life activity, of the world. She owns the world, holding it in a strange, complex, and most effective control which needs no armies.

She acts with a fierce precision and absolute immunity reminiscent of ancient dynasties and despots. She reached as far as Australia and Canada to penalize the two men who gave false testimony against her; she had them castrated and blinded and then enlisted them in her service – chattels of completed transactions, mere objects of settled accounts, acquired and dispensed with at will. They are not trophies of past victories, reminders of cruel conquests; such feudal romanticism is alien to her. Nor is her primitive, almost biblical revenge executed secretly, like a crime. She acts as an absolute master. Her two sedan-chair bearers are ex-convicts, for a second example. They were about to be executed in Sing Sing, when she petitioned for them to be freed as her bearers. It cost her one million dollars per petition.[6] Cer-

---

4 For example: Eisenhower, Nehru, the French President, Onassis, the Riviera crowd, film stars, high society, financiers are in her social circle. She has been a guest in Buckingham Palace; once she was married by a Pope.

5 The incident with the ticket inspector is indicative of her use of money to remove irritating obstacles. Dürrenmatt forces the issue of the magic of wealth to an extreme in another instance: 'Quite a fantastic' salary lures the Lord Chief Justice, who had arbitrated her paternity claim, to her service as her butler. This symbolizes justice as the servant of wealth; this is not a case of an official who succumbed the temptation of a bribe; he is a transformed individual, a transvaluated consciousness; he is just what the townspeople are about to become.

6 That she had to petition and pay should not be interpreted as a sign of the limitation of her power. We should have no doubt that she can always have her way. Her power is diverse and complex but always effective. She strikes with primitive violence (e.g., against the two men who gave false testimony). The President of the World Bank flies in from New York to visit her; she refuses to see him: 'I'm not at home. Tell him to fly away again.' Unlike ancient barbaric despots she employs logic and procedures to get what she wants. Her power is not directly

tainly, other millionaires could afford two million dollars. But surely the government of the United States would not consider such petitions! Her petition was considered and granted. Herein rests the difference between ordinary wealth and her wealth: her wealth is not just money as purchasing power in the market. It is the logic and structure of the market itself.

It is a bankrupt, demoralized town that she visits. Its factories and businesses are shut down. Its railway station was once a busy stop for famous express trains; now only three commuter trains a day stop here. Watching the express trains go by is the last remaining pleasure of the townspeople. Perhaps it is also a source of sorrow, a reminder of better days and of vibrant life elsewhere. The poverty here is extreme and generalized, engulfing the entire population and tarnishing every domain of public and private existence. Individual dreams, promising future careers are destroyed or abandoned.

These are people who have experienced a higher standard of living. They know of poverty only as loss. Unlike those born into poverty whose whole life is consumed by it and who are defeated and broken, these people are agitated, planning their escape from poverty. Their basic values were founded outside a life of poverty.

Their crisis does not become an occasion for serious speculation regarding poverty. Poverty as such is taken for granted; it is never questioned; probably they view it as an ancient reality, an ineradicable feature of life, just like death. It is their own poverty that troubles and concerns them. The town has not been driven, after all, into the very darkness of poverty, into the region of hunger and physical pain, the loss of self-identity, the distortion of biological drive. The people have not been touched by the lethargy of emptiness and nothingness. They are not fragments of humanity, isolated atoms of private misery and anguish. Violence is absent. Existence is not questioned. Suicide is not contemplated. Theirs is a community under siege; it is an hour of emergency and not the moment of the disintegration of their social world. A sense of collective fate unites them.

Not only was the town once prosperous and famous, a city of the arts – Goethe spent a night and Brahms composed a quartet there, such were the glorious moments of the past – but furthermore the economic ruin of the town takes place in the midst of a national economic boom. In the accurate diagnosis of the mayor, the town's poverty is 'a real economic enigma'. Though they feel the significance of the economy, they have no actual

---

aggressive like an invading army; it is economic, hidden in the foundation of the existing social structure. She does not command; she requests. But her requests are effective, dominating as no command can be. Her power is smooth and efficient like a business transaction. Her desire is the dynamics of the system. Her will is for others their desire.

understanding of it. Their only wish is to escape their present situation and to restore the past. They long for a return to familiar, normal comforts.

They are apprehensive and anxious; they experience anger, a sense of victimization. The very poor have simplistic, truncated explanations of the enigma: a conspiracy by the Jews and the Communists (Dürrenmatt's sardonic sense of humour is superb: he includes the Free Masons too). Such are the mental acrobatics of the poverty-stricken. The less poor, more sophisticated, are perplexed, cunning. The leaders of the community are at work to save themselves and their town. A sense of deserving a better life prevails. Chronically empty stomachs extinguish such aspirations and useless thoughts; the psychological death of the poor occurs when their condition is perceived as an inescapable fate. Dürrenmatt's didactic tale does not deal with poverty which reduces individuals to the living dead, beyond hope and temptation, the kind of poverty under which everything ceases, even desire. Dürrenmatt concerns himself with a poverty that dehumanizes, exposes human fragility and weakness, denies heroic action, undermines consciousness, and forces the surrender of freedom.

Neither their present poverty implies the lower depths nor did their past prosperity imply opulence. Regarding the past, we hear of an incident involving the police and a beggar; we are told of a poor hungry widow. False testimony at the paternity suit was secured by a mere pint of brandy. Ill abandoned Claire for someone of substantive means – the daughter of the owner of the general store. Claire was driven away from home; she became a prostitute. Such was life for the less privileged in the idealized past.

The nature of their society has not been transformed. Poverty did not level everything. Old hierarchies and privileges still linger on. The town doctor drives his old Mercedes. The mayor, the schoolmaster, the priest, the police inspector are the elite. Other citizens are poor enough to be on relief. The entire town senses the invisible hand of economic death. All are condemned. But not all suffer equally. Generalizations – past prosperity, present poverty – obscure social reality.

What we see here now are anxious, limited people. There is nothing noble about them in their dreams, hopes, and strategies. But there is nothing sinister or satanic about them either. They maintain their social respectability. They are willing neither to steal nor to beg. But neither are they able to rebel.

Zachanassian has a global financial empire at her disposal, stretching from West to East.[7] She has no aversion towards philanthropic gestures: a hospital

7 The foundation of her economic empire is oil. Perhaps there is a cryptic irony in Dürrenmatt's insistence to relate her wealth to Armenia, a country and a people who have suffered immensely; a reminder that wealth and suffering are connected.

here, a kindergarten there, a memorial church. And she is one of them, a native of the town. Childhood bonds could prove stronger than social roles. Simple thoughts of ordinary people. The elite are calculating. For example, the mayor's adjustment of the true facts of Claire's childhood is an attempt to flatter, to avoid anything offensive. But such flattery is transparent, at times comic. His version of Claire's childhood is not an Orwellian re-writing of history; it is simply a pathetic performance.

With Ill it is another story. He is a merchant. For him life is a sequence of business deals in pursuit of profit. He uses the system; he knows of human needs and material possessions; he has mastered the psychology of the most basic human transactions. Upward mobility is his talent. He is a practical man wounded by poverty. We must see him for what he is now. His brief retelling of his love affair should not mislead us; an old man's memory speaks of youth and sexuality, devoid of genuine sentiments. He is now significant and vital to the town's mission. He has been promised the mayoralty.

The extreme flattery with which he addresses Claire, in private, exceeds that of the mayor. Whenever he believes that he is manipulating her, he is elated. He wants her to pity him and the town. Offensive and repulsive he can be, though he is neither vicious nor sinister. Life is like any other transaction for him – some improve themselves and others do not. His merchant's mind cannot think beyond the master metaphor of buying and selling. Profit and self-interest coincide in blissful harmony and define the meaning of humanity. There are no ideals here; all is pure practical commercial reasoning: 'mine and thine' exhaust the universe of merchant Ill.

Zachanassian owns the world; but she does not seem impressed by it. Ultimately it is a meaningless possession; money can buy everything, except meaning.[8] The memory of her simple, youthful love seems to be the only tender, human moment in her opulent life. She recalls Ill's treachery without fury or rage. Her demand for his death does not disclose any passionate sense of ruthless vengeance. It is a deal, a matter of emotionless facts.

Zachanassian is capital itself. She refers to herself as 'unkillable'; obviously she has no illusions of immortality, but, as capital, she cannot be killed because she is not a living being. Emptiness, a non-human state of being, and

---

8 Claire declares: 'Everything can be bought' including justice. Dürrenmatt concentrates on the ability of wealth to possess everything, to convert everything into an object. The belief that 'you can get anything you want with money' is repeated in the play. But Ill's wife says, 'Money alone makes no one happy', and a reporter says, 'That's a truth we in this modern world ought to write up in the sky of our hearts'. Zachanassian herself is the ultimate and complete refutation of the false identification of opulence with happiness, of possessive individualism with meaningful, human existence.

not cruelty, is her main feature. She has become mechanized functions. Even Ill's death gives her no satisfaction, no excitement, no true sense of revenge. 'Justice for a million,' she says. But her justice, as revenge, is deflated, empty. She is not intoxicated with her wealth and power; she is bored.[9]

Her kingdom is arid, her power the function of a system. She declares, 'the world turned me into a whore. I shall turn the world into a brothel'. This is her 'new world order'. Ill's death is only another of the means whereby all are forced to become citizens, subjects, prostitutes of the Brothel of Capital.

The town is thus visited by none other than the spirit of capitalism with all its monstrous, devouring power.[10] She moves about not with arrogance but with a force well beyond human will. As in ancient Greek tragedy, the rhythm of inevitability accompanies her utterances.[11]

The town's impoverishment is not an accident; nor is it natural. It is the result of a scheme. A calculated, systematic pursuit of wealth does impoverish others; the genesis, maintenance, and increase of wealth must victimize others. Dürrenmatt wishes to show the inherently coercive, exploitative, dehumanizing character of the relations of market society: they are violent, unjust, and unfree just like her power and revenge. The casualties of the market society are not accidents – they are an inherent feature of the system.

The suffering of the casualties is not rooted in life itself; it belongs to specific historical structures of human existence. Dürrenmatt shows how

9 During her first conversation with Ill, she indicates that the world, her possession, is not worth seeing. She does not recall who is who of her many ex-husbands; sometimes she filed for divorce immediately after the ceremony – that is how meaningless the whole process was. She is not an eccentric. Beyond boredom and meaninglessness she defines herself: 'I've grown into hell itself'. She is not simply evil; she is the source of evil – suffering. Symbolic of capital, she is presented as made up of non-human parts: she has an artificial leg and an artificial hand. Dürrenmatt tells us that she should be 'represented as a stone idol'.

10 In the original text all currency remains unspecified. We hear only numbers. The only reference to specific currency occurs with the two million dollars paid to the United States government. The absence of specificity conveys the universality of capital. Mr Bowles subscribes to Samuel Beckett's theory of translation: to render the original as if it had been written in the language in which it is being translated. This attitude can yield admirable results. But in this instance the translator obscured a significant feature by insisting on referring to pounds.

11 The inevitability of Ill's death is intimated repeatedly: Zachanassian's first words to the policeman, the priest, the doctor, the gymnast; the allegorical-surrealistic use of the black panther, its hunt and ultimate death (Claire used to call Ill during their love affair 'black panther'); the presence of the coffin. Dürrenmatt refers to her as 'something like Medea', precisely what the schoolmaster calls her. The schoolmaster with intuitive accuracy speaks of her as 'horror', 'a gruesome vision', 'an avenging Greek goddess', and as one 'of the Fates'. This genuine insight will be forgotten subsequently.

arbitrary and dehumanizing impoverishment can be. But so too is wealth. Murder is shown as the indispensable nexus between poverty and wealth.[12] Wealth II creates poverty; poverty seeks salvation in wealth; poverty reduces human beings to saleable objects, commodities in the command of wealth. Humanity is sacrificed.

Dürrenmatt forces us to see that poverty is a condition of powerlessness, of denied freedom. Poverty is nasty and brutish,[13] and one's only wish is to escape it. To be sure, there is natural poverty, a poor environment, an inhospitable terrain. But in capitalism, there is a different poverty, unnatural, historically created.

It is the co-existence of poverty and wealth that here constitutes the human drama. Poverty being hell, its opposite appears as paradise. The townspeople originally complain about their current poverty, measured against a past higher standard of living. The temptation of wealth – an even higher standard of living – kills the nostalgia for simply restoring the past. The desire for increase emerges. Dürrenmatt demonstrates that the 'either/ or' of poverty and wealth is false; it is predicated upon an artificial choice. The townspeople are confronted with the haunting reality of a wretched existence and the lure of prosperity. Between poverty and prosperity the human mind and psyche are mobilized towards the obvious superiority of the latter. The accessibility of wealth, within a context of poverty, forces them to change their desires and wishes. No other alternatives are visible.

The townspeople engage in an accelerating spree of purchasing and consuming. The thought process that initiates such activity remains invisible. The experience of poverty and the temptation of wealth are blended silently, imperceptibly.[14] Their purchasing is characterized by an insistence on ac-

12 The connection between crime and wealth is stressed visually: she is held up high by the two criminals, who carry her sedan-chair.
13 In a final plea to her, the schoolmaster says, 'We're only human'. He begs, 'don't try us till we break'. And to Ill, later on, he says, 'The temptation is too great and our poverty is too wretched'. The priest earlier told Ill 'Flee! Lead us not into temptation with your presence.' The play emphasizes the temptation of wealth in a context of poverty; fear of further impoverishment is not an issue. As Dürrenmatt puts it: 'The temptation is too strong, the poverty too wretched.' Those who yield to the temptation, the new consumers, wear yellow shoes – the colour of gold, the symbol of opulence. Ill, witnessing the town's economic boom – Zachanassian had said 'a boom for a body' – says, 'Everything's yellow. The autumn's really here. The leaves on the ground are like layers of gold.' Zachanassian speaks of her 'golden millions'.
14 Act II introduces the purchase-frenzy. It is sudden, without any preliminaries as if it were an on-going process. The schoolmaster in a lucid statement to Ill says, 'I can feel myself slowly becoming a murderer', and is aware of the implications. Yet he adds, 'perhaps in a few hours, I shall have lost that knowledge'. In effect this would apply to the whole town. Ill's own family are actively participating in the

quiring the more expensive and the higher-quality superior commodities. Old habits and past preferences are renounced. They act as if they are rich. These are not hungry people who decide to feed themselves; these are middle-class citizens in the paradise of commodities, celebrating life, their rising standard of living.

They do not consume because they think they will get the million; they consume as if they have the million. It is under such circumstances that Ill begins to fear for his life. He reasons that the townspeople are incurring debts for which he must be killed if the million is to be collected and the debts paid. He demands Zachanassian's arrest for incitement to commit murder. His demand is thwarted by the police inspector in a marvellous exercise of legal formalism. The mayor does likewise on political grounds.[15] The priest advises Ill to examine his conscience and repent; finally he tells him to flee. Ill attempts to do so, but at the railway station he encounters the townspeople led by the mayor, the schoolmaster, the doctor, and the policeman. Without ever forcing him physically, in ominous tone and movement they in effect prevent him from leaving the town, even though they proclaim him free to depart. A gradual, generalized indignation against Ill is manifest.

Dürrenmatt does not suggest either recklessness or sinister hypocrisy on the part of the townspeople. Nowhere do we witness any conspiracy; they do not act secretly. On the contrary, Dürrenmatt portrays the naturalness with which the townspeople assume their new behaviour – thoughtlessly, in unison. They act as if they are rich. Simple as that. They incur debts which logically lead to the killing of Ill. The rich become murderous, imperceptibly. There is no agony, no crisis of the conscience, no satanic excitement.

Opulence presupposes, demands, and generates poverty. The difference in the two conditions is behavioural, not ontological. The poor *are* now rich; the habits of poverty are discarded, the manners of the rich assumed.

The townspeople do not first break down, surrender, give in, and then change. They *become* their opposite. They internalize Zachanassian's command. They act as if they had chosen their actions, hence their intense moralization and rationalization. Having left the actual hell of poverty, they now breathe the air of their false freedom, false paradise. Dürrenmatt presents them as if they indeed are self-determined, autonomous, authentic individuals. Thoughtless but not idiotic, they enter the paradise of possessions, fetishes, and consumption. They are oblivious to their condition.

joys of material possessions. The knowledge that the town's impoverishment is a deliberate act is never made public. Also the initiation of the purchase-frenzy preceded the disclosure by Zachanassian.

15 The policeman and the mayor are among the new consumers. The mayor tries later to persuade Ill to commit suicide – a neat elimination of the mayor's problem. Ill refuses but agrees to abide by the decision of the townspeople.

They moralize and ideologize. Their actions are transvaluated, altered, falsified. As rich people they react indignantly. Their collective conscience is offended. The injustice and monstrosity of their impending act must disappear. Hence their commitment to justice and their moral resentment towards Ill. The wealthy are moral, philanthropic, pragmatic, but essentially they build upon murder and suffering. We do not see here hungry, poverty-stricken people who kill in order to become rich. It is the reverse behaviour that Dürrenmatt stresses: these are rich people who kill. They falsify their actual killing; it is called justice. It is not even an execution; it is declared a natural death.

All are oblivious to the true dynamics of their historical reality. The locus of their perception is the realm of appearance. Take the case of the schoolmaster. He, as the intellectual of the town, recognizes the logical inevitability of the debts of the townspeople. In an attempt to avert a tragic resolution he, in the doctor's company, proposes to Zachanassian that she invest in the town, develop it, and thus help them pay their debts and recover economically. He stresses the natural wealth of the town: oil, minerals. He makes a business proposition. It is then that he is informed that she already owns the whole town and has impoverished it on purpose. In that context, Dürrenmatt forces us to recognize that in the dominion of capital those without it are at the mercy of those who do. Capital sets the rules. The fact of material resources or natural wealth does not alter the reality of dependence. The utilization of the natural resources requires capital, but the solution of the town's economic condition cannot take place outside the structure of the economy of the world: capitalism. The schoolmaster is a naive intellectual. He fails to grasp the essentials: Zachanassian's *secret* ownership of the town symbolizes the *public* power of capital and the inequality of negotiation. He fails to realize that the town cannot be freed from the tentacles of the monster – capitalism – symbolically presented as an inhuman old woman: the town can offer nothing material that she does not already have. They cannot appeal to her humanity: there is none.[16] They cannot tempt her with any profitable offers. She literally owns their world.

Ill the merchant, a man without conscience, seeking his material self-interest, willing to betray for money and social mobility, comes to a realization. He admits guilt. His moral awakening is an idealist, indiscriminate embrace of all sorrow, a martyrdom rooted in an exaggerated personal guilt. It is a desperate attempt to redeem the world of suffering without ever

16 When asked to let her 'feeling for humanity prevail', she answers, 'Feeling for humanity, gentlemen, is cut for the purse of an ordinary millionaire; with financial resources like mine you can afford a new world order'.

understanding its working mechanism. Ill, more admirable now, is as wrong about the world as when he was treacherous, devious, and selfish.

Zachanassian, in the poverty of her youth, ends as a whore; in her super-opulence, she wants to turn the world into a brothel. The dialectics of poverty and wealth, of deprivation and domination, escape her. The brothel she once inhabited and the new world order she proclaims – the world as brothel – constitute the world of capital. She does not impose a new order on that world; she only reaffirms vividly its original order.

Her revenge is nothing but the actual workings of capital. She, in her omnipotence, chooses nothing outside the world of capital. She only confirms the prostitution of the market society. She is its prisoner at a higher level. The world did not turn her into a whore. A specific historical structure of the world permits, indeed warrants, that some destroy others. She thinks that Ill chose his life and forced her into hers. His 'choice' and his 'freedom' were as empty and false then as the 'choice' and 'freedom' of the townspeople under her conditions. These are preordained roles which devour individual lives.

In a last encounter between Claire and Ill, Dürrenmatt allows them to reflect on their condition and its inner meaning. During that encounter Ill speaks of his meaningless life; he has grown now into a solitary and sad figure, neither pathetic nor heroic. The full human being has not emerged. It cannot be born in Ill's world. But the merchant in him has died. Claire speaks of her utterly empty, non-human existence. She inhabits that strange twilight zone devoid of human passion, the zone that mimics life and transvaluates it. Then, in a simple, precise, concise non-melodramatic statement she confesses his death as inevitable but meaningless, her own life empty, meaningless, and unfree. Dürrenmatt demolishes any notion that her power corresponds to freedom. No one is free in the dominion of capital.[17] There are hierarchies of command, there are circles of fierce, horrible poverty juxtaposed to centres of opulence, possessions, and freedom from poverty; but all are interconnected, all are subject to a single iron

17 Ill originally viewed life and history as coterminous. More precisely, he has no notion of history. He says, 'Life tore us apart. Life. That's the way it is.' To Claire he says, 'If only life hadn't put us asunder'. Now he accepts responsibility for everything. Still, he is incapable of recognizing history. It is the meaning of history that eludes Claire too. The priest had said to Ill, 'Because you once betrayed a young girl for money, many years ago, do you believe the people will betray you now for money? You impute your own nature to others'. It is precisely that original betrayal that is re-enacted. It is not a question of human nature; it is a question of the circumstances under which a fragile human nature is forced to deny itself.

master – capitalism. No human being can survive its rule. It is alien to humanity. The kingdom of capital is the kingdom of murder and death. In Claire's words, her encounter with Ill ends in 'a dead man beside a stone idol'. No signs of human life.

Claire's accurate self-reflection precedes the intense and ritualistic self-delusion of the townspeople. The wealthiest woman in the world confesses the emptiness of her life – her unhappiness. It is in this context that we must see the townspeople and their material paradise. In their newly acquired universe they can be seen for what they really are: miniatures of Claire. No genuine happiness exists for either of them. Freed from poverty, they have not entered a humanized world.

The play reaches its climax when the townspeople and their elite moralize in a grandiose justificatory ideology the impending killing of Ill. It is not a case of a reversal of positions now cast in highly moral terms; this would be hypocrisy or lunacy. Dürrenmatt is more merciless than that. What we have here is quite distinct. A public ritual altering the meaning of their activity takes place. The Zachanassian Endowment is proclaimed. Ill accepts. The schoolmaster, the intellectual, delivers a triumphant speech regarding the ideals of humanity. He who resisted this travesty is the most systematic ideologue of the whole group. Dürrenmatt carefully shows us that Ill's murder, which is declared a heart-attack, is an act that involves planning, manipulation, deception – and, above all, self-deception.

These individuals, in Dürrenmatt's portrayal are neither fools nor liars – they are serious, ordinary citizens praising the material dimension of their dehumanized world, their victory over poverty. They do not recognize themselves as victims. They perform their roles. They are their roles.

The play ends in a scene where the people in choruses and as individuals proclaim their good fortune. This final scene declares prosperity as the way of life. In this sense any semi-awareness about Ill's murder disappears into amnesiac bliss. Verging on a paean the final scene discloses the meaning of the whole play. Many are the monstrous things on earth, we are reminded – volcanoes, earthquakes, wars – but

> These monstrous things / do not exceed
> The monstrous plight / of poverty
> Which excites / no tragic deed
> Is not heroic / but condemns
> Our human race / to barren days
> After hopeless / yesterdays.

Dürrenmatt's parable is about an ancient human plight, poverty, which is the root of a modern plight, domination, the paradise of the bourgeoisie. The actual, devastating misery of poverty is not a natural phenomenon for

Dürrenmatt; it is a human creation. The riches of some are the poverty of others. Wealth has its whims, granted, but its whims do not run contrary to the market society. They are not destructive of its principles and workings. They are commands or seductive calls to the rest of the world. Poverty is a monstrosity, Dürrenmatt tells us, a monstrosity beyond courage and heroics. There, in its darkness, human survival denies human essence. The victims of poverty survive, dreaming of wealth; the wealthy witness poverty and its curse and regard themselves as being in a state of grace. Poverty and its misery are not imaginary, they are painfully actual. But their actuality does not disclose immediately or spontaneously their root, wealth. Poverty and wealth stand apart. Dürrenmatt wants us to remember that the poor are made poor. Seemingly, it is a world of victors and vanquished, rich and poor. Dürrenmatt shows us how in reality all, rich and poor, are defeated, dehumanized, dead. There are no victors in the dominion of capital. The poor, desperate in their actual wounds and concrete misery, dream of relief in the heaven of opulence. The rich dread the misery of the poor and rejoice in their many blessings. The wounds of poverty are visible and tangible; the deformity of opulence is invisible, or embellished. Poverty and wealth asphyxiate humanity in an artificial, false 'either/or.' Poverty initiates the fear. It bestows an excessive significance on wealth. In its oppressive character, poverty paves the way for the inauthentic world of domination, its false paradise, its empty abundance, its mere defeat of hunger.

Dürrenmatt refutes the naive identification of history with ontology. He elicits different actions, behaviour, and speech from the *same* individuals by shifting them from poverty to wealth. It is not the human essence that is paraded before us. When freedom is denied and consciousness is deformed, then, in historical masks and guises, we witness the grand defeat of humanity, visible in poverty but utterly obscured in wealth.

Dürrenmatt mercilessly exposes the cruelty of poverty, the inhumanity of wealth, and the falsehood of opulence. The world in its historical dehumanization is symbolized for him by the brothel.

In his precise, Aristophanic manner, Dürrenmatt speaks of inhuman temptations and desperate, humiliating survivals. Poverty is hell; wealth is a false solace, a sorrowful paradise. Claire in her youth is exiled in the poverty and misery of a brothel, a social outcast; at the pinnacle of her power she is a stone idol, a non-human agency of death. Dürrenmatt's parable teaches us that Claire the whore and Claire the stone idol are two modes of dehumanization, two modes of the denial of human freedom. But in the world of history Claire the stone idol disguises and masks her true identity, her emptiness.

Whenever appearance is graced with the aura of reality, the voices of truth must once again differentiate them.

Crawford Brough Macpherson:
A Bibliography

This bibliography contains a listing of all the scholarly publications of C.B. Macpherson (to September 1979). Correspondence, including letters to editors and
similar public submissions, and reported versions of addresses, speeches, and inter-
views have not been included. Categories for the internal organization of this
bibliography are: books (including books edited by c.b.m. and his own chapters
contained therein); articles, review articles, and chapters in books (edited by others);
and book reviews. Listings are arranged chronologically within each category, except
for book reviews, where the entries are arranged alphabetically by the last names of
the (first) author being reviewed and include entries for all books treated principally in
review articles (this is the only case of double entries). Where the title of a review or
review article is different from that of the book under review, both titles are given
within the same entry, with the title of the review directly following the title of the
book under review. Translations, revised editions, and reprints are noted along with
the original work (reprints on a selective basis only).

The following abbreviations are used: *CJEPS* for the *Canadian Journal of Economics and Political Science*; and *CJPS* for the *Canadian Journal of Political
Science/Revue canadienne de science politique*.

BOOKS

Democracy in Alberta: The Theory and Practice of a Quasi-Party System. Toronto:
  University of Toronto Press, 1953. Pp. x, 250
  Second edition with revised subtitle, *Social Credit and the Party System*. Toronto:
  University of Toronto Press, 1962. Pp. xii, 250

The Political Theory of Possessive Individualism: Hobbes to Locke. Oxford: at the
  Clarendon Press, 1962. Pp. 303
  Translations

Die politische Theorie des Besitzindividualismus: Von Hobbes bis Locke.
Frankfurt: Suhrkamp Verlag, 1967
La teoria politica del individualismo posesivo. Barcelona: Editorial Fontanella,
1970
La théorie politique de l'individualisme possessif. Paris: Gallimard, 1971
*Libertà e proprietà alle origini del pensiero borghese: la theoria dell' indi-
vidualismo possessivo da Hobbes a Locke.* Milan: Instituto Librario Inter-
nazionale, 1973
A teoria politica do individualismo possessivo de Hobbes até Locke Rio de Janiero:
Paz e terra, 1979

The Real World of Democracy. Toronto: Canadian Broadcasting Corporation, 1965.
Pp. 67
English edition   Oxford: Clarendon Press, 1966
Japanese edition   Osaka: Aoyama Shoten, 1968
US edition   New York: Oxford University Press, 1972
Translations
Japanese   Tokyo: Iwanami Shoten, 1967
Drei Formen der Demokratie. Frankfurt: Europaische Verlagsanstalt, 1967
La realidad democratica. Barcelona: Fontanella, 1968
Den mångtydiga demokratin. Stockholm: Aldus/Bonniers, 1968
Demokratiets ansigter. Copenhagen: Steen Hasselbalchs Forlag, 1970
Le véritable monde de la démocratie. Montréal: Les Presses de l'Université du
Québec, 1976

The Future of Canadian Federalism/L'avenir du fédéralisme canadien (edited with a
joint introduction by C.B.M. and P.-A. Crépeau). Toronto and Montreal: University of Toronto Press and Les Presses de l'Université de Montréal, 1965. Pp. x, 128

Thomas Hobbes' *Leviathan* (edited with an introduction and a note on the text [pp.
9–70] by CBM). Harmondsworth: Penguin Books, 1968. Pp. 729
Democratic Theory: Essays in Retrieval. Oxford: Clarendon Press, 1973. Pp. xii,
255. This volume contains fourteen essays, five of which were not published
previously.
Translations
Demokratietheorie: Beiträge zu ihrer Erneuerung. Munich: Beck'sche, 1977. Pp.
255. This contains only essays 1–6 and 10.
Italian edition in preparation   Milan: Etas Libri
Japanese   Tokyo: Aoki Shoten, 1978

The Life and Times of Liberal Democracy. Oxford and New York: Oxford University
Press, 1977. Pp. 117.
Translations

A democracia liberal: origens et evolução Rio de Janiero: Zahar Editores, 1978
Italian edition in preparation   Milan: Mondadori (Il Saggiatore)
Japanese edition in preparation   Tokyo: Iwanami Shoten

Property: Mainstream and Critical Positions (edited, with preface, chapter 1, 'The
Meaning of Property', and chapter 12, 'Liberal-Democracy and Property', by
C.B.M., the latter substantially 'Liberalism and the Political Theory of Property', in
A. Kontos, ed., *Domination*, 1975). Toronto and Buffalo: University of Toronto
Press; Oxford: Basil Blackwell, 1978. Pp. 207

ARTICLES, REVIEW ARTICLES, AND CHAPTERS IN BOOKS

Pareto's 'General Sociology': The Problem of Method in the Social Sciences. *CJEPS*.
    III, 1937, pp. 458–71
On the Study of Politics in Canada. In H.A. Innis, ed., *Essays in Political Economy in
    Honour of E.J. Urwich* (Toronto: University of Toronto Press, 1938), pp. 147–65
The Ruling Class. *CJEPS*, VII, 1941, pp. 95–100
The History of Political Ideas. *CJEPS*, VII, 1941, pp. 564–77
The Meaning of Economic Democracy. *University of Toronto Quarterly*, XI, 1942;
    pp. 403–20
The Position of Political Science. *Culture*, III, 1942, pp. 452–9
Sir William Temple, Political Scientist? *CJEPS*, IX, 1943, pp. 39–54
Hobbes Today. *CJEPS*, XI, 1945, pp. 524–34. Reprinted as 'Hobbes's Bourgeois
    Man', in Keith Brown, ed., *Hobbes Studies* (Oxford: Blackwell, 1965), pp.
    169–83; and in *Democratic Theory: Essays in Retrieval*
The Political Theory of Social Credit. *CJEPS*, XV, 1949, pp. 378–93
A Disturbing Tendency in Political Science. *CJEPS*, XVI, 1950, pp. 98–106
Locke on Capitalist Appropriation. *Western Political Quarterly*, IV, 1951, pp. 550–66
The Social Bearing of Locke's Political Theory. *Western Political Quarterly*, VII,
    1954, pp. 1–22. Reprinted in C.B. Martin and D.M. Armstrong, eds., *Locke and
    Berkeley* (New York: Doubleday Anchor, 1968); and in Gordon J. Schochet, ed.,
    Life, Liberty, and Property (Belmont CA: Wadsworth, 1971). Translation: El
    contenido social de la teoria politica de Locke. *Teoria*, no. 5–6, Diciembra, 1975,
    pp. 51–71
I partiti politici. *Studi Politici*, III, 1954; pp. 108–13. Original version in English,
    Notes on the Requirements of a General Theory of Party Systems, mimeo, pp. 9, a
    paper presented at the International Political Science Association roundtable on
    comparative government, Florence, April 1954
L'enseignment de la science politique au Canada. *Revue française de science
    politique*, IV, 1954
The Deceptive Task of Political Theory. *Cambridge Journal*, VII, 1954, pp. 560–8.
    Reprinted in *Democratic Theory: Essays in Retrieval*

World Trends in Political Science Research. *American Political Science Review*, XLVIII, 1954, pp. 427–49. Translation: Les tendances mondiales de la recherche en science politique. *Revue française de science politique*, IV, 1954

Democracy in Alberta: A Reply. *Canadian Forum*, January 1955, pp. 223–25 (Reply to S.M. Lipset's review of *Democracy in Alberta*, in *Canadian Forum*, November–December 1954)

A Jubilee of Good Taste. *The Financial Post* (Toronto), 26 May 1956

The Social Sciences. In Julian Park, ed., *The Culture of Contemporary Canada* (Ithaca: Cornell University Press, 1957), pp. 181–221

The Treadmill. *Canadian Forum*, January 1958, pp. 230–2

Political Science. *Encyclopedia Canadiana* (Ottawa, 1958)

Edmund Burke and the New Conservatism. *Science and Society*, XXII, 1958, pp. 231–9

Edmund Burke. *Transactions of the Royal Society of Canada*, LII, third series, 1959, pp. 19–26

Harrington's 'Opportunity State'. *Past and Present*, 17, April 1960, pp. 45–70

Technical Change and Political Decision. *International Social Science Journal*, XII, 1960, pp. 357–68. Translation: Progresso tecnico e democrazia. *Mercurio* (Milano), IV, 15 Luglio 1961, pp. 55–62

Market Concepts in Political Theory. *CJEPS*, XXVII, 1961, pp. 490–7. Reprinted in *Democratic Theory: Essays in Retrieval*

Reluctant Duellists? Nuclear Arms for Canada: A Strong Case Examined. *Our Generation against Nuclear War* (Montreal), II, 1962, pp. 7–14

Harrington as Realist: A Rejoinder. *Past and Present*, 24, 1963, pp. 82–5 (Response to J.F.H. New, 'Harrington, A Realist?' ibid.)

Positive Neutralism for Canada? *Commentator* (Toronto), VII, 1963, pp. 9–11

Scholars and Spectres: A Rejoinder to Viner. *CJEPS*, XXIX, 1963, pp. 559–62 (Response to J. Viner, 'Possessive Individualism as Original Sin', ibid.)

Beyond the Nuclear Arms Issue. *Canadian Dimension* (Winnipeg), December–January 1963–64, pp. 14–16 (attributed to 'C.B. McPherson')

Post-Liberal-Democracy? *CJEPS*, XXX, 1964, pp. 485–98. Reprinted in *Democratic Theory: Essays in Retrieval*; in the *New Left Review*, no. 33, 1965; and in Robin Blackburn, ed., *Ideology in Social Science* (London: Collins, 1972)

Yardsticks for Canada's Future. *Saturday Night* (Toronto), July 1965

A New Kind of History. *New Statesman*, 4 March 1966, pp. 299–300

Revolution and Ideology in the Late Twentieth Century. In Carl J. Friedrich, ed., *Revolution* (Nomos VIII) (New York: Atherton, 1966), pp. 139–53. Reprinted in *Democratic Theory: Essays in Retrieval*

Halévy's Century Revisited. *Science and Society*, XXXI, 1967, pp. 37–47

Historians' Sabbath. *The Listener*, 28 September 1967, pp. 399–400

Quandary of Positive Liberalism. *New Statesman*, 3 November 1967, p. 591

The Maximization of Democracy. In P. Laslett and W.C. Runciman, eds.,

Philosophy, Politics and Society (Third Series) (Oxford: Blackwell, 1967), pp.
83–103. Reprinted in *Democratic Theory: Essays in Retrieval*

Democratic Theory: Ontology and Technology. *In D. Spitz, ed., Political Theory and Social Change (New York:* Atherton, 1967), pp. 203–20. Reprinted in *Democratic Theory: Essays in Retrieval*

Natural Rights in Hobbes and Locke. In D.D. Raphael, ed., *Political Theory and the Rights of Man* (London and Toronto: Macmillan, 1967), pp. 1–15. Reprinted in *Democratic Theory: Essays in Retrieval*. Translations: Los derechos naturales en Hobbes y en Locke. *Revista del Instituto de Ciencias Sociales.* (Barcelona), 1965; Prirodna prava u Hobsa i Loka. *ARHIV* (Belgrade), April–June 1966

The Historian as Underlabourer. *The Listener*, 11 January 1968, pp. 53–4

Elegant Tombstones: A Note on Friedman's Freedom. *CJPS*, I, 1968, pp. 95–106. Reprinted in *Dissent*, January–February 1969, pp. 69–78; and in *Democratic Theory: Essays in Retrieval*

The Nature of the Contemporary University. *Proceedings, Annual Meeting of the Association of Universities and Colleges of Canada*, 1968, pp. 97–100

Rejoinder to E. van den Haag, *Dissent*, May–June 1969, pp. 287–8 (Response to letter in same issue)

Interpretation *vs.* Criticism: A Rejoinder to Professor Crowley. *CJPS*, II, 1969, pp. 356–8 (Response to Crowley's 'Comment on Prof. Macpherson's Interpretation of *Capitalism and Freedom*', in previous issue, ibid.)

The Violent Society and the Liberal University. *Bulletin of the Canadian Association of University Teachers*, XVIII, 1968 (Canadian Association of University Teachers, Presidential report, reprinted in *AAUP Bulletin*, LV, 1969)

Bow and Arrow Power. *The Nation*, 210, 19 January 1970, pp. 54–6

Progress of the Locke Industry. *CJPS*, III, 1970, pp. 323–6

The University as Multiple Fool. *Bulletin of the Canadian Association of University Teachers*, XIX, 1970, pp. 3–7

The University as Critical Capital. *Queen's Quarterly*, LXXVII, 1970, pp. 389–94

Clifford Hugh Douglas. In *Dictionary of National Biography, 1951–1960* (London, 1971)

The Currency of Values. *Transactions of the Royal Society of Canada*, IX, Series 4, 1971, pp. 27–35

Towards 2000: The Future of Post-Secondary Education in Ontario: A Note. *Stoa* (Montreal), I, 1971, pp. 58–60

The Criticism of Concepts and the Concept of Criticism. *CJPS*, V, 1972, pp. 141–5 (Response to B. Wand, 'C.B. Macpherson's Conceptual Apparatus', ibid. IV, 1971)

Reflections on the Sources of Development Theory. In Manfred Stanley, ed., *Social Development: Critical Perspectives* (New York: Basic Books, 1972), pp. 206–20

Marxism in Canada: A New Beginning. *Canadian Forum*, IX, July–August 1973, pp. 69–72

Rawls's Models of Man and Society. *Philosophy of the Social Sciences*, III, 1973, pp. 341–7

After Strange Gods: Canadian Political Science 1973. In T.N. Guinsburg and G.L. Reuber, eds., *Perspectives on the Social Sciences in Canada* (Toronto: University of Toronto Press, 1974), pp. 52–76

Commentary on H.G. Johnson's 'Current and Prospective State of Economics in Canada'. Ibid., pp. 125–8

Liberalism and the Political Theory of Property. In A. Kontos, ed., *Domination* (Toronto: University of Toronto Press, 1975), pp. 89–100

Capitalism and the Changing Concept of Property. In E. Kamenka and R.S. Neale, eds., *Feudalism, Capitalism and Beyond* (Canberra: Australian National University Press; London: Edward Arnold, 1975), pp. 104–24

Individualist Socialism? A Reply to Levine and MacIntyre. *Canadian Journal of Philosophy*, VI, 1976, pp. 195–200 (Response to A. Levine, 'The Political Theory of Social Democracy', and A. MacIntyre, 'On *Democratic Theory: Essays in Retrieval* by C.B. Macpherson', ibid., pp. 183–93 and 177–81)

Comment on Lorenne Clark's 'Politics and Law: The Theory and Practice of the Ideology of Male Supremacy'. In D.N. Weisstub, ed., *Law and Public Policy* (Toronto: Osgoode Hall Law School, 1976), pp. 55–8

Humanist Democracy and Elusive Marxism: A Response to Minogue and Svacek. *CJPS*, IX, 1976, pp. 423–30 (Reply to K. Minogue, 'Humanist Democracy: The Political Thought of C.B. Macpherson', and to Victor Svacek, 'The Elusive Marxism of C.B. Macpherson', ibid., pp. 377–94 and 395–422)

Human Rights as Property Rights. *Dissent*, Winter 1977, pp. 72–7

Hampsher-Monk's Levellers. *Political Studies*, XXV, 1977, pp. 571–6. (Response to I. Hampsher-Monk, 'The Political Theory of the Levellers: Putney, Property and Professor Macpherson', in ibid., XXIV)

Do We Need a Theory of the State? *European Journal of Sociology*, XVIII, 1977, pp. 223–44

Needs and Wants: An Ontological or Historical Problem? In R. Fitzgerald, ed., *Human Needs and Politics* (Sydney: Pergamon, 1977), pp. 26–35

The Economic Penetration of Political Theory. *Journal of the History of Ideas*, XXXIX, 1978, pp. 101–18

Class, Classlessness and the Critique of Rawls. *Political Theory*, VI, 1978, pp. 209–11

The False Roots of Western Democracy. In F.R. Dallmayr, ed., *From Contract to Community* (New York and Basel: Marcel Dekker, 1978), pp. 17–27

Second and Third Thoughts on Needs and Wants. *Canadian Journal of Political and Social Theory*, III, 1979, pp. 46–9 (Comment on A. Kontos, 'Through a Glass Darkly: Ontology and False Needs', ibid., pp. 25–45)

On the Concept of Property. *Archiv für Rechts- und Sozialphilosophie*, Beiheft neue Folge Nr. 10. n.d., pp. 81–5

Reply to Professor Weaver, *Journal of the History of Ideas* (forthcoming) *Re* F.S.
  Weaver, 'Exploitation vs. Inequality in Political Theory', ibid., 1978)
By Innis out of Marx: The Revival of Canadian Political Economy. *Canadian Journal
  of Political and Social Theory*, III, no. 2 (1979), pp. 134–8
Property as Means or End. In A.J. Parel and Thomas Flanagan, eds., *Theories of
  Property: Aristotle to the Present* (Waterloo, Ont.: Wilfrid Laurier University
  Press for Calgary Institute for the Humanities, 1979), pp. 3–9

BOOK REVIEWS

Trevor Aston, ed., *Crisis in Europe: 1560–1660* (*New Statesman*, 12 November
  1965)
Ernest Barker, *Principles of Social and Political Theory* (*CJEPS*, XIX, 1953)
Brian Barry, *The Liberal Theory of Justice* (*CJPS*, VII, 1974)
Samuel H. Beer, *The City of Reason* (A Disturbing Tendency in Political Science,
  CJEPS, XVI, 1950)
A.A. Berle, *Power* (Bow and Arrow Power, *The Nation*, 210, 19 January 1970)
Charles Blitzer, *An Immortal Commonwealth: The Political Thought of James
  Harrington* (*Canadian Historical Review*, XLIII, 1962)
John Bowle, *Hobbes and His Critics: A Study in Seventeenth Century Con-
  stitutionalism* (*CJEPS*, XIX, 1953)
H.N. Brailsford, *The Levellers and the English Revolution*, ed. Christopher Hill
  (*Canadian Historical Review*, XLIII, 1962)
Horace L. Brittain, *Local Government in Canada* (*Letters in Canada*, 1951)
Canadian Institute on Economics and Politics, *Canada: The Empire and the League*
  (Canada and the League, *New Frontier*, 1, 1937)
Canadian Society for the Study of Higher Education, *Towards 2000: The Future of
  Post-Secondary Education in Ontario* (*Stoa*, 1, 1971)
George Catlin, *The Story of the Political Philosophers* (The History of Political Ideas,
  CJEPS, VII, 1941, and *University of Toronto Law Journal*, IV, 1941)
G.E.G. Catlin, *Systematic Politics: Elementa Politica et Sociologica* (*CJEPS*, XXIX,
  1963)
H. McD. Clokie, *Canadian Government and Politics* (*Food for Thought*, February
  1945)
Alfred Cobban, *Rousseau and the Modern State*, second ed. (Halévy's Century
  Revisited, *Science and Society*, XXXI, 1967)
Bernard L. Cohen, *The Case for Conservatism* (*Letters in Canada*, 1951)
Carl B. Cone, *Burke and the Nature of Politics: The Age of the American Revolution*
  (Edmund Burke and the New Conservatism, *Science and Society*, XXII, 1958)

– *Burke and the Nature of Politics: The Age of the French Revolution* (Halévy's Century Revisited, *Science and Society*, XXXI, 1967)

J.A. Corry, *Democratic Government and Politics* (*Letters in Canada*, 1951)

Richard H. Cox, *Locke on War and Peace* (*CJEPS*, XXVIII, 1962)

Maurice Cranston, *John Locke: A Biography* (*CJEPS*, XXVIII, 1962)

Maurice Cranston, and R.S. Peters, eds., *Hobbes and Rousseau: A Collection of Critical Essays* (*American Political Science Review*, LXVIII, 1974)

R.H.S. Crossman, *Government and the Governed* (The History of Political Ideas, *CJEPS*, VII, 1941)

Alexander P. D'Entrèves, *The Notion of the State* (Quandary of Positive Liberalism, *New Statesman*, 3 November 1967)

H.T. Dickinson, *Liberty and Property: Political Ideology in Eighteenth Century Britain* (*Journal of Modern History*, 51, no. 2, 1979)

Graeme Duncan, *Marx and Mill* (*British Journal of Sociology*, XXVI, 1, 1975)

John Dunn, *The Political Thought of John Locke* (Progress of the Locke Industry, *CJPS*, III, 1970)

James Eayrs, *Northern Approaches: Canada and the Search for Peace.* (Reluctant Duellists? Nuclear Arms for Canada: A Strong Case Examined, *Our Generation against Nuclear War*, II, 1962)

William Ebenstein, ed., *Man and the Modern State: Modern Political Ideas* (*CJEPS*, XV, 1949)

G.R. Elton, *The Practice of History* (The Historian as Underlabourer, *The Listener*, 11 Jan. 1968)

Jean-Charles Falardeau, ed., *Essais sur le Québec contemporain* (*Queen's Quarterly*, LX, 1954)

Benjamin Farrington, *Science and Politics in the Ancient World* (The History of Political Ideas, *CJEPS*, VII, 1941)

Zera S. Fink, *The Classical Republicans: An Essay on the Recovery of a Pattern of Thought in Seventeenth Century England* (*CJEPS*, XIV, 1948)

John L. Finlay, *Social Credit: The English Origins* (*Journal of Modern History*, XLVI, 1974)

Joseph Frank, *The Beginnings of the English Newspaper* (*Canadian Historical Review*, XLIII, 1962)

Milton Friedman, *Capitalism and Freedom* (Elegant Tombstones: A Note on Friedman's Freedom, *CJPS*, I, 1968; *Dissent*, Jan./Feb., 1969; and *Democratic Theory: Essays in Retrieval*)

Igor Gouzenko, *This Was My Choice: Gouzenko's Story* (*International Journal*, IV, 194)

J.A.W. Gunn, *Politics and the Public Interest in the Seventeenth Century* (Progress of the Locke Industry, *CJPS*, III, 1970)

William Haller and Godfrey Davies, eds., *The Leveller Tracts: 1647–1653* (*CJEPS*, XI, 1945)

John H. Hallowell, *Main Currents in Modern Political Thought* (*Western Political Quarterly*, IV, 1951)

Joseph Hamburger, *James Mill and the Art of Revolution* (Halévy's Century Revisited, *Science and Society*, XXXI, 1967)

F.A. von Hayek, ed., John Stuart Mill's *The Spirit of the Age* (*CJEPS*, IX, 1943)

Gertrude Himmelfarb, *On Liberty and Liberalism: The Case of John Stuart Mill* (*Mill News Letter*, Winter 1976)

Richard Hirsch, *Soviet Spies: The Story of Russian Espionage in Canada* (*International Journal*, III, 1948)

Arthur N. Holcombe, *Dependent Areas in the Modern World* (*Canadian Forum*, February 1942)

Arthur N. Holcombe, *Human Rights in the Modern World* (A Disturbing Tendency in Political Science, *CJEPS*, XVI, 1950)

René Hurtubise and Donald Rowat, *The University, Society and Government: Report of the Commission on the Relations between Universities and Governments* (*CAUT Bulletin*, XIX, Winter 1971)

Charles S. Hyneman, *Bureaucracy in a Democracy* (*Western Political Quarterly*, IV, 1951)

Paul Johnson, *The Offshore Islanders* (The White Cliffs of Liberalism, *The Listener*, 28 September 1972)

Bertrand de Jouvenel, *The Pure Theory of Politics* (*Political Science Quarterly*, LXXXII, 1967)

Karl W. Kapp, *The League of Nations and Raw Materials 1919–1939* (*Canadian Forum*, February 1942)

P. King and B. Parekh, eds., *Politics and Experience: Essays Presented to Professor Michael Oakeshott* (*Political Science Quarterly*, LXXXVI, 1971)

J.D. Kingsley and D.W. Petegorsky, *Strategy for Democracy* (*Canadian Forum*, August 1942)

Leopold Labedz, ed., *Revisionism* (*Political Science Quarterly*, LXXVIII, 1963)

Harold J. Laski, *The Dilemma of Our Times* (*Political Studies*, II, 1954)

Harold J. Laski, *Faith, Reason, and Civilization: An Essay in Historical Analysis* (*CJEPS*, XI, 1945)

Peter Laslett, *The World We Have Lost* (A New Kind of History, *New Statesman*, 4 March, 1966)

V.I. Lenin *et al. The Soviet Union and the Cause of Peace* (The Soviets and Peace, *New Frontier*, I, 1937)

Shirley Robin Letwin, *The Pursuit of Certainty* (Halévy's Century Revisited, *Science and Society*, XXXI, 1967)

George Lichtheim, *Marxism: An Historical and Critical Study* (*International Journal*, XVIII, 1963)

Benjamin E. Lippincott, *Victorian Critics of Democracy: Carlyle, Ruskin, Arnold, Stephen, Maine and Lecky* (*CJEPS*, VI, 1940)

Henry Meyer Magid, *English Political Pluralism: The Problem of Freedom and Organization* (*CJEPS*, VIII, 1942)

Herbert Marcuse, *Soviet Marxism* (*Political Science Quarterly*, LXXIV, 1959)

J.P. Mayer et al., *Political Thought: The European Tradition* (The History of Political Ideas, *CJEPS*, VII, 1941)

H.B. Mayo, *Democracy and Marxism* (*International Journal*, XI, 1956)

J.D.B. Miller, *The Nature of Politics* (*Political Science Quarterly*, LXXIX, 1964)

S.I. Mintz. *The Hunting of Leviathan: Seventeenth Century Reactions to the Materialism and Moral Philosophy of Thomas Hobbes* (*Journal of Modern History*, XXXVI, 1964)

A.G. Meyer, *Leninism* (*Political Science Quarterly*, LXXIII, 1958)

A.G. Meyer, *Marxism: The Unity of Theory and Practice* (*Political Science Quarterly*, LXX, 1955)

Gaetano Mosca, *The Ruling Class: Elementi di Scienza Politica* (The Ruling Class, *CJEPS*, VII, 1941)

Michael J. Oakeshott, ed., *Social and Political Doctrines of Contemporary Europe* ('The History of Political Ideas, *CJEPS*, VII, 1941)

Leo Panitch, ed., *The Canadian State: Political Economy and Political Power* (By Innis out of Marx: The Revival of Canadian Political Economy, *Canadian Journal of Political and Social Theory*, III, 1979)

B. Parekh and P. King, eds., *Politics and Experience* (*Political Science Quarterly*, LXXXVI, 1971)

Vilfredo Pareto, *The Mind and Society* (Pareto's 'General Sociology': The Problem of Method in the Social Sciences, *CJEPS*, III, 1937)

Charles Parkin, *The Moral Basis of Burke's Political Thought* (Edmund Burke and the New Conservatism, *Science and Society*, XXII, 1958)

Alan T. Peacock, ed., *Income Distribution and Social Policy* (*Western Political Quarterly*, VIII, 1955)

S.G. Peitchinis, *Financing Post-Secondary Education in Canada* (*CAUT Bulletin*; XXI, October 1972)

J.B. Pike, ed., John of Salisbury's *Frivolities of Courtiers and Footprints of Philosophers* (*University of Toronto Law Journal*, III, 1940)

John M. Robson and Michael Laine, eds., *James and John Stuart Mill: Papers of the Centenary Conference* (*Canadian Forum*; December–January 1976–77)

William A. Robson, ed., *University Teaching of Social Sciences* (*International Journal*, X, 1955)

Wilhelm Röpke, *Civitas Humana: A Humane Order of Society* (A Disturbing Tendency in Political Science, *CJEPS*, XVI, 1950)

George H. Sabine, *A History of Political Theory*, rev. ed. (*Western Political Quarterly*, IV, 1950)

John T. Saywell, *The Office of Lieutenant-Governor* (*Canadian Public Administration*, September 1958)

George Seldes, *Sawdust Caesar: The Untold Story of Mussolini and Fascism* (Debunking Mussolini, *New Frontier*, I, 1936)

Martin Seliger, *The Liberal Politics of John Locke* (*Political Science Quarterly*, LXXXVI, 1971)

K.B. Smellie, *Reason in Politics* (*University of Toronto Law Journal*, III, 1940)

C.W. Smith Jr, *Public Opinion in a Democracy: A Study in American Politics* (*CJEPS*, VI, 1940)

Thomas A. Spragens Jr, *The Politics of Motion: The World of Thomas Hobbes* (*New Statesman*, 26 October 1973)

Kathleen M. Stahl, *British and Soviet Colonial Systems* (*Western Political Quarterly*, VI, 1952)

Piero Sraffa and Maurice Dobb, eds., *The Works and Correspondence of David Ricardo*, vols. I–IV (*Western Political Quarterly*, V, 1952); vols. V–IX (ibid., VII, 1954); vol. X (ibid., VIII, 1955)

W.J. Stankiewicz, *Politics and Religion in Seventeenth-Century France: A Study of Political Ideas from the Monarchomachs to Bayle, As Reflected in the Toleration Controversy* (*CJEPS*, XXVIII, 1962)

Peter J. Stanlis, *Edmund Burke and the Natural Law* (Edmund Burke and the New Conservatism, *Science and Society*, XXII, 1958)

John B. Stewart, *The Moral and Political Philosophy of David Hume* (Halévy's Century Revisited, *Science and Society*, XXXI, 1967)

Leo Strauss, *On Tyranny: An Interpretation of Xenophon's Hiero* (A Disturbing Tendency in Political Science, *CJEPS*, XVI, 1950)

J.L. Talmon, *The Origins of Totalitarian Democracy* (*Past and Present*, 2, November 1952)

Gary Teeple, ed., *Capitalism and the National Question in Canada* (Marxism in Canada: A New Beginning, *Canadian Dimension*, IX, July–August 1973)

H.M. Tomlinson, *Mars His Idiot* (*New Frontier*, I, 1936)

Hugh Trevor-Roper, *Religion, The Reformation and Social Change* (Historians' Sabbath, *The Listener*, 28 September 1967)

Pierre Elliott Trudeau, *La grève de l'amiante: une étape de la révolution industrielle au Québec* (*CJEPS*, XXIII, 1957)

Adam B. Ulam, *The Unfinished Revolution* (*Political Science Quarterly*, LXXVII, 1962)

Howard Warrender, *The Political Philosophy of Hobbes: His Theory of Obligation* (The Treadmill, *Canadian Forum*, January 1958)

Ian M. Wilson, *The Influence of Hobbes and Locke in the Shaping of the Concept of Sovereignty in Eighteenth-Century France* (*Modern Language Notes*, May 1974)

Donald Winch, *Adam Smith's Politics* (*History of Political Economy*, XI, no. 3, 1979, pp. 450–4)

Don M. Wolfe, ed., *Leveller Manifestoes of the Puritan Revolution* (*CJEPS*, XI, 1945)

Leonard Woolf, *After the Deluge: Volume 2: 1830–1832* (The History of Political Ideas, *CJEPS*, VII, 1941)

John W. Yolton, ed., *John Locke: Problems and Perspectives* (Progress of the Locke Industry, *CJPS*, III, 1970)

Alfred Zimmern, ed., *Modern Political Doctrines* (The History of Political Ideas, *CJEPS*, VII, 1941)

(various authors) *International Bibliography of Political Science. Volume One* (UNESCO *Publications Committee (Canada) Review*, no. 4, January 1955)